TYING
WARMWATER
FLIES

C. Boyd Pfeiffer

©2003 by C. Boyd Pfeiffer
All rights reserved.

No portion of this publication may be reproduced or transmitted in
any form or by any means, electronic or mechanical, including
photocopy, recording, or any information storage and retrieval system,
without permission in writing from the publisher, except by a reviewer
who may quote brief passages in a critical article or review to be
printed in a magazine or newspaper, or electronically transmitted on
radio or television.

Published by

krause publications
An F&W Publications Company

700 East State Street • Iola, WI 54990-0001
715-445-2214 • 888-457-2873
www.krause.com

Please call or write for our free catalog of publications.
Our toll-free number to place an order or
obtain a free catalog is (800) 258-0929.

Library of Congress Catalog Number: 2002113140
ISBN: 0-87349-514-4

Editor: Kevin Michalowski
Designer: Jamie Griffin

Printed in China

Dedication

To Brenda,
who continues to inspire me

Acknowledgments

Shortly after learning the rudiments of tying trout flies, I began adding warmwater patterns to my fly boxes. Back then, warmwater patterns were mostly for bass and panfish. Fifty years ago, not too many people thought of, tried, or wrote about fly-fishing for pike, pickerel, freshwater drum, catfish, carp, crappie and the other warmwater species. The old bachelor next door who taught me fishing as a boy, including fly-fishing and fly-tying, encouraged me with my warmwater fly-tying.

Along the way I learned not only about using cork and balsa for hard-bodied bugs, but also spinning and stacking deer (and other) hair for bugs, and trying some strange designs. Some of these were successful; most were not. But they were still part of the learning process. The same friends who helped me by example and encouragement with trout flies, also helped with my interest in bass and panfish flies and ultimately flies for all warmwater species. Close friends, then and now, such as Chuck Edghill, Lefty Kreh, Ed Russell, Norm Bartlett, Joe Zimmer, Irv Swope, Joe Messinger Jr., Vern Kirby, Bill May, Jack Goellner, Jim Heim, and others – all fly tyers and excellent fishermen – have served as both sounding boards for some crazy ideas and also mentors and instructors in fly-tying techniques.

I also appreciate the help of friends in the industry and tyers who provided advice, help, or flies for inclusion in the book and for photos. These include: Lefty Kreh, Joe Messinger Jr., Chuck Edghill, William Tapply, Greg Webster, Bob Clouser, Scott Sanchez, Poul Jorgensen, Carl Blackledge, John Shewey, John Mazurkiewicz of Catalyst Marketing, Bill Black of Spirit River, Dave Hall of Umpqua, Tom Eggler of Gaines, Rod Yerger, Bill Skilton, Blane Chocklett, Tony Spezio, Rainy Riding of Rainy Riding Flies, McKenzie Flies, Spirit River, Umpqua, Brookside Flies, EdgeWater Flies, Riverborn Flies, Holly Flies, and others.

My longtime fishing companion and close friend, Chuck Edghill, deserves special mention and thanks. As he has done with past books, he served as unofficial consultant and also did the thankless but necessary task of reading the manuscript to correct typos, spelling mistakes, and grammar. In general he added his wisdom and experience to the book to make it better than it would have been without his thoughtful advice. Naturally, any errors and faults that remain are my responsibility, but this is a better book because of Chuck Edghill. In addition, I thank my wife, Brenda, for her encouragement, thoughts, and for the time to complete the book. Finally, my thanks for the patience and interest by Don Gulbrandsen, Kevin Michalowski, and others at Krause Publications for their continued help and encouragement.

C. Boyd Pfeiffer
November, 2002

Table of Contents

About the Photographs

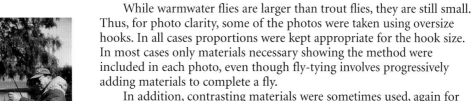

While warmwater flies are larger than trout flies, they are still small. Thus, for photo clarity, some of the photos were taken using oversize hooks. In all cases proportions were kept appropriate for the hook size. In most cases only materials necessary showing the method were included in each photo, even though fly-tying involves progressively adding materials to complete a fly.

In addition, contrasting materials were sometimes used, again for photo clarity. Many flies are tied using a thread that matches, or is complimentary to, the body or fly color. In all cases here, thread and other material colors were chosen for contrast so the method illustrated would be clear.

Similarly, some photos of the 100 top patterns, mostly of small flies for panfish and carp, have been tied larger than normal or with oversize hooks for photo clarity.

Introduction

Our interest in fly-fishing in this country came from our English heritage, with the initial emphasis on trout. While trout fishing and the fly-tying styles for trout of the Catskills were immediately popular, fly fishermen were experimenting with new methods to take warmwater species. One of these ideas came from Florida Indians. They used what was later described as a "bob," which was a wrap of deerskin on three hooks tied "back to back" (the precursor of a treble hook?). It was similar to bushy flies that have since been developed for bass.

The precise formula, mentioned in William Bartram's 1764 writing, described the hook as being covered with "… the white hair from a deer tail, shreds of a red garter, and some particoloured feathers, all of which form a tuft, or tassel, nearly as large as one's fist …" This "bob" was skittered along the shore near bass cover; the angler was in the front of the canoe and a steersman in the rear. In 1951, Jason Lucas of *Sports Afield* described using a long pole/short line/bass bug rig for a fishing method he called "spatting."

Today's anglers fish with a smaller offering, tied more expertly, and cast with a fly rod instead of being flipped or pitched on the surface with a reed or cane pole. But this early "fly," even though over 200 years old (and perhaps much older – no one knows when the Indians developed this technique), would undoubtedly work today if cast into some lily pads.

Early on, American fly anglers found bass, pike and other warmwater species worthwhile game. There are records of fly-fishing for bass early in the 1830s and fly-fishing for pike began about the same time. The flies for such fishing were large. An 1800 account mentions fly-fishing for pike using a fly the "size of a wren."

Dr. James Henshall capitalized on warmwater fly-fishing with his 1881 tome, *Book Of The Black Bass*, covering both largemouth and smallmouth. In addition to the usual and expected information on fishing with bait-casting tackle, bait, and early lures, it also included a fair amount on fly tackle, flies, and fly-fishing. A much later development was the deer-hair bug with black- and yellow-banded body, yellow hair tail, and yellow bucktail wings that was known as a "Henshall Bug." In later editions of his book, Henshall wrote of the use of cork as a bass bug body. He also wrote about and illustrated the many bass flies that were popular at that time, many of which were variations of standard wet flies popular at the turn of the century, but with exaggerated, overly large wings.

"Flies" and "fly-fishing" for bass in the early 1900s was often done with what we today would call lures, as evidenced by John Muma's *Old Flyrod Lures*, which documents the metal, plastic, and wood offerings that began 100 years ago. Some of these, of course, did double duty in the late 1940s and early 1950s as lures for ultralight spinning tackle. They were most popular in the 1920s through the 1940s. One expert on the history of the sport estimates that there were as many as 25,000 tyers or "manufacturers" of warmwater bugs and flies during this period. Some of these were the large companies such as Glen L. Evans, Eppinger, Weber, Accardo, and Peckinpaugh. Others were smaller companies or individual tyers tying only for one local tackle shop, fly shop, gas station, or general store.

Over time, fly fishermen began to tie more frequently for other species, such as pike, carp, perch, crappie, pickerel, muskie, freshwater drum, white bass, buffalo, bowfin, catfish, gar, redhorse, shad, walleye, and sunfish. These and others have all become a part of the warmwater fly-fisherman's targeted species. Indeed, the International Game Fish Association includes all of the above – and a lot more – in their listings of freshwater fly rod records.

After the surge of interest in spinning that began in the early 1950s, the popularity of fly-fishing for some warmwater species seemed to wane. Fortunately, that is changing. Bass fishing with standard tackle has grown in interest, media attention, and popularity.

But there have also been recent upswings of interest in fly-fishing for all warmwater species. The seminal book on the subject was Joe Brooks' *Bass Bug Fishing*, published in 1947. While only 69 pages, the book covers the topic well and includes directions on tying half a dozen different bugs.

Also important has been the explosion of tying techniques that can often apply equally to trout, salmon, saltwater and warmwater patterns. These do not usually break the bounds of fly-tying, but often bend them into new directions as tyers develop varied and different ways to make old patterns and to create new ones previously unimagined.

Fly-tying and fly-fishing specialty sport shows, symposiums on fly-tying and fly-tying exhibitions have also helped. The Conclaves of the Federation of Fly Fishers have paved new ways of tying flies for all species. There is now also a greater understanding of the habits, habitats, and foods of all the species for which we fish. This has brought about innovation in design of warmwater flies by some of the most imaginative tyers.

One aspect of a book like this that simultaneously makes it both easier and more difficult to produce is the multitude of species covered. Its precursor *Tying Trout Flies*, covered only trout – different species, but all with similar habits and food requirements. That's a little different from this book on flies designed for pike and pumpkinseed, carp and crappie, bass and bluegill. A cottonwood seed fly on a size 14 hook that you throw to a surface summertime carp would be of no interest at all to a pike, nor would the 6-inch long baitfish fly twitched through the weeds of pike cover ever be taken by a carp.

For the beginning tyer, or one new to warmwater flies, this brings a wealth of diversity, innovation, and imaginative materials available to the process of fly design, and also a blurring of the boundaries of the past.

These new fields of fly-tying should not discourage anyone. Rather they should open the floodgates to working with new materials and exploring new tying methods. They should allow the imagination to create new patterns that no other fly tyer has yet thought of or devised, or tried on warmwater species.

Naturally, the enclosed list of 100 top patterns will no doubt engender thought, some controversy, and even some disagreement. Note that it is not the "top 100 flies" since that would suggest that any other flies are not worthy of this listing of 100 patterns. Each fly on the enclosed list is designed to show a particular tying style or an example of a fly that will work in all parts of the country or perhaps be specific to a certain area of the country or even specific to a certain species of fish.

Some flies are general and, with modification in size and style, will work for a number of species. Some will be specific to a particular species, or for working particular types of water or levels in the water column. That's the challenge of fly-fishing and of tying warmwater flies.

Realize that many of the designs here may also differ slightly from the same "pattern" that you see in other books, particularly older books on fly-tying. The development of synthetics and the loss of some natural materials require this, while many tyers have developed their own slight variations of standard classic patterns. Realize also that unlike trout flies that often develop from a very specific initial pattern, many warmwater flies are more design than pattern. The difference is important. A pattern describes particular materials and colors for each part of the fly. A design describes a general way of tying a fly, which may vary widely in color and sometimes even materials, provided that the end result resembles the original design. An example of a pattern would be an Adams or McGinty trout fly, while a design would be a Woolly Bugger or Lefty's Deceiver, which can be tied in any color imaginable, sometimes even with slight materials changes.

Once you know the basics, it is just a matter of practice, imagination, and innovation. After all, reduced to its elements, fly-tying is all pretty much just winding string on a hook, and tying stuff down on it to make something attractive to fish.

Chapter 1

Essential Tools and Accessories

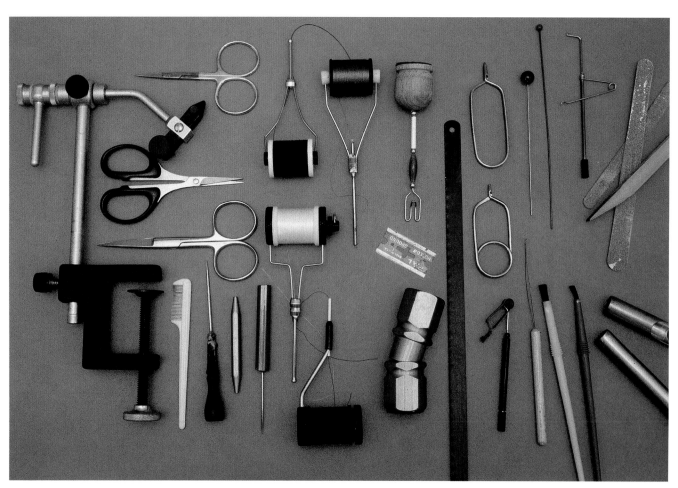

Tools for fly-tying warmwater flies. In columns, left to right and top to bottom: fly-tying vise; scissors (top), comb, half hitch tool, and bodkins (bottom); bobbins (top to bottom, two standard, adjustable tension Merco and adjustable-tension Griffin); dubbing spinner, double edge razor blade, and stacker; hacksaw blade; hackle pliers; bobbin cleaners, whip finisher, bobbin threader, and disposable brushes; emery boards, sanding stick, and tubing cutters for foam.

ESSENTIAL TOOLS

Even though most warmwater flies are larger than those tied for trout, you still need the proper tools. While the hooks are larger and more material is used, tools make the job go easier and quicker, resulting in far better flies than most of us could tie freehand. Good tools need not be expensive and some can be easily made from materials commonly found in any home or hardware stores. Since warmwater flies run the gamut from panfish and pike to carp and catfish, with bass and bream in the mix somewhere, your tying may need only a narrower range of tools than might be required by a tyer embracing all species and tying for all situations. Get good tools for your initial fly-tying interests and you are off to a good start.

Essential tools include the following:

VISE – A good vise is a must. It does not have to be expensive and does not have to have fine-point jaws, as do vises used for tying tiny patterns. Some very good, reasonably priced vises are available. Basic choices include rotary or stationary, the method of jaw closure and the type of base. True rotary styles allow turning the vise jaws with a crank or knob. The hook shank stays on the axis of rotation to allow feeding the material to the turning hook. Those vises that allow movement in which the hook does not stay horizontal allow some tying adjustments, but are not true rotary. True rotary vises are a help when tying flies in which a lot of body material is added, or if making stacked deer-hair bugs, where it allows the 180-degree switching for stacking the back and belly of the fly.

Traditional vise jaws close by a cam system in which the jaws, by means of a lever, are pulled back against a collet at the end of a sleeve to tighten the jaws on the hook. Some modern vises close using a pivotal thumbscrew system that levers the jaws together to hold the hook. Both systems work well and both systems allow for jaw adjustment to hold a large range of hook sizes. If you are making large flies for bass and pike, make sure that you get a vise that will take large hooks.

Basic vise types come in two styles. A "C" clamp that fastens the vise post to a table or bench makes the unit very stable and solid, but it must have a table of the right thickness to clamp securely. An additional thumbscrew adjustment on the "C" clamp allows vertical positioning of the vise. The pedestal style has a shorter post holding the jaws, and fits into a heavy base. It can be positioned anywhere on a table or bench, and does not depend upon table style or thickness. The pedestal style vise is useful for tying in a motel room, although the weight of the base makes it a disadvantage for air travel. Most vises allow interchangeability between "C" clamp and pedestal base.

Manufacturers that make true rotary and rotary-style vises include Norlander, Renzetti, Dyna-King, Griffin, BT's Fly Fishing Products, Abel, Anvil, HMH, Regal, D. H. Thompson, and others. Those that make vises with interchangeable jaws include HMH and Thompson. If you have one of these with fine jaws for trout flies, consider adding heavier jaws for the larger flies used for warmwater fly-fishing.

LIGHT – Adequate light is a necessity for tying any fly. My favorites are the small halogen lights. These are available in stand-alone models from fly shops and general stores. There are also specialty models that clamp onto the vise post.

Just make sure that any lamp stands high enough above the vise jaws to give you good clearance for all wrapping and tying operations and is not too hot to work around.

BACKGROUND PLATE – A background contrasting with the fly color helps in seeing the materials and improves the end result. I like white for dark flies and black for light-colored flies, but I also switch to other colors just for a change of pace when doing a lot of tying. A Profile Plate from Dyna-King will fasten to any vise post, and comes with five color plates for varied flies. Lacking this, you can set up matte-finish blotter paper at an angle behind your vise. Blotter paper is best to prevent distracting light reflections.

HACKLE PLIERS – These are designed to hold hackle while winding it around a hook, either when making a collar-style hackle for wet flies, or when palmering hackle over the body. Several styles are available. The most recent of these styles is a rotary type, with a small spring clamp fixed to a universal joint on the end of a thin handle. This allows holding the handle and winding the hackle, without changing the hackle pliers' position with each turn. This helps prevent twisting the hackle. I like this style best for most of my tying.

A more traditional design is the standard, or English, style that is made of spring steel bent so that two opposing jaws formed on the ends of the spring wire clamp together to grip the hackle. These are also made in a flat steel style with rubber buttons on one or both inside ends of the jaws to better grip the hackle. TIP – on any hackle pliers lacking soft jaws, it is easy to add a short length of thin surgical tubing, or a short length of shrink tubing, heated to hold it in place.

SCISSORS – Get good fly-tying scissors. Those with fine tips available from drug and cosmetics stores are not of good enough quality or have small finger holes that will not fit the

average man. Also, buy two pairs of scissors. One pair must have very short fine tips that are ideal for cutting hackle and thread only and for fine work on the fly. The other pair should be larger, with tips about 1-1/2 inches long. Use these for any coarse cutting of lead wire, tinsels, metals, coarse thread and any mono or Kevlar thread. For most warmwater flies, you will probably use the coarser scissors more than the fine-blade pair. I prefer my scissors with one serrated jaw for better gripping and less slipping of the materials being cut – again particularly important with many of the materials used in warmwater flies.

BOBBIN – While you don't really need a bobbin, it does make it far easier to precisely position thread on a fly. It also makes it easier to control thread tension. I would not work without one. Originally, they were only available with a straight metal tube. Today, the best of these have a full ceramic tube, or a small ceramic ring (like a guide ring) fitted into the end of the tube, through which the thread passes. Even though these are more expensive, they are well worth it to prevent fraying the thread. The straight metal tube bobbins will groove in time and damage thread. Avoid them. Bobbins are also available in short- and long-tube styles. Buy the long-tube style, since it can be used for small flies, and is far better for clearance and reach when working with large flies or bugs for bass, pike and such.

Relatively new bobbins by Griffin, Merco/Rite and Norlander have adjustable tension control on the spool holder.

BODKIN – Bodkins are basically needles on the end of a thin handle. They are useful for adding head cement to a finished fly, adding glue to fly parts, separating hackle fibers bound down by thread, pulling whip finishes up neatly and many other tasks. TIP - To make them, use pliers to carefully force the dull end of a needle into a wood dowel handle. Use different size needles for different purposes. Fine needles are good for separating hackle fibers and working on fine flies; coarser points are good for mixing glue and applying head cement.

HALF-HITCH TOOL – Half-hitch tools are nothing more than small tapered tools (like a pencil point with a hole where the pencil lead would be). To use, loop the thread around the tool and hold the hole against the hook eye to slide the looped thread from the tool and onto the fly head to create a locking hitch on the fly head. Some half-hitch tools have very deep holes so that the tool can be slipped over the hook eye and shank to place half hitches when tying down each material in turn. These are particularly handy when locking thread in place with each step of tying hair bodied-bugs. A whip finish should be used to complete each fly.

ADDITIONAL/ACCESSORIES

If you are not tying deer-hair, you won't need a stacker or packer. If not working with cork, you won't need razor blades, hacksaw blades, and paintbrushes. If you are always going to use head cement or nail polish and never add epoxy to the head of the fly, then you will not need a fly turner. If you can make a whip finish with your fingers, you will not need a whip finisher. The list goes on. Here, then are some suggestions of additional tools that should be added only after you make your initial selection of basic tools, and have mastered the basics of fly-tying.

TOOL RACK – Many of the vise and equipment

manufacturers make various racks of wood, foam, or plastic for holding fly-tying tools. Similar racks for thread and other supplies are available from craft and sewing supply stores. You can make your own tool holder for scissors, bobbins, and the like by drilling out a block of wood with the appropriate size holes, or cutting holes in a block of craft foam.

BOBBIN THREADER – Bobbin threaders are made to help pull the thread through the bobbin tube. Some are a stiff looped wire; others are straight pins with small hooks on the end. In time, most bobbins get clogged with wax from the thread, making these a great help when changing threads.

BOBBIN CLEANER – Bobbin cleaners are nothing more than a rod by which to push accumulated wax out of a bobbin tube. They are available commercially, but a short length of heavy mono from a Weed Whacker tool works fine for this also.

HAIR STACKER – These are sometimes called hair eveners, which is perhaps a more descriptive term. These are used to stack hair by the tip end to make it even. Stackers come in several different styles, but most include a flared open tube that fits into a capped butt section. In use, add the hairs tip end down into the stacker, pound the closed end of the stacker several times on the bench, and then hold the stacker sideways to pull out the open tube with the hairs made even. Stackers come in several different diameters. Large ones are best for the larger warmwater patterns you will be tying.

HAIR PACKERS – Hair packers are designed to pack hair tightly when making hair-bodied flies. Prime examples would be deer-hair bugs for warmwater fishing. These push the wrapped hair towards the back of the hook shank to get maximum density to the body. TIP – One simple tool available from a hardware store is a fender washer. These are small hole/large diameter washers that are easy to hold and pack hair. Pick sizes with small holes that will just fit over the hook eye.

WHIP FINISHER – Whip finishers are mechanical tools that allow easy rotation of the thread around the head of the fly when making the whip finish to tie off the fly. There are several different principles of use involved, depending on the brand that you purchase. All work well. Some allow positioning a whip finish only at the head of the fly, while the well-known Matarelli allows placing a whip finish anywhere on the fly. This is particularly helpful with warmwater flies where you can make a whip finish in back of a cork, balsa, or foam bug body. An alternative to this is to learn to make a whip finish with your fingers, which is not difficult to do with the larger patterns usually tied for warmwater fishing.

COMB – Fine-tooth combs are a must for removing the underfur from wing material such as deer hair, bucktail, and other fur where you want only the long guard hairs. You can use any small comb. Those used for combing mustaches and used by women for eyelashes and eyebrows are ideal.

DUBBING TEASER – These are designed to slightly fray dubbing materials to make the body of a fly – usually a nymph – more suggestive of the natural insect. Most available commercially are similar to the small wire rasps used by dentists for root canal work. TIP - You can make your own using a Popsicle stick to which is glued a section of the hook side of hook-and-loop (Velcro) fastener material.

DUBBING SPINNER – One way to add dubbing to a fly is to bind it into a spun thread loop before wrapping it around the hook shank to form the body. Dubbing spinners allow twisting the thread loop to accomplish this. The same thing can be done with hackle pliers or the similar electronic grips or weighted heat sinks. Dubbing twisters come in simple hook style (like an open screw eye on a weighted handle) or wire loop style that holds the thread loop slightly open.

FLY TURNER – If tying streamer flies or other large patterns for warmwater fishing, an epoxy finish on the head will often be quicker to add than multiple coats of head cement or clear nail polish. It is also more durable. For this, you will need a slow-turning motor mounted with a foam disk or cylinder to hold the completed flies. Turning the fly this way will keep the thick epoxy from sagging and dripping. Some tyers make their own, but they are available commercially from most fly shops and material supply catalogs.

MATERIAL CLIPS – Material clips sometimes come with fly vises, but are available separately. They consist of a small spring collar that fits around the vise sleeve to hold long materials out of the way of the tying operation.

MATERIAL DISPENSERS – Material dispensers come in two different styles. One is a compartmented plastic box (like a lure or fly box) with holes in the bottom of each compartment through which dubbing can be pulled.

The second type of dispenser is for spooled materials. For this, the Spirit River All Around dispenser is ideal, since it comes with six spools that fit into a compartmented, locking-lid box that has a slot for pulling out each of the spooled materials. They also make other dispensers and racks for dubbing, lead eyes, or hooks and the like.

WASTE CONTAINERS – Waste containers that clamp onto the fly-tying bench at the vise are designed to catch any waste that falls from the vise. They are handy and keep the floor clean when using a clamp-style vise. They generally aren't needed when using a pedestal-style vise

FLY-TYING BENCHES, DESKS, LAPTOP ORGANIZERS, AND CARRYING CASES – Many companies make fly-tying work areas and carrying cases in a variety of styles and price ranges. I use a specialized tying bag that holds all (well, most) of the fly-tying tools and materials that I need on the road for shows and club meetings. It is the Scientific Anglers, J. W. Outfitters model TOTL Tying Bag. A portable unit like this is ideal when you might wish to tie up new or replacement patterns in a motel room while on a fishing trip.

RAZOR BLADES – Razor blades are useful for trimming and shaping cork, foam, and balsa, and also for trimming deer hair in hair-bodied bugs. The best for trimming hard body materials are the single-edge style, available in industrial packs of 100. The thinner metal and sharper taper in double-edge blades makes them preferable for trimming deer-hair bodies. TIP – One way to protect yourself from cuts when using double-edge blades is to carefully break them in half and then tape the broken edge with masking or electrical tape.

HACKSAW BLADES – A fine-tooth hacksaw blade is best for slotting the belly of a cork or balsa bug for inserting the hook shank. Use 24- or 32-tooth blades for this. TIP – To make a wider slot for inserting hooks wrapped with coarse thread or chenille, use two or more hacksaw blades taped together, alternating the tooth direction.

AWL – Awls are nothing more than thicker bodkins, but are ideal for making the pilot hole through the belly of a foam bug body for inserting and gluing the hook. If you have, or have made, a bodkin with a thick enough shaft, that will do fine also. TIP – To make an awl for this purpose, drill a small hole in the end of a 4-inch length of wood dowel and glue in a thick yarn needle, eye first.

PAINT BRUSHES – Cork and balsa (and some foam) bug bodies are painted. For this, you will need paint brushes. To avoid clean up, I like to use disposable brushes. The best and cheapest that I have found come in bulk packs from Flex Coat.

DRYING RACK – Drying racks are a must for bug bodies that have been painted. They are available commercially, or can be made of wires or bead chain strung horizontally on a framed support. The bead chain will prevent the bug bodies from sliding together and sticking while the paint cures.

FOAM AND CORK/BALSA CYLINDER CUTTERS – Cork and foam cylinder cutters are similar in that they both cut cylinders from the material. Both are basically brass or steel tubes, sharpened on one end, to cut through the foam, balsa or cork. Those for balsa must be hammered through; those for cork and foam can be pushed through by hand. They are available commercially, or can be made.

OTHER TOOLS – There are tools for folding hackle for making wet flies, for making dubbing brushes for nymphs, plug cutters for making foam cylinders for trout terrestrial bodies, wing cutters, vision magnifiers, dubbing blenders, bobbin rests, tweezers, etc. More tools are being developed all the time.

Chapter 2

Fly Tying Materials

Some of the many materials used in tying warmwater flies. Left to right, and top to bottom: spools of thread, hanks of yarn, spools of floss, cards of chenille, dubbing, dispenser, cards of dubbing and saddle hackle. Second row: stranded flash, marabou, deer body hair, foam sheets, zonker strips foam cylinders, and peacock herl. Third row: bucktails, synthetic wing material (Super Hair), turkey feather, spools of tinsel, blocks and sheets of balsa, chenille, paints, bead chain and lead eyes, cork bodies and cylinders.

While the tools are necessary to tie flies, it is the combination of hook, thread, and other materials that make the fly come to life. Today, there is a vast assortment of materials available and by the time this book is published, there will undoubtedly be more on the market.

HOOKS – Fly-tying hooks are available from great companies such as Mustad, Eagle Claw, Dai-Riki, Daiichi, Tiemco, Gamakatsu, Partridge, VMC, and others. For warmwater flies, the range and style of the hooks will vary greatly. For example, you might use a size 14 dry fly hook for a cottonwood seed pattern for carp, but a long-shank 4/0 extra heavy hook for a large pike fly. In addition, you might use standard hooks for small flies, but some of the larger, extreme bend "stinger" hooks for hair-bodied bass flies. While these would be straight-shank hooks, hard-bodied bugs of cork and balsa require kinked or hump shank hooks. The name refers to a bend in the center of the shank, which while slightly different with several hook styles, is basically designed to help prevent the body from rotating on the hook shank. Thus, fly hooks for the broad range of species covered here would include everything from about a size 14 through a 5/0.

For cork and balsa surface bugs, hump-shank hooks will be necessary. Several hook companies make these, but it is important to choose a hook that has a long shank for maximum hooking ability. I like a Mustad 33903 that is available in sizes 12 through 1/0. In all cases, the diameter of the bug used should match the hook gap for maximum hooking ability.

While the "standard" size of each type and brand of hook varies, most hooks come in a regular-length shank for most warmwater flies and longer shank lengths for longer-bodied flies and streamer flies. The system for calculating wire size and length is based on an "X" system in which 1X is the equivalent of the next size hook, even if the next size (an odd number) is not be made. Thus, a 2X long-shank size 4 hook would have the shank length of a size 2 hook of the same style. The same measurement system would apply to short, stout, and fine-wire hooks, although these nuances are generally not used in warmwater flies. Bends on hooks vary, with the Model Perfect (round bend) often the best for the maximum strength of the bend. The even bend also makes it best if tying flies in which a bead is threaded onto the hook shank. The extreme-bend stinger hooks are also becoming more popular, particularly for their better hooking ability with surface bugs. They provide maximum gap for hair-bodied and hard-bodied bugs. Most hooks for warmwater fly-fishing have straight shanks. Hooks also have straight, turned-

Below is a list of suggested hook sizes for many of the species covered in this book. Note that these sizes might have to be adjusted larger or smaller, depending upon the game available to you. Some fish – such as catfish and buffalo – get very large and could require larger hooks.

SPECIES	HOOK SIZE
Bass, largemouth	6 to 2/0
Bass, smallmouth	12 to 1
Bass, white	10 to 1
Bass, yellow	12 to 2
Bass, inland striper	2 to 4/0
Bass, rock	8 to 4
Bluegill	14 to 8
Bowfin	1 to 2/0
Buffalo, bigmouth	1 to 4/0
Buffalo, smallmouth	1 to 4/0
Bullhead	10 to 6
Carp	14 to 1
Catfish, white	2 to 3/0
Catfish, flathead	2 to 3/0
Catfish, channel	2 to 3/0
Crappie (white and black)	10 to 4
Drum (freshwater)	10 to 2/0
Gar (all varieties)	1 to 4/0
Muskie	1 to 5/0
Muskie, tiger	1 to 4/0
Perch, white	10 to 6
Perch, yellow	8 to 2
Pickerel (chain and redfin)	4 to 1/0
Pike	1 to 4/0
Pumpkinseed	12 to 8
Redhorse (and other suckers)	10 to 2
Sauger	8 to 1
Shad and herring	10 to 4
Sunfish (green, redear, redbreast, etc.)	14 to 8
Walleye	4 to 1/0
Warmouth	12 to 6

up, and turned-down eyes, with straight and turned down the most commonly used for warmwater flies. If you like to tie on your flies with a Turle knot, you must have a turned-up or turned-down eye for the leader to align with the hook.

Consider stainless steel hooks for some of your fly-tying. Some species, such as largemouth bass, white perch, yellow perch, catfish, stripers, and even pike live in brackish water where flies are more susceptible to corrosion. Tying a fly on a stainless steel hook, and washing it well in fresh water after fishing it, will insure that the fly and the hook will last longer and look better.

THREAD – There are a number of thread companies making a wide range of thread types in an almost unlimited range of colors and many sizes. As a general rule it is best to use the color thread called for in the pattern, or a color that will complement the fly if you are designing your own.

It is also best to use the finest thread possible for the fly being tied. "Letter" size threads (A, C, D, and E) are used for rod building while the number threads 1/0, 2/0, 3/0 up to

10/0 and rarely 15/0 are common for fly-tying. Most warmwater flies are tied using size 3/0 for large flies and hair-wing/hair-body flies, with 6/0 a standard size for most small patterns such as those used for panfish and perch. Some very large patterns might be tied using 1/0 thread.

WAX – Wax is used on thread to help capture dubbing when working with a single thread or dubbing loop. Much thread comes waxed, but more wax is necessary when making dubbing. Waxes vary widely from hard to soft, with most fly tyers developing a brand loyalty. Avoid the very hard waxes or those that are very soft and sticky.

SEALERS – Commonly called head cement when applied to the head of the fly – sealers are designed to prevent the thread wrap from unraveling and to preserve the life of the fly. Many types are available in both petroleum and non-toxic solvent bases. Most are clear, but colors are available. Standard head cement is usually solvent-based, but companies such as Loon Outdoors make environmentally safe finishes. Many fly tyers use nail polish; specifically, clear Sally Hansen Hard as Nails finish. It dries hard and protects well.

In addition to these sealers, some fly tyers use epoxy on larger flies. While there is no exact formula as to when to use each product, generally use epoxy on those flies larger than about size 4, or which have a clean head to which epoxy can be easily applied. Epoxy is also ideal for protecting plastic, sequin, or self-stick eyes when they are added to fly heads. Most epoxies turn yellow over time. Consider this before sealing flies with epoxy, or tie seasonally so that you are

constantly restoring your box with new flies.

FLOSS – Floss is available in silk or synthetics and is nothing more than a bundle of fine strands of material. It comes in several sizes and many colors. It does require care to work with properly so that the fine strands do not frizz out. It also requires smooth fingers so as to not catch on rough skin. Some fly tyers keep a pumice stone to smooth their fingers before working with such materials.

YARN – Yarn comes in natural or synthetics and in different diameters and many colors. With its frizzy, fuzzy look, yarn can be tightly wrapped to make a hard body, or untwisted slightly to make a looser wrap with a buggier look. Polypropylene yarn in clear, white, and light colors can be used for bodies and, if necessary, colored with permanent felt-tip pens. Leech Yarn and mohair have long fibers that will make for a very buggy appearance when tying nymphs and some wet flies. Since all yarns absorb water, they are used primarily for wet flies and nymphs.

CHENILLE – From the French word for caterpillar, chenille is a velvety, tufted material of short strands twisted around a central core for use as body material. There are several varieties, but the stiffer grade usually called Ultra Chenille or Vernille is best reserved for trout flies.

DUBBING – Traditionally, dubbing is any material that can be wrapped onto a waxed thread that is then wound around the hook shank to make a fly body. It is less used in warmwater flies than in trout flies, and for warmwater would be primarily used for making nymphs and wet flies for smallmouth and panfish. It can be synthetic or natural materials, or a mix of both. Whether natural or synthetic, it is almost always fine. Some fur has long guard hairs that can be left in or combed out, depending upon the desired buggy/leggy look of the fly body. Some newer synthetic "dubbing" material is stranded and is designed to be used more as a yarn and wrapped on rather than cut, teased, and spun onto waxed thread for wrapping.

HACKLE – WET AND DRY – The term hackle refers to the feathers from the neck, cape, and throat of a rooster. Roosters provide the best dry fly hackle since it has very little webbing (which will absorb water). "Webbing" is the mesh of

fine barbules between the fibers that helps to lock them together. Hen hackle has more and wider web on each hackle feather, is softer, soaks up water better, and is the hackle of choice for tying wet flies, some soft-hackle wet flies, and nymphs. Holding hackle to the light readily shows the amount and location of the webbing.

Hackles are sold loose or on a neck or half neck. A neck will have a range of hackle sizes, from small hackles at the upper end (toward the head of the bird) for tying tiny flies to successively larger hackle for larger flies. Saddle hackle is a longer hackle, generally from the back or cape of the bird and is typically used for making streamer wings on warmwater and saltwater streamers.

OTHER FEATHERS – Feathers from partridge, grouse, woodcock, and other game birds (also domesticated guinea hens) are also used for hackle, particularly when tying soft-hackle, sparsely tied wet flies.

Duck and goose wings are commonly used, taking a matching feather (quill) from each wing and then cutting an identical section from each quill to make the matched (right and left) wings used on many wet flies. They can be used natural, or obtained in dyed colors. Turkey is used to make wings similar to duck quill wings along with tent-like wings when tying caddis, stonefly or hopper imitations.

STRANDED FLASH MATERIALS – Stranded flash materials include an ever-increasing range of fibers such as Flashabou, Krystal Flash, Crystal Splash, Tie Well, Flash in a Tube, and others. They are mostly plastic strands, available in a wide range of colors and occasionally twisted for more body, action and flash.

STRANDED WING MATERIALS – Materials such as Super Hair, Ultra Hair, Aqua Fiber, Unique, Poly Bear, FisHair and others are used widely for warmwater flies. Any of these can be used in place of natural bucktail or other furs.

TINSELS, WRAPPED FLASH MATERIALS, AND WIRE – In the past, only metallic tinsels were available, usually in flat, round, and oval, in gold or silver, each in several sizes. Today a much wider range of flat plastic and Mylar "tinsels" is available. The plastics will not tarnish as will metallic tinsels, but they are also a little more likely to be cut by the fine teeth of a fish. All types of tinsel are used for fly bodies and also for body ribbing.

Metallic wire is also available in a wide range of diameters and colors. In large sizes, they have the advantage of adding weight to nymphs and wet flies, and in all flies will make a body material (for weight) or a body ribbing.

LEAD WIRE – Lead is available in diameters from about 0.010 to 0.035 inches. It is used to weight streamers and nymphs, usually by wrapping around the body, but sometimes in straight lengths, laid along the hook shank and wrapped in place. More and more companies and tyers are also going to lead substitutes, since California, through the restrictive Proposition 65, prohibits lead and a number of other materials in products sold in the state. Body material always covers lead wire, since its only function is to help the fly get deep.

FURS – Rabbit fur is widely used, often available as thin "Zonker strips" for making Zonker flies. It comes in dyed colors for any application. Many other furs can be used in fly-tying, but seem to be less used today than in the past. Typically the specific furs are used for only certain patterns or for just one part of a fly. Often they are used for dubbing

only, or mixed with other furs for a dubbed body. These are in addition to the seal, opossum, Angora goat, and buffalo that are used primarily for dubbing material.

HAIR FOR WINGS – Bucktail is typically used for the wings of bucktail-style streamers and for the tails and legs of many hard-bodied and hair-bodied bugs. Bucktail is just what it says, the tail of a deer. It can be used natural, using the brown or white fur from the tail, or it can be dyed. It makes for a nice, streamlined streamer in which one color can be used, or in which stacked colors can be used as with the popular Mickey Finn. Calf tail is also a popular wing material for some smaller panfish flies. Bear is sometimes used when available, although the popular polar bear, favored for the translucency of the fur, is now prohibited for importation or sale. Squirrel is used for small dark-wing streamer flies.

BODY HAIR – Body hair is hollow hair from the bodies of deer, elk, antelope, moose and caribou. Deer, antelope, and elk are most often used for tying the many hair-bodied flies used for bass, pike and other patterns. The hair varies widely in length, color, texture and coarseness, with moose mane very long and coarse and coastal deer hair short and fine. Hair choice is important for the size and style of fly being tied.

LEAD, NON-LEAD, PRISM, AND OTHER EYES – While the terms dumbbell and hourglass are sometimes used interchangeably, there are differences. Dumbbell eyes are shaped like a miniature dumbbell and thus sometimes

difficult to center exactly on a hook shank. Hourglass eyes, shaped like the namesake, self-center on the hook. They are available in lead, lead substitute, chromed, brass, and other finishes, as well as painted and with painted pupils.

Prism eyes can be placed on the head of any streamer fly or baitfish pattern (they must be coated with head cement or epoxy to stay on), small ball-monofilament eyes for nymphs are available, as well as bead-chain eyes as a lighter-weight substitute for lead hourglass eyes on streamers and the Clouser Deep Minnow.

MARABOU, CHICKABOU – Marabou, originally from the African marabou stork and now available from turkey feathers, is very soft and has a lot of action in the water. If used in the wing of a fly, it mats down, but on a pause, will fluff out or blossom to attract fish. It is used in simple streamers and also in dark colors as the tail of Woolly Buggers. A similar more recent material is Chickabou, soft chicken hen fibers that have action in the water similar to that of marabou.

PEACOCK HERL, OSTRICH, AND EMU – Fish seem to like flies made with peacock herl. Some panfish patterns (and many trout patterns) include these materials, but they can also be used in tying bodies on streamers, heads on nymphs, and as topping for the wings of typical streamer flies.

VINYL/PLASTIC BODY MATERIAL AND RIBBING – Larva Lace is just one of many plastic body materials that can be used for fly-tying. Larva Lace is very thin, colored translucent tubing that can be stretched and wrapped around

a hook shank to make a life-like segmented body. A similar flat (really half round) material also works well as a tough plastic ribbing on flies. Some tyers use thin strips of latex for the same purpose when tying nymphs. When tying large warmwater flies, the thicker plastic lacing available from craft stores can be used the same way.

RUBBER/SILICONE LEGS – Flexible, synthetic legs are used when tying bass and panfish flies. They can also be used as legs and additional attraction when tying terrestrials such as hoppers, crickets, beetles, etc.

BODY TUBING – Body tubing consists of braided plastic materials such as Corsair and E-Z Body. The tubing comes in many diameters and several colors. It is ideal for making baitfish-like bodies for streamer flies by slipping it in place over the hook and tying off at both ends.

MYLAR TUBING – Mylar tubing is shiny, thin-walled, braided tubing that is also used for making streamer bodies and is available in several sizes. It is sold with a core that must be pulled out before use. The most common use for this is when tying bodies for Zonkers and Matukas.

FOAM – Both closed-cell and open-cell foam are used in tying flies. Open-cell foam will absorb water and is commonly used as a body or underbody on some patterns. Closed-cell foam will not absorb water and is ideal for making floating terrestrials. It is available in a wide range of colors and styles. If using cylinders, always use a body no larger in diameter than the hook gap, with the hook close to one side of the cylinder to provide maximum hooking.

CORK AND BALSA BODIES – Hard-bodied bugs can be made of cork or balsa. These are available as plain or tapered cylinders, and shaped (bullet) and painted bodies. Several sizes are available to make poppers from about size 14 up through about 2/0. Balsa in shaped or rough bodies is less readily available. To make your own, buy blocks of balsa from a hobby shop, and cut or punch out the desired shape. As with any bug body, the cork or balsa should be no larger in diameter than the hook gap. The cork should be glued onto the hook with maximum hook gap clearance.

PAINTS – Acrylic-based paints are best. Some of these are designed for hard bodies, while others can be used on soft foam without risk of the paint cracking. Paints can be added to bugs by brushing, dipping, or spraying, and scale finishes can be added by spraying through a net cloth wrapped around the side of the body. In most cases, the best and truest colors are made over a base of several coats of white paint.

OTHER MATERIALS – There are a host of other materials available from fly shops and craft stores. One of the flies in this book is made from velvet tubing that is used in sewing and available from sewing shops. You might also want stainless steel pins (sewing stores) or stainless steel wire (hardware stores) for making bent kicker legs on frogs, lamb's wool floor polishing pads (hardware stores) for "Zonker" type tails, rattles (tackle shops), large plastic beads (craft stores) for making large eyes/heads on large flies, etc. Be open to ideas wherever you shop and look for materials that can be substituted or used to develop a new fly or new design.

Chapter 3

Fly Tying Methods

The assumption is that the fly tyer is right-handed and will have the jaws of the vise facing the right. Where right or left hands are mentioned, it is based on this premise. These methods are not the only ways to accomplish what is needed. They are among many proven methods that work well and which allow the creation of good-looking, effective flies. For encyclopedic information on the many ways of working with fly-tying materials and accomplishing fly-tying tasks, check out the excellent 444-page book, The Fly Tier's Benchside Reference To Techniques And Dressing Styles, *by Ted Leeson and Jim Schollmeyer.*

ORDER OF TYING – Many beginners don't think of an order of tying – they just start by tying the thread onto the hook. This is a mistake. Where and how you start, and in which order you place the materials, can make a big difference in the appearance of the completed fly and the ease with which it is tied. The recipes for our 100 top patterns will contain a suggested order of tying. Some general suggestions are as follows:

Surface hair-bodied bugs – These are best started at the rear, tying down the tail or legs, then adding the spun or stacked body hair to build up the body going towards the hook eye. In this, the body hair is tied down over the wrap of the tail or legs to hide it, and then the thread is used to secure and spin or stack the hollow body hair. Since this is done by adding a small bundle at a time, the thread can only be wrapped forward a little at a time – just enough to wrap down the next bundle of body hair. Near the head end, it may be necessary to add wings or rubber legs, which can be tied in before continuing with the body hair. Since this method requires careful trimming of the body hair later to avoid cutting the wings or legs, an alternative method is to finish the body, trim it, and then re-attach thread at the appropriate points to add the wings, rubber legs or other additions.

Surface hard-bodied bugs and foam bugs – These present a challenge with a combination of materials tied to the hook and a hard body glued in place. If you paint the body (already glued to the hook) first, then you have to do all tying around this body. If you add the body after tying the tail material, you can hide the tying wraps in the hard body, but must then paint the body. If a collar hackle is used, this requires making or using a sleeve to hold the collar out of the way to avoid getting paint on it. There is no right or wrong order to tying tails and gluing bodies. Go with the method you prefer. The easy way (and the way used by most bug manufacturers) is to glue the hook into the bug and paint the bug body, then tie on the tail and other materials.

When tying foam bugs (assuming that they are not to be painted – some paints are available that will work on the soft foam), the best method is to tie in all the tail materials first, then wrap the shank with coarse thread for the best glue bond. Make a hole with a large bodkin through the belly of the bug, slide it in place for a test fit, then add CA glue (cyanoacrylate glue) to the hook shank and slide the bug body onto the hook so that the body covers the hook shank and all the wraps securing the tail. Align the body with the hook quickly before the glue sets.

Streamers and bucktails – To make a simple streamer without a tail, tie the thread on at the head, add the tinsel or body material, and then wrap the body material down to the hook bend and back up again to tie off at the head. A body and ribbing can be handled the same way, or begun at the tail of the fly and wrapped forward. Add the wing or wing components, including any topping, followed by the throat. The wing may be two sets of saddle hackles (streamer) or a bucktail wing (single or stacked bucktail colors). After trimming, complete the head and tie off the fly. A variation of this for streamers with a tail is to tie in at mid-shank, wrap thread to the rear to tie in the tail, and then tie in the body material and ribbing (if used). Wrap the thread forward, followed by the body material and ribbing. The remainder of the fly with wing, topping, and throat is completed as above.

Simple streamers are sometimes tied without a body and only a wing tied onto the head of the fly. In addition, some large streamers for bass and pike are tied with long tails and a simple body, and no standard wing tied in at the head of the fly.

Wet flies – Begin your wet fly by tying on at about the middle of the hook shank, then wrap the thread to just forward of the bend. Tie in any tail material, then tie in the ribbing/body material, wrap the thread forward, follow with the wrapped body and any ribbing, then tie them off. Tie in a hackle, wind it collar-style, and then tie in paired wings clipped from duck quills. Trim the excess and tie off at the head. An alternative to the full hackle is to tie in hackle or other throat fibers underneath the fly at the head and then finish as above.

Nymphs – Tie in at mid-shank, then wrap to the bend to tie in any tails. Tie in any ribbing and body material, and then wrap the thread 2/3rds up the hook shank. Then wrap up the body, followed by the ribbing. Tie off, and then tie in a section of quill (often turkey quill), followed by the stem of a short length of a game feather. Add more body material and wrap it forward to just in back of the hook eye. Wind the game feather forward and tie it down. At this point, the tips can be pulled under to make a beard hackle, or pulled to the side to make legs or a semblance of gills. Follow by folding over the quill to make the wing casing. Trim and tie off to complete the fly. This is just one example of a nymph, since others may include a bead head, or a simple tie of tail, body material, legs, and wrapped head. Nymphs vary widely in patterns, designs, and tying styles.

Terrestrials – Beetles, ants, hoppers, and crickets are usually started in the middle of the hook shank. Following this, wrap back or forward to build up the body or to add the foam, deer hair, or other body materials with ants or beetles. For crickets and hoppers, tie on in back of the hook eye, then add the deer hair or foam for the body, then any turkey quill for wings, and any hackle to finish the fly. Some terrestrials, such as the McMurray ant, are tied completely in the middle to hold the previously prepared balsa or foam abdomen and thorax and the wound hackle.

Miscellaneous – Many miscellaneous flies require long tails with no traditional wings, folding of foam, and other materials, adding materials in non-traditional ways, gluing of materials, etc. The best way to consider an order of tying any fly or bug is to look at or visualize the finished product. Consider what must be tied on in which order for the tying method to progress easily and allow you to complete the fly properly. If there is a general rule, it would be to begin by tying on the thread in the middle of the hook shank, since this then makes it possible to wind to the head of the hook for tying down barbell eyes or securing previously-placed cones or beads, or winding to the rear of the hook shank for a smooth addition of a tail and securing one end of body materials and ribbing or palmered hackle. Most flies are tied by working from the rear of the fly to the head, finishing with a neat head of the working thread, which is then secured with a whip finish and sealed with head cement of epoxy.

TYING THREAD ONTO THE HOOK – Thread can be tied on at any point, but always involves the same method. For best results, hold the tag end of the thread in the left hand below the hook and the bobbin in the right hand above the hook. Make a few turns of the thread around the hook shank so that the wraps are parallel. Then make a few additional wraps around the hook shank in which the thread crosses over the previous wraps. It is this wrapping method, and the constant tension on the thread, that maintains the tight wrap. For a more secure wrap, add a little head cement to the hook shank before tying to prevent the thread and subsequent body materials from slipping.

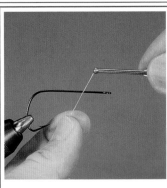

Step 1 – To tie the thread onto the hook, first hold the tag end and the bobbin (if used) over the top of the hook shank as shown.

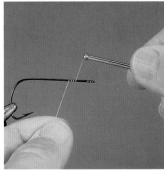

Step 2 – Then wrap the standing end of the thread (bobbin) around the hook shank two or more times. Gaps are shown here for clarity – normally the thread wraps would be tight.

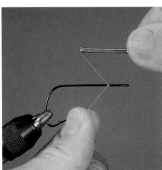

Step 3 – To lock the thread in place, wrap or wind over (cross over) the previous wraps with the thread as shown here.

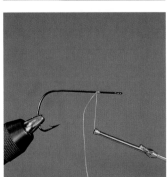

Step 4 – Pull the thread down and make several more winds of the thread to securely lock the thread in place on the hook shank.

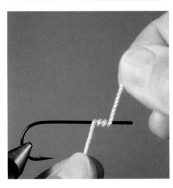

Close-up views – close-up of the initial thread winding shown here with heavy cord on a large hook.

Close-up views – Close-up as left, but here the thread has been crossed over the previous wraps to lock the thread and wrap in place on the hook shank. Shown with heavy cord and oversize hook.

USING THREAD AS RIBBING – If using thread as ribbing, make the tag end of the tie-down process several inches longer than normal and do not clip it. Then tie in the tail or tag followed by the body material or the addition of dubbing to the working thread. Then, after the body is wrapped in place, use this tag end for the ribbing to spiral wrap up the shank and over the body. Tie off this tag end with the working thread. In some cases, you may want to reverse the ribbing wrap (counterwrap) to help secure and protect the body material. Naturally, this technique of using thread for ribbing only works if the desired ribbing thread color is the same as the working thread.

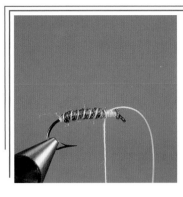

To use thread as a ribbing, leave a long tag end at the end of the hook when tying down and when tying on the body. Yarn is used here for the body. Then tie down the body and wind forward, then wrap the thread over the body in a spiral winding as shown here.

TYING BODIES – After tying in tail materials, begin a body by tying down the ribbing first (if applicable) then the body material, using a tag end of the body material as long as the hook shank. Then wrap the thread forward to the tie-off point, wrapping over the tag end of the body material. Wind the body material around the hook shank to the tie down point, and secure with two or more wraps of thread. Then follow with a spiral wrap of the ribbing to the tie-down point and secure the ribbing (if used). An alternative method is to start at the mid-point of the hook shank to build up more bulk there before wrapping to the tail and then back up to tie off with the thread. This works best with floss and dubbing; not as well with chenille except on very large flies. With the ribbing tied down at the rear of the fly, wrap it forward and tie off where the body ends.

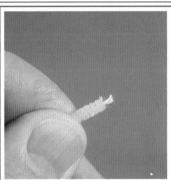

Step 1 – To tie in a body of chenille, first use the nails of your thumb and index finger to strip a little of the chenille from the central cork. This is not necessary when tying with other body materials such as yarn, floss, prepared spun fur, etc.

Step 2 – To tie in a chenille body, tie in the stripped end at the point just above the tie down spot for the tail (if included). Other materials are tied down the same way, but may have a long tag end to lie along the hook shank to provide a level base for the wrapped body.

Step 3 – To continue winding the body, wind the thread forward to the tie down point, them follow with the winding of chenille. Chenille is always wrapped so that the wraps do not overlap each other to make an even body as shown here.

Another way to wind a body is to wind the thread forward first and then tie down so that the body material can be wound down and then back up the hook shank. It is also possible to tie down the body material at about the midpoint of the hook shank (as shown here) to build up a tapered body that is thick in the middle and thin at both ends. Here, yarn is being used.

To complete the above, first wind the thread forward to the hook eye, then wind the yarn body down to the tail position, and then back up to hook eye to tie off the completed body.

TYING TAILS – Begin the thread wrap on the hook shank farther forward (where the body will cover it) and then wrap the thread to the tail area before adding the tail fibers. For best results, use the full length of tail material to cover the hook shank even if tying down only a short tail. This allows making properly a tapered body. Use the soft loop method outlined above for this. This keeps the tail straight and on top of the hook shank, rather than cocked to one side. It may be advantageous to add the body material and ribbing to the hook shank before adding the tail to get a smooth transition from the tail to the body and up the hook shank. For the same reason, do not clip the tail materials immediately forward of the tail tie-down point. Instead, clip them so they will extend forward and will be covered by the body.

To tie tails in place, leave enough of the tail forward of the tie down point that any subsequent body material will have a level base for tying. Failure to do this can result in a "stepped" appearance to the body, particularly when using thin materials such as tinsel or a thin floss body.

TYING RIBBING – Ribbing is spaced wraps of tinsel, wire, thread, or other material that adds flash or color to a body and/or simulates the segmented body of the fly. Tie down the tag end of the ribbing immediately after tying the tail in place, assuming a tail is added to the fly. Then tie the tag end of the body material down. This allows wrapping the body material forward (after wrapping the tying thread forward first) so that the ribbing follows naturally over and around the body from the first wrap. In some cases, the ribbing may fall into the spacing between the body material wrap. This can happen with chenille and some yarns. If you don't want this, an alternative is to wrap the ribbing in the opposite direction (counterwrap) so that the wrap is angled, rather than parallel to the body wrap. An alternative method of adding ribbing is to tie it in with the body material at the middle of the hook shank, then wrap the body over the ribbing to the rear of the fly before tapering and completing the body. Then spiral the ribbing forward over the body and tie off.

Step 1 – To tie in ribbing, first tie in the ribbing (metallic tinsel is being used here) and then tie down the body. Here a chenille body is being tied down with the tag end the length of the hook shank to provide a level base for the body and ribbing.

Step 2 – Before working with the ribbing, first wind the thread forward followed by the body material, which is then tied off.

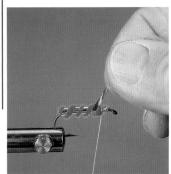

Step 3 – Grasp the ribbing and spiral wind it forward over the body to make a segmental appearance as shown.

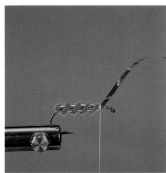

Step 4 – Once at the head of the fly, tie off the tinsel with the working thread and then clip any excess tinsel.

MAKING THE SOFT LOOP TO TIE MATERIALS IN POSITION

POSITION – What fly tyers typically call a soft loop is a method by which any material can be positioned properly on the hook. In warmwater flies, it is typically used to position tails, streamer wings, and throat hackle. It can also be used when stacking deer hair. It allows placing a material so that it will not slip to the side or become cocked or angled. Hold the material in place on top of the hook shank with the left hand using the thumb and index finger. Bring the thread straight up

with the right hand, pinch it with the left hand (thumb and finger), then bring it straight down on the far side of the hook before pulling tight. An easy way to do this is to rock your left index finger and thumb back and forth to open and close their grip on the material. Repeat several times. This keeps the material straight and on top of the hook shank, rather than cocked to one side. This method is important to master – and it is easy to master – to secure all types of materials.

Step 1 – Making a soft loop to properly position wing materials begins by holding the material (in this case, bucktail), and then bringing the thread straight up alongside the material as shown.

Step 2 – Roll the fingers forward to grasp the thread as shown here and secure both the wing material and the working thread.

Step 3 – Then bring the loose thread down on the far side of the hook shank and the material being tied in place.

Step 4 – Make one or two soft wraps like this, then pull the thread tight to secure the material as the bucktail wing is being secured here. Note that the bucktail is on top of the hook – not skewed to one side.

Step 5 – A top view of the above step shows that the material (bucktail) is in alignment with the hook and properly positioned.

Step 6 – A top view of the bucktail tied in place without using the soft loop. In these cases, the material (wing material – bucktail) will be pulled to one side and skewed out of line as shown here.

Step 7 – A side view of the bucktail tied in place without the soft loop shows the material pulled to one side of the hook.

TYING WET FLY THROAT HACKLE – A throat hackle is a small bundle tied in at the throat directly under the fly. In streamers it is often tied red to simulate gills. Length varies with the pattern, but it is generally shorter than the hook shank or at least does not extend beyond the hook point. There are two ways to tie in a throat since it is not wound around the hook shank as with traditional collar hackle. One way is to keep the hook in the basic fly-tying position and add the throat. To do this, pull the working thread down, and hold the throat material under the fly. Use the fingers of your left hand to pinch the thread, and then pull up straight on the thread to capture the throat with the thread loop. This step, identical to the soft loop method used on top of a fly hook to mount a streamer wing, is necessary to keep the throat straight and in line with the hook shank. Make a second identical wrap and then several final wraps. Trim the material in front of the thread wraps, and then complete the head of the fly, since adding a throat is often the last step in tying. A second method is to remove the hook from the vise and remount it hook point up. (A variation to this, with a rotary vise, is to rotate the vise 180 degrees to position the hook point up.) Then pull up the thread, position the throat material, and then pull down on the thread on the backside of the hook shank to capture the material.

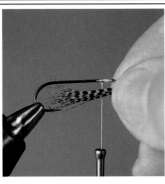

Step 1 – To tie a wet fly throat hackle, hold the hackle fibers in place under the hook shank as shown here.

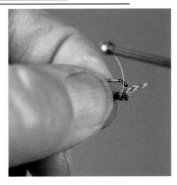

Step 2 – Make a soft loop to hold the hackle, but in this case make it down and then up to secure the throat hackle directly under the body and in line with the hook shank.

Step 3 – Use a fine-tip scissors to clip any forward excess fibers from the throat hackle as shown here, and then complete the rest of the fly or the head of the fly.

Another way to make a throat hackle is to turn the hook point up in the vise, or use a rotary vise to turn the hook 180 degrees. Then use the same method as above to attach the throat hackle, working from the top instead of underneath. This will be easier than working under the fly.

TYING WET FLY WINGS – Wet fly wings are usually tied on after the throat or collar hackle is added to the fly. Basically, the wings are the last material added before the fly is finished. Wet fly wings are tied facing the rear, the position they will have in the completed fly. Most often, wet fly wings are quill sections, and these can be tied in four different ways. Since the quill sections have a point to them, and since they have a curvature to each section, the wings can be tied point up or point down, and with the concave side of the quill flared out or facing each other. Most wet flies are tied with the wing tips or points down so the wing has a smooth curve to it, rather than a peaked, pointed look. Also, most are tied with the concave side flared out, to give the wing more body and lifelike appearance. Wings from hackle fibers are also possible. These are tied as a bundle placed on top of the fly and tied down to give the fly a winged appearance. Hackle fiber wings like this are not as noticeable as are quill wings, and give more of a nymph-like appearance to the fly. In tying down all of these wing styles, use the soft loop to secure and position the wing directly on top of the hook shank.

Step 1 – Tie in wet fly wings by holding the wing quills (most often used) over the head of the fly and securing with a soft loop method with the thread.

Step 2 – Finish the wings by clipping the excess wing quill in front of the working thread.

TYING OFF – WHIP FINISH – The technique of tying off with a whip finish is no different than the method used to make a whip finish on the end of a rope. To make a whip finish, make a large loop with your index and middle fingers, and then lay the working thread parallel to the hook shank. Use the loop to make wraps with your fingers around the head and the working thread. After four or more turns, pull the working thread to draw the loop tight against the head and complete the whip finish. TIP – Use a bodkin to hold the loop while drawing it up to keep the thread from twisting. Twisting may make it impossible to pull all of the thread under the whip finish wraps. It is also possible to use one of the several brands of whip finishers to accomplish the whip finish. For this, follow the directions included with these tools.

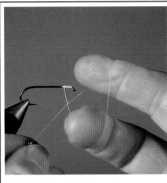

Step 1 – To tie off with a whip finish, make a large loop with the thread and then fold it over with your fingers as shown here.

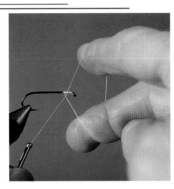

Step 2 – Continue to make the whip finish as above, and rotate your hand to place the pads of your fingers away from you so that one finger can rotate the loop of thread around the hook shank.

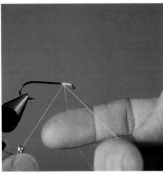

Step 3 – Bring the thread up and over the hook shank and then back to the original position of the thread loop as shown. Repeat several times to make a secure whip finish.

Step 4 – Make a number of these turns or wraps (four to six) and then use a bodkin to hold the loop and pull it up tightly to the head of the fly. Using a bodkin prevents the thread in the loop from twisting and tangling.

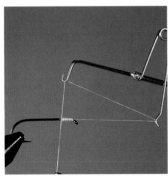

It is also possible to use a whip finish tool to make the whip finish. Several styles are available, but all come with instructions for their proper use. They work well.

SEALING THE HEAD – HEAD CEMENT – To keep the fly head and whip finish from unraveling, a coating of cement is a must. Many sealers (called head cements) are available. For small panfish flies, use a bodkin to apply a small drop to the head of the fly. Make sure that the liquid cement is distributed evenly over the fly head without touching the rest of the fly or the hackle. Larger heads on streamer flies can be coated with a small brush, such as is available with nail polish bottles. Many anglers use clear nail polish for coating fly heads, with Sally Hansen Hard As Nails a favorite. Note that with any sealer, multiple coats are necessary.

To seal the head to protect it, use head cement or fingernail polish. Dip a bodkin into the head cement or nail polish as shown and carefully apply a drop to the wrapped head of the fly as shown here.

TYING OFF – HALF-HITCHES – Half-hitches are just what they sound like and just what they look like in any knot book. They are a loop taken around the head of the fly with the loop capturing one strand of the standing thread. To make a half-hitch, maintain tension on the thread and loop it around the half-hitch tool. Then place the tool on the eye of the hook, and slide the loop off of the tapered end of the tool and onto the fly head. It is possible to tie one without a half hitch tool by maintaining tension on the thread wrapped around the hook, folding a loop in the thread and positioning it on the head of the fly. This method also makes it possible to add a half-hitch anywhere on the fly as an added security lock after each material is added. A final alternative is to make several loops with the thread around the half-hitch tool before pulling it all tight. If doing this, the basic result is the same as a whip finish, although it may not pull up quite as nicely.

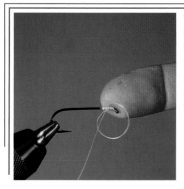

To make a half-hitch around the hook shank, fold the thread over as for the whip finish, but do not wrap it around hook shank. Instead, position the loop over the hook shank as shown and pull the thread to secure this locking knot.

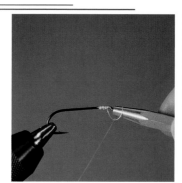

It is also possible to make a half-hitch in the end of a fly (around the fly head) using a half-hitch tool. These are shaped like the end of a pencil, but with a hole in the end to fit over the hook eye. They come in various sizes to fit all hook eye sizes.

PALMERING HACKLE – Palmered hackle is tied on at the rear of the fly and then spiral-wrapped forward over the body to give it a buggy, leggy appearance. The technique is characteristic of a Woolly Bugger and Woolly Worm. After tying on the tail of the fly, tie down a hackle by the tip in which the fibers have been splayed out at right angles to the main stem. Next, tie down the fly body and wrap the thread, then the body forward. Secure the body material with thread. At this point, use hackle pliers to grip the end of the palmering hackle and spiral-wrap it forward over the body, tying off at the head or with sufficient space to add any additional materials required by the pattern being tied. If not using rotary pliers, you will have to rotate the hackle pliers once with each turn to prevent the hackle from twisting. If wrapping over chenille, as with a Woolly Bugger, it helps to use the same spiral wrap as used for the chenille so that the palmered hackle can follow in the spaces between the chenille wraps to help protect the hackle. It is also possible to reinforce palmered hackle by first adding a length of thread and then counter wrapping with this thread over the palmered hackle and tying off at the head of the fly.

Step 1 – To palmer a fly (spiral wrap the hackle around the body – standard for flies like the Woolly Bugger), first tie in the hackle to be used, followed by the body as shown here.

Step 2 – Wrap the thread forward to the tie off point, followed by the body wrap. Here, chenille is used for the body.

Step 3 – Begin to palmer the hackle around the body by spiral wrapping the hackle around and over the body material, leaving the body material to show through the spiral wraps of the hackle.

Step 4 – Palmer the hackle up to the tie off point and tie off with the working thread. Clip any excess hackle and then continue or finish the rest of the fly.

SEALING THE HEAD – EPOXY – Larger heads on streamer flies, bass flies, pike flies, and such are best sealed with epoxy. This is not recommended for small flies, since epoxy is thick and may cover the hook eye, or mat the hackle. Any good clear epoxy will work, but most epoxies turn amber in time. First measure and mix the proper amounts of resin and hardener. Mix until you can no longer see the swirls of the two different liquids in the batch. Use a bodkin and carefully coat all parts of the head without touching the hook eye or soiling the materials with epoxy. Once coated, rotate the fly until the epoxy cures. This will prevent sagging. Most fly tyers use five-minute epoxy. The advantage of using epoxy is that only one coat is necessary.

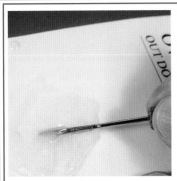

Step 1 – To use epoxy to seal the head of large flies, first thoroughly mix the two parts of a five-minute two-part epoxy using a bodkin as shown here. Measure and mix thoroughly to assure a good seal and curing or the epoxy.

Step 2 – Use a bodkin to apply a drop evenly to all parts of the fly head as shown, saturating and soaking the head without getting any epoxy on the body or wing materials.

Step 3 – To keep the epoxy on the head of the fly from sagging and curing unevenly, place the fly on a fly rotator (this one from Flex Coat) and rotate the fly closely until the epoxy is cured.

STACKING (EVENING) HAIR BUNDLES – Evening the tip ends of most fur will make for a better appearance of the fly. This is especially important in streamer wings and tails, but also helpful when gathering body hair for making clipped, hair-bodied flies. First remove the underfur as above. Then place the hair, tip down, into a hair stacker. Bang the hair evener hard several times on the bench. Carefully remove the hair from the stacker, check to make sure that the ends are even enough, and then tie in place as required. Another way to do this if you do not have a stacker is to hold the bundle by the cut base, then grab the long ends and pull them free. Relax your grip on the bundle and lay the long hairs on top, with the ends even with the bundle. Repeat this several times until the tips are even enough for your use. Add a little talcum powder to the hair to make it slide and stack more easily.

Step 3 – Here, a stacker is used to even the bucktail. The bucktail has been placed tips down in the stacker and then the stacker pounded on a table to shake all of the tips to an even length.

Step 4 – Once the tips are even, remove the bottom cup of the stacker to expose the even tips. Grasp the wing by the tip ends and remove from the stacker. If the tips are not sufficiently even, reassemble the stacker and even the tips some more before removing to tie onto the fly.

REMOVING UNDERFUR – Most fur has fuzzy, finer, shorter underfur which you must remove. To do this, clip the fur very close to the skin. Then use a small comb (moustache comb, eyelash comb or fly-tying combs sold for the purpose) to comb out all the underfur. Comb several times, turning the fur each time and repositioning the comb to get rid of all the underfur. The removed underfur can be used for dubbing.

HANDLING PEACOCK HERL FOR BODIES – Because peacock herl is a natural material that comes in 5- to 6-inch lengths, it is handled a little differently than other body materials. On some small flies, one strand of peacock herl is sufficient. On larger flies, or on streamer flies tied on long-shank hooks, more peacock herl will be required. You can tie in two to four strands of the herl, then wrap all the strands at once, with each wrap covering more of the hook shank than would one individual strand. Or you can use one strand, wrap and tie off, then tie in a second to wrap, then a third, etc., until reaching the final tie-off point. For this, the thread can only be advanced to the tie off/tie down point of the herl, thus requiring working on the body in segments. Another method is to use two or more strands and twist them with the working thread to create a reinforcing strand through the herl. If not doing this, it helps to use a ribbing or a long tag end of thread to counter wrap (wrap opposite to the normal fly-tying wrap) around the body and tie off at the forward end of the body.

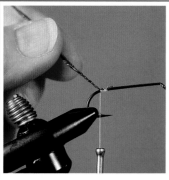

Step 1 – To make a peacock herl body, tie in a single strand of peacock herl at the end of the hook shank as shown. Wrap the thread forward part way on the hook shank for tying down the peacock herl later.

Step 2 – Wrap the peacock herl to the end (or until it is too short to comfortably hold any more) and then tie down with the previously wrapped thread.

Step 3 – At this point, tie off the peacock herl and add a second strand, then wrap the thread forward. Continue this way, a strand at a time, to cover the hook shank and complete the body.

An alternate method of wrapping a peacock herl body is to tie in two to four or more strands (four are used here) of peacock and then wrap them together forward after winding the thread forward over the hook shank and to the tie down point.

Here, the four strands of peacock herl are being wrapped up the hook shank to more rapidly cover the hook shank and form a body. Twist the peacock herl with the working thread and wrap the two together. In this, the working thread in the center of the peacock herl strands will reinforce the delicate peacock herl and make for a tougher fly – particularly good for panfish.

TYING WET FLY COLLAR HACKLE – Wet fly collar hackle is wound completely around the hook shank. Tie in the hackle in front of the body and then use hackle pliers to wind the hackle several times around the hook shank at the same point. Tie off with the working thread, and clip the excess hackle. Use the fingers of your left hand to fold and flare back the hackle, then wrap around the forward part of this with the thread to keep the hackle flared towards the rear. A second way is to fold the hackle over itself along the center quill. Then tie down the butt end of the folded hackle. With the hackle fibers facing to the rear, use hackle pliers to wind the hackle around the hook shank, and then tie off and finish as above. With most wet flies, wings are added on top of the hackle after this step.

Step 1 – To tie in a wet fly collar hackle, tie in by first securing the butt or tip end of the hackle feather chosen for the hackle.

Step 2 – Then wind the hackle around the hook shank, using hackle pliers to hold the end of the hackle.

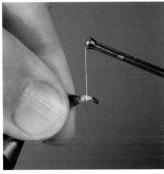

Step 3 – Use your thumb and fore finger to pull back the hackle and hold it in place while winding the thread in front of the hackle to help flare it into a rear-angled position.

Step 4 – If wings are not added (some wet flies, panfish flies and nymphs lack them), you can finish the fly with a whip finish as shown here. The whip finish has been made and the bodkin is holding the loop open while the loop is being pulled tight.

SPINNING DEER HAIR – Basic spinning requires hollow body hair (deer, antelope, caribou) that will spin around the hook shank when wrapped with the tying thread to form a 360-degree flare that, when clipped, becomes the body or head. Begin by tying on the thread, then pick, clip, comb and, if necessary, even (stack) a small bundle of hair. Hold it at an angle on top of the hook shank, then make a soft loop of thread straight up and then straight down on the backside of the hook. Pull the thread gently and then make a second wrap of thread like the first while still holding the bundle of deer hair. Gradually pull the thread tight while beginning a third wrap of thread around the bundle. This will spin (rotate) the body hair around the hook shank and flare it at right angles at the same time. Make one or two more wraps, then use a hair packer to push the hair together and tight before repeating the process again immediately in front of the first bundle. To pack the hair, take care to hold the fly at the rear of the hook shank with your left hand, while pushing on the hair bundle at the hook shank with the right hand. Otherwise, the hook may bend or slip out of the vise, or you may push the body hair around the bend of the hook. Bring the thread forward to just in front of the packed hair to add a second bundle. Continue this way to fill up the hook shank. The result will be a hook shank fully covered with flared body hair. Once all the deer hair is in place, tie off with a half-hitch or two. Trim the deer hair before adding additional materials such as wings or hackle. Trim the fly with scissors and make any final adjustments with a new, sharp razor blade. Make sure that the belly is trimmed close to allow for maximum gap of the hook. (Wide-gap stinger hooks are often used for hair-bodied bugs for the added hook gap clearance.) Then add any additional wings, front legs, hackle, or other materials and complete the fly with a neat head and whip finish.

Step 1 – To spin deer or other body hair to make flies such as deer hair bass bugs, first cut and comb out a small bundle of fur as shown and position over the end of the hook shank.

Step 2 – Use soft loops over the hook shank as shown here to hold the fur in position before pulling the loops tight to flare the fur.

Step 3 – Pull on the working thread while continuing to make turns of thread around the hook shank to spin and flare the body hair as shown here.

Step 4 – Once a bundle of fur is spun, wrap the thread through the fur to in front of the bundle and make several turns of thread to push the fur back as far as possible as shown here.

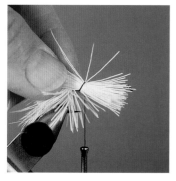

Step 5 – Continue the above steps with more bundles as shown here. Once the hook shank or body is filled with fur, tie off or finish the rest of the fly.

STACKING DEER HAIR – Stacking deer hair when tying does NOT refer to evening hair in a hair stacker. In this case, it is a variation of spinning body hair (see above) to make a fly body of clipped deer hair in which the belly color differs from the back color. Examples can be found in many hair-bodied patterns such as those by Joe Messinger. Any pattern or design with spun hair can be tied with a two-color body using this stacking technique. For this, two different colors of body hair are used. The tying method involves keeping each color of body hair in place to make the two-tone body. Follow the basic directions of hair preparation as above, and then hold the small bundle of hair on top of the hook while making the two soft loops of thread. Continue to hold the bundle in place while you pull the thread tight so that the bundle does NOT spin around the hook shank, but stays on top to cover only half of the hook shank while still flaring out. Once the first bundle is in place, turn the hook over (rotary vises are ideal for this), pick the second color, and repeat the above in the same spot. Continue this, with one color on top of the hook shank and a second, lighter color on the bottom. Once finished, trim and complete the fly as above.

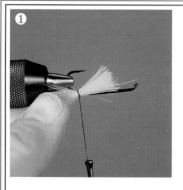

Step 1 – To make a stacked body (as with Messinger Bucktail Frog), use two different colors of body hair. One of these will be placed and positioned on the top of the hook shank to form the back and the other on the bottom of the hook shank to form the belly of the bug. This fly is begun by positioning the hook point up (use a rotary vise or reposition the hook from normal position) and then adding a clipped and combed out bundle of deer hair on the bottom of the fly. Hold the bundle at an angle as shown here and then make a thread wrap or two and pull to position the bundle on one side (the bottom here) of the hook shank. Note that a rotating vise is used here with the jaws extended horizontally so that the vise can be rotated to position the hook alternately point up and point down. Here the fly is point up. Stacking can also be accomplished by positioning the hook point down (normal position) and adding the belly hair to the bottom of the hook shank and pulling it tight to maintain this hair position.

Step 2 – Pull the thread tight while holding the body hair to make it flare. To keep it from flaring and spinning around the hook shank, hold the fur in position while pulling the thread tight.

Step 3 – Rotate the hook (or remove the hook out of the vise and reposition it) and add a second bundle of a different color or deer hair, using the same method described above.

Step 4 – Flare out this bundle of fur just as you did with the first, positioning it on top of the hook shank to make the back of the bug. This should be directly opposite the previously place belly bundle.

Step 5 – Wrap the thread in front of this bundle and push the hair back, as was done previously with the spinning technique.

Step 6 – Continue in this fashion, alternately placing the hook point up or point down (or position the bundles on the top or bottom if keeping the hook in one position) and placing the appropriate colors of body hair on the hook without spinning the fur around the hook shank. Here the shank has been filled with the two colors of body hair.

Step 7 – Once the fly is complete, finish by trimming, first with scissors and then a final trim with a new double-edge razor blade.

The finished bug with the stacked body should look like this, with a yellow belly and brown back. This shows only the body, since a stacked or spun bass bug or pike bug would normally include a tail and perhaps wings.

INSERTING BODY HAIR SPOTS AND STREAKS – Spots and streaks can be added to any hair-bodied fly by inserting a different color of hair into the previously spun or stacked body. This is most frequently done for frog bodies or sunfish and baitfish patterns. Hold a bundle of the new color of hair and fold it over the working thread. Then hold the bundle by the fold and pull the thread down to position the folded hair bundle in the exact position desired in the previously wrapped body. This can be repeated with a second, smaller bundle in a different color to make for a two-tone concentric spot. Thus, you could have a green frog body enhanced with red within yellow spots or a yellow sunfish pattern with a green barred body.

Step 1 – To add spots, stripes, or streaks of color to a bug, prepare a bundle of contrasting color by clipping and combing it. These bundles of contrasting color can be added after the rest of the bug is complete, or as you work your way forward tying in each body bundle.

Step 2 – Fold the prepared bundle over the working thread when the working thread is in position where you want the contrasting spot. Hold the bundle while you pull the thread into position and pull the bundle into the hair body.

Step 3 – Pull the bundle down to the body as shown here.

Step 4 – Bundle of red hair in position on the back of the light brown deer hair body.

Step 5 – Here, a body has been partly trimmed, with the body tied with a large white spot and a central red spot in the center of the brown body. In this case, the white spot was made first and then the red spot pulled down into the center of the white spot to get this effect.

MAKING TINSEL BODIES – Tinsel bodies are used primarily on streamers. If a tail is not added to the streamer, nor ribbing used, the simple way to do this is to cut the tinsel to a point and tie it down at the head of the fly, right where the wing will later be tied in place. Then wrap the tinsel down to the bend of the hook, reverse the direction of the wrap and wrap back up again to tie off at the head of the fly. If making a streamer with a tinsel body and a tail or ribbing, a different approach is required. For this, tie on at the head of the fly and wrap the thread evenly down to the bend of the hook, then wrap the tail fibers in place. Tie in the tinsel, then wrap the thread tightly and smoothly over

the tail fibers to create an even, smooth base on which to subsequently wind the tinsel. With the thread at the tie-down point, wrap the tinsel forward without gaps or overlapping and tie off. If using ribbing over tinsel with or without a tail, the ribbing is tied on before the tinsel and spiral-wrapped after the tinsel body wrap has been completed. Usually such ribbing would be wire or different color/finish tinsel. To assure getting a tight wrap of metallic tinsel, slightly overlap each wrap with the tinsel, then pull it forward and down until you can feel or hear the tinsel "click" into place as it drops into place tight against the previous wrap.

Step 1 – To make a tinsel body on a fly that has a tail, tie in the tail and then the tinsel. Wrap over the forward part of the tail to make for an even base on which to wrap the tinsel as shown here.

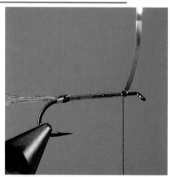

Step 2 – If you cut the forward part of the tail short and do not make an even base wrap of thread, the tinsel body can result like this – uneven and with gaps where the level of the base wrap changes.

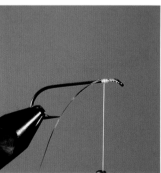

Step 3 – To make a tinsel body on a fly that lacks a tail, the best way is to tie the tinsel in at the head of the fly and then wrap the tinsel up and down the body. Here, the tinsel has been wrapped in place where the wing of the fly will be later tied in place.

Step 4 – Once the tinsel has been tied down, wrap the tinsel down the hook shank to the bend and then back up (reverse the wrap direction) as shown here, tying off at the head of the fly.

ADDING FLASH MATERIAL TO WINGS AND TAILS – Flash materials such as Krystal Flash, Crystal Splash and Flashabou supplement the look of the fly. For this, the best solution is to cut two small bundles and tie in one on each side of the fly after the wing has been added and secured. TIP – an alternative to the above is to cut a long bundle (two times the length needed for one side), tie it in at the halfway point on one side of the fly. Then bring the forward end around the hook shank of the fly to the opposite side. Continue wrapping to secure the flash material in place on that side. This can be added to standard wings on top of a streamer fly or to a throat or to the long large tails that are used on some bass and pile flies.

Step 1 – One way to tie in flash material to the side of a wing is to tie in a length of flash that is twice the length that will be used. Tie this in at the center as shown.

Step 2 – Fold the forward part of the flash material around and over the top of the tie down point and position it on the opposite side of the head as shown here. Use the working thread to hold the flash on the opposite side in this position.

Step 3 – With more wraps of thread, the flash will be held and secured on the sides of the wing as shown here. This is a top view of the fly, showing the flash on both sides.

MAKING MYLAR/PLASTIC MESH TUBING BODIES – Make some baitfish streamers with tubing slipped over the hook shank to make the body, rather than wrapping the body material or tinsel around the hook shank. This technique is possible using plastic translucent tubing materials such as Corsair and E-Z Body or Mylar. Mylar comes in several sizes and finishes, and always with a thread core. The plastic tubing materials do not have a core, but are available in several sizes and finishes. To use, remove the core from the tubing (Mylar). Then cut the tubing to the length required. If making just the body, make this about the length of the hook shank. If fraying out some of the tubing to make a tail, add about 1/4 to 1/3 the length of the hook. To make a simple body, slip the prepared cut sleeve over the hook shank. Push the tubing a little to the rear and then tie on the thread in back of the hook eye and clip the excess. Move the tubing back into proper position (slide forward) and then tie down with the working thread. Once the head is complete, tie off and cut the excess thread. Then retie on at the bend of the hook over the tail of the tubing, tie down, and then complete with a whip finish. If making a tail, tie the tail on first, then slide the tubing in place and tie down at the rear before tying off and retying at the head of the fly.

Step 1 – To make a Mylar body streamer fly, first pull the central cord from the Mylar tubing as shown here. Discard this central cord.

Step 2 – Begin to make a Mylar body fly by cutting the tubing to the length of the fly (longer will leave room for a tail of frayed body material) and then slide the tubing over the hook shank. Tie down the thread in back of the hook eye and then slide the tubing forward to tie down the front end of the tubing with the thread as shown here.

Step 3 – Tie off the head of the fly and the wrapped Mylar body with a whip finish before turning to the tail of the fly and completing that part.

Step 4 – Tie the thread on again at the tail of the fly to secure the Mylar tubing. Then clip the excess thread before making a whip finish to complete the fly. At this point, the tag end of the thread has yet to be cut.

Step 5 – Once the tail of the fly has been tied off with a whip finish and the thread cut, use a bodkin to fray out the fibers (this is if the body material has been made long enough to accomplish this step) to make a tail. In addition, flies can be tied without this tail and with a previously wrapped tail of other natural or synthetic materials.

MAKING REVERSE-TIE MYLAR/PLASTIC MESH TUBING BODIES – Mylar or plastic tubing can be tied so that the head tie of the material is hidden. Cut a length of tubing about 1-1/4 to 1-1/2 times the length of the hook shank. Remove the core (Mylar) and then tie down, with the length of the tubing extending in front of the hook (to your right). Once it is securely tied down, tie off with a whip finish and clip the thread or wrap the thread to the rear and tie on any tail material. Then use your fingers to roll the tubing back over the hook shank, turning it inside out. Once it is reversed, tie on at the rear of the hook shank and tie down the other end of the tubing. Complete with a whip finish. This is an effective tie for making blunt-head minnow imitations, since the thread wrap is hidden under the inverted tubing body.

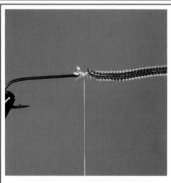

Step 1 – To make a reverse tied Mylar streamer fly, remove the cord and cut a length of Mylar as shown. Tie in the thread in back of the hook eye. Then slip the end of the Mylar tubing over the hook eye with the body extending in front of the hook (to the right). Tie down with thread as shown. Make sure that the thread wrap is immediately in back of the hook eye so that no thread shows when the Mylar is reversed on the hook.

Step 3 – Once the Mylar is pushed to the rear, use the thread to secure the tail of the fly as shown here.

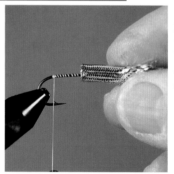

Step 2 – Once the Mylar is tied in place, wind the thread to the bend of the hook and push the Mylar back over itself to turn it inside out and push the Mylar to the rear as shown here.

Step 4 – Fray out the Mylar in back of the wrap to make the tail of the fly as shown. Then complete with a whip finish. You can also make the fly without this frayed Mylar tail, and separately tie in a natural or synthetic tail. This is done after the thread is wound to the hook bend and before the Mylar is reversed on the hook shank.

ADDING EYES TO STREAMERS – To add painted eyes, first completely finish the head of the fly with several coats of head cement. Then use small bottles of enamel (Testor's or Model Maker are good) to make the eyes. Shake the bottle, and then remove the cap and work from the small amount of paint on the inside of the cap. Apply the paint with two sizes of pinheads or finishing nails. Use the larger of the two for making the eye color (usually light). Dot on each side of the head of the fly and allow to cure. Once cured, use the smaller applicator to make a smaller pupil of black or red. To add prism eyes, just peel the eye from the backing and stick it on the fly head. Then coat the eye with several layers of head cement or a single layer of epoxy. To add plastic or rattling doll eyes, use a small dot of glue in the back of the eye to glue the eye to the head of the fly.

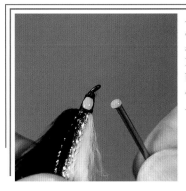

Add painted eyes to streamer flies or other flies with large heads by using a painting tool or nail head or pin head to dip into paint and form the basic eye. This should be in a color contrasting with the head of the fly. Allow to cure before the next step.

Use a smaller nail head or pin head dipped into a contrasting paint to dot the eye and make the pupil of the eye on the fly.

TYING DUMBBELL/HOURGLASS EYES – Dumbbell and hourglass eyes have revolutionized deep fly-fishing for all manner of fish. To tie them down, first make a series of wraps around the hook shank and the center of the eye. This will place the eye cockeyed, but this is fine since it will allow you to get a tight wrap on the eye. With the eye canted at an angle, take your fingernail and pull the eye back into a right angle alignment with the hook shank. Then wrap over the hook shank and eye to hold the eye in this position. This creates tension to help hold the eye in the proper position. Add more tension by making wraps around these bindings. If desired, add a drop of CA glue (any brand of the super glues) or a drop of epoxy to the eye at this point to secure it. For most weighted flies, it helps to use a turned-down eyehook and place the hook point down in the vise to tie the eye on the shank. Then place the fly in the vise point-up to tie the fly, which is how the fly will be fished anyway. The eye in this position with a turned-down eye (which will ride up when fished) makes the fly almost weedless on the bottom.

Step 1 – To tie in a dumbbell or hourglass eye on a fly such as a Clouser Deep Minnow, wrap over the eye and the hook shank as shown. Note that, initially, the eye will be at an angle to the hook shank, rather than at 90 degrees to the shank, as it will be in the final position.

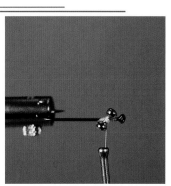

Step 2 – Close-up of above. Note that the angle of the dumbbell will change to 90 degrees once a cross wrap is made over the eye.

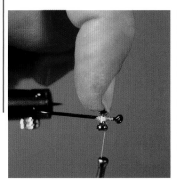

Step 3 – To straighten the eye on the hook shank to a 90-degree position, use your fingernail or thumbnail to pull back on the forward part of the eye and then wrap over this in the opposite direction with the tying thread. Complete by running thread around the base between the eye and the hook shank to tighten and secure this eye position.

ADDING BEADS AND CONEHEADS – Beads and coneheads are available in metal (for weight and flash), plastic and glass (mostly for color – only slight weight) and are ideal for sinking nymphs for sunfish, crappie, and even carp (beadhead) and in streamers (conehead) for bass, pike, and walleye. Ideally, you want a bead that will slide onto the point of the hook (with the barb bent down) and slide around the bend to seat against the back of the hook eye. Usually, the thread is tied down in back of and after the bead or beads are positioned on the hook. With some flies, beads are also added as part, or all of, the body. In these cases, the beads are added all at once, with the thread then added and the rest of the fly tied around these beads. Use Model Perfect or round-bend hooks when tying beadhead flies, since the sharper bends in Limerick, O'Shaughnessy, and other hook styles limit the size of the beads that will easily slide onto the hook.

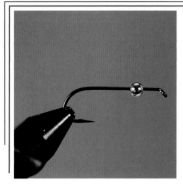

Add cones or beads to hooks by first bending down the point of the hook and sliding the cone or bead over the hook point and up onto the shank. Perfect or round bend hooks are best for this since they have an even radius to the hook bend.

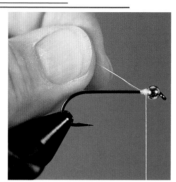

To position the bead or cone onto the hook, begin the thread wrap in back of the bead and wrap a bump of thread here to hold the bead or cone in place as shown.

ADDING LEAD – Lead and lead substitutes are used for weighting streamers, wet flies, and nymphs. While we will use the term lead throughout, lead substitutes are available and required in some states and on some waters. The simplest way to add lead is to wrap the lead around the hook shank, then tie on the thread and wrap over this, with spiral crisscross wrappings to secure the lead. It is also best to make a small tapering "ramp" of thread at each end of the lead wrap for smoothly adding tapered body materials. If tying a fly with a white or light-colored body, add a coat of head cement to the lead before going further to prevent the lead from bleeding through and discoloring the light body.

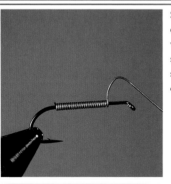

Step 1 – One way to wrap lead wire onto a hook shank is to make tight wraps of the lead (or lead wire substitute) around the hook as shown here. Any excess lead can be cut off.

Step 2 – To secure the head onto the hook, wrap over it with thread as shown and make a small "ramp" of thread at each end to taper the body material that will subsequently be added.

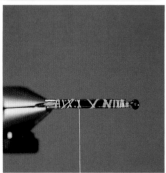

Step 3 – One other way to add lead to a hook shank is to cut two lengths equal to the shank length and wrap them in place on each side of the hook shank using the working thread.

ADDING SHEET LEAD AND WEIGHT TO FLIES – Self-adhesive backed sheet lead or soft metal can be added to a hook to make flattened nymph bodies as well as the beer-belly shape of Zonkers. First, cut the metal to the length desired and double the width desired in the underbody. Fold the tape in half before removing the backing, then remove the backing, position the hook between the folded metal like a sandwich, and squeeze with pliers. For nymphs, the metal body will be flat – at right angles to the hook plane. Then use your coarse scissors to trim and taper the metal body to shape. Tie on the thread and wrap the body with thread from one end to the other and tie off. To secure the wrap, coat with head cement, or better still, thinned epoxy or CA glue. Then tie the thread back on and tie the fly using standard fly-tying materials. To make a Zonker body, use the same method to measure and fold the metal. In this case, the metal body will be in the same plane as the hook, and the hook shank will be placed at the fold in the metal. Remove the backing, position the hook shank against the fold, and squeeze with pliers. Use coarse scissors to trim the ends to a belly shape. You can wrap the metal with thread as with nymph bodies or leave it bare, since it will be covered with the Mylar tubing to complete the Zonker.

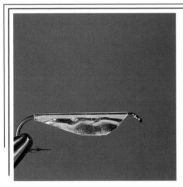

Step 1 – Add sheet lead to flies to make Zonkers or other weighted patterns by using self-adhesive lead tape made for this purpose. To do this, fold and cut the tape into the size and shape desired for the hook, then remove the backing and fold onto the hook as shown. Mylar tubing is usually used as a covering for this lead sheet.

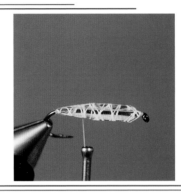

Step 2 – Tape can also be folded and cut to make flattened bodies for nymphs and other bottom crawlers for bass and other species. Use the same technique previously described, only fold the sheeting at right angles to the hook plane and taper the body evenly.

TYING FOAM BODIES – Closed-cell foam, available in sheets or strips, is primarily used for terrestrials such as ants, beetles, jassids, hoppers, crickets, ladybugs, and the like. Open-cell foam, which will absorb water, is used for some nymph patterns both as a body and underbody. Round cylinder foam (closed-cell) is usually prepared as a short cylinder and tied on at the center of the hook shank and center of the foam cylinder to make flies such as the foam McMurray Ant and similar bees and wasps. Cylinder foam makes great cricket or hopper bodies by tying on at one end of the foam and in back of the hook eye. Strips cut from sheet foam can also be tied on at the rear of a hook shank and then folded over to the make a beetle body or segmented parts of an ant.

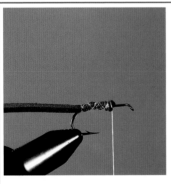

Step 1 – One way to make a simple foam body for a beetle or other sponge bug is to tie the thread at the rear of the hook shank and then tie in a strip of closed cell foam as shown here. Then wrap the thread forward to tie down the foam when the foam is folded over to make the body. Legs are often added to the hook shank as you wrap the thread forward.

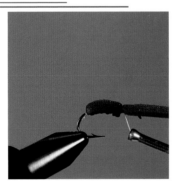

Step 2 – Make the foam body of the beetle or sponge bug by folding over the foam and then tying it into place with the working thread as shown here.

Step 3 – Wrap the thread forward again to the head of the fly and then tie down the end of the foam to make a thorax or body. Clip any excess foam and then tie off the thread and whip finish. To make a complete beetle or foam bug, add legs of deer hair, hackle, or rubber to the body as later described.

TYING STREAMER HAIR WINGS – Traditional streamer wings involve bucktail tied directly on top of the hook shank and immediately in back of the hook eye. Wings are generally added after adding all other materials, although a throat can be added before or after adding the wing. First clip the bucktail from the skin and use a small comb to remove any underfur. Then, place the wing material, tip down, into a stacker or evener. Trim the butt ends relative to the length needed for the fly wing. Position the wing over the head of the fly, taking care that the length of the wing is proportional to the fly and hook size. Generally, a wing of about 1-1/4 to 1-1/2 times the length of the hook shank is standard. Use the soft loop method to get the wing on straight and securely. Trim any excess wing material in front of the wrap, tapering it to correspond with the final shape of the tapered head. Complete more thread wraps to cover the wing butts and prepare the head for finishing. This method will assure that the wing will be tied correctly and straight on top of the hook shank.

Step 1 – To make a bucktail streamer wing on a fly, first comb out the fur as shown to remove all the underfur and then stack to make the tips even.

Step 2 – Place the bucktail in position on top of the hook shank and use the soft loop method to secure the bucktail. Then clip the forward ends of the fur (not yet done here) before completing the head and tying off.

STACKING HAIR WINGS OR TAILS FOR STREAMERS – Some streamers have stacked wings of different colors of bucktail. An example is the Mickey Finn, with a wing of alternating yellow/red/yellow bucktail. To tie this, first add the base wing of yellow, following the directions above. Then repeat with a smaller bundle of red, again following the above directions to place the red directly on top of the yellow wing. Then finally add a wing of yellow over the red, again following the directions as above. When complete, the three parts of the wing should be separated by color and look the same on both sides of the fly. This technique can be used for making long multicolored tails on bas0s and pike flies.

Step 1 – To stack a hair wing, first complete the above step to make a wing base of one color of bucktail, as shown here, then repeat the above step with a different color of bucktail, using the soft loop method to secure and stack the second color directly on top of the first as shown here. Clip the forward part of the added wing.

Step 2 – Add a third wing color if desired, repeating the above steps in terms of using the soft loop to position the wing and then clip the forward part of the bucktail. Here red has been added over a wing of white and yellow.

Step 3 – In this wing, a fourth wing color has been added with the black topping. The wing is added using the soft loop method and then the forward part is clipped before the head is wrapped and the fly tied off with a whip finish.

TYING STREAMER HACKLE WINGS AND TAILS – Saddle hackle (long hackle feathers) is used for many streamer wings and tails for surface bugs and large bass and pike flies. To tie these in you will need hackle matched by width, shape and length. For most flies you will use two pair – two hackle feathers on each side. For large flies, you will need more hackle, but they must be matched in pairs. All hackle feathers have a natural curve to them. For a streamlined appearance, match the feathers so that the concave side (dull side) of each feather faces the middle of the fly. For saddles that flare out for more action with each pause on a retrieve, tie the hackles so that the concave side of each pair faces out. Measure the feathers for length, making the wing or tail about 1-1/2 times the length of the hook shank, or follow specific pattern instructions. Cut off the excess feather at the butt end and then cut the fibers back about 1/8 inch on each side of the main feather stem. This creates some "tooth" to the main stem for more secure binding. Place the entire feathered wing on top of the hook shank, with the feathers parallel to the hook shank and the plane of the feathers parallel to the hook plane. For a wing, the thread must be back far enough from the hook eye to allow proper tying of the wing. Then bring the thread straight up on the near side of the hook with your right hand, pinch the thread and the feathers with your left thumb and index finger, and then pull the thread straight down on the far side of the hook. Pull tight and repeat. Then trim any excess feather stems. Add any topping (if used) at this time. Then continue wrapping with thread to build up a smooth and uniform head.

To make streamers with saddle hackle wings, first choose two pairs of hackle feathers equal in appearance, length and width. Position them with one pair on each side of the hook shank, concave side out as shown so that the wings will flare and pulse in the water on retrieve.

To complete the streamer wing, position the wing hackles on the top of the hook shank as shown and tie in using the soft loop method. This will assure that the wings stay on top, are not flared to one side, or twisted. Wing length can vary from about 1-1/4 to 2 times the hook shank length.

TYING SYNTHETIC WING MATERIAL FOR STREAMERS – Synthetic materials such as Unique, Super Hair, Ultra Hair, Neer Hair, Aqua Fiber, Poly Bear, and others can be used for wings, or Krystal Flash, Crystal Splash, or Flashabou can add flash and sparkle. The synthetics are more slippery than natural materials, so use the soft loop to position the wing and make tight wraps to hold it. If making a thick wing, it often helps to add several small bundles rather than one large bundle. To trim the tail ends of the synthetic fibers for a more tapered appearance, do selective cutting with standard scissors or trim with a pair of barber's thinning scissors that have one toothed blade. Similar special fly-tying thinning scissors are also available.

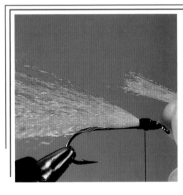

Tie in synthetic wing material (Super Hair used here) the same way that you tie in bucktail. Use the soft loop method to keep the wing material on top of the hook shank as shown here. Finish by clipping the excess synthetic material and then wrap the head to complete the fly.

TYING TOPPING OVER STREAMER WINGS – Topping over streamer wings is typically peacock herl, but can be other materials including ostrich, synthetics, or bucktail. This is simply held in place over the previously tied wing with the thread in the same position as when first tying the wing in place. Then, just as with a wing, bring the thread straight up on the near side of the hook, pinch the thread and the topping with your left index finger and thumb, and bring the thread down on the far side of the hook shank. Pull tight, repeat two or more times, then trim the excess topping and wrap with thread to complete a uniform head.

Step 1 – One way to tie in flash material to the side of a wing is to tie in a length of flash that is twice the length that will be used. Tie this in at the center as shown.

Step 2 – Fold the forward part of the flash material around and over the top of the tie down point and position it on the opposite side of the head as shown here. Use the working thread to hold the flash on the opposite side in this position.

Step 3 – With more wraps of thread, the flash will be held and secured on the sides of the wing as shown here. This is a top view of the fly, showing the flash on both sides.

Topping of peacock herl, color colors of wing materials of synthetics can be added to any streamer fly to make the fly look more natural and like the dark shaded natural minnow it imitates. To do this, use the soft loop method to tie down the topping of peacock herl after the rest of the wing material is secured. Clip the excess and then complete the fly.

HANDLING MARABOU – Marabou is great on simple streamer flies and as the tail in Woolly Buggers. But because of its fluffy nature, handling marabou is often difficult. First, carefully cut the marabou from the stem of the feather as close to the stem as possible. You can then pull this strip of material away and fold it over several times to make a bundle. To keep the marabou from floating around and interfering with the tying process, wet your fingers and smooth back the marabou. Do not moisten the area where you will be tying the marabou in place, since this may not allow complete penetration of the head cement when you finish the fly.

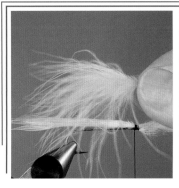

Fluffy marabou or the similar chickabou is difficult to handle and tie down properly. One tip to doing this is to lightly moisten the marabou wing material so that it will straighten out and be easier to handle. Here, for comparison purposes, fluffy marabou is held over the top of the moistened marabou, which has been tied to the hook shank.

TYING REVERSED-WING BULLET HEADS – This method, first used by Carrie Stevens at the turn of the 20th century and later popularized by Keith Fulsher with his Thunder Creek series of flies, uses a reverse tie of the wing to make a bullet head. The method is simple. After tying on the rest of the fly (tail, body, ribbing) tie in a wing of bucktail with the tips facing forward rather than back over the body. Also, tie this so that the wing (which extends to the right of the fly) surrounds the hook shank. After tying this wing on, wrap the thread back to a point about 1/3 the way back from the hook eye. Then fold the wing back over the tie-down point so that the wing surrounds the hook shank and body. Use the tying thread to tie down the wing and secure it with a whip finish, then seal with head cement. This type of bullet head and wing can be made full or very sparse. It can also be made in two parts, with a dark top and light belly or bottom, with the two parts pulled back to make the light belly/dark back camouflage of a typical minnow.

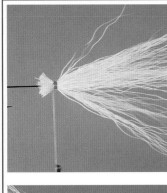

Step 1 – To make a bullet head streamer (Keith Fulsher Thunder Creek series or Carrie Stevens style), you must first tie in the tail and the rest of the fly before adding the head. Here, the method is shown with the thread and the wing tied down, without the rest of the fly in place. The thread has been tied to the hook shank, wrapped forward to the hook eye, and then the prepared (clipped, combed and stacked/evened) bucktail wing tied down so that it surrounds the hook shank. Note that this wing is tied forward of the fly, with only the butts tied down at the head of the fly. If using two different materials rather than one as shown here, tie in the two colors, using a stacking technique to keep each color on the top or bottom of the fly.

Step 3 – Use a straw or tube (in this case a flared brass tube is used) to flare the wing material and reverse them so that they will flare and surround the hook shank.

Step 2 – To continue the head, wrap the thread back partway down the hook shank to a point where you will want to tie in the reversed head. It is best, as in this case, to wrap over the butt ends of the wing as a base for tying the head.

Step 4 – Once the wing is flared back and held in place, use the working thread and soft loop method to make one or two turns around the wing to hold it in place. Note that with this example, red thread has been used to simulate a gill on the fly. Make a whip finish with only a few turns and clip the thread, then use head cement to seal the wraps.

SHAPING CORK AND BALSA BODIES – There are several ways to shape cork and balsa bodies prior to gluing them onto the hook. If necessary, first consider preliminary shaping using a single edge razor blade, sharp hobby knife, or a fine saw such as an X-Acto saw. Use extreme care if using any cutting tool. You can then sand the body to shape with a sanding board or emery board. Note that balsa and cork have a completely different feel. Cork is made up of small "cells" and has a slightly spongy-soft feel to it. This means that it has a tendency to crumble and crack. Balsa is a soft wood, but does have a straight grain. This makes it a little easier to work with.

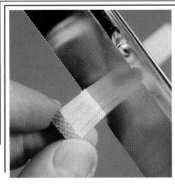

Step 1 – One way to make easy balsa bodies for warmwater flies is to buy strips of balsa in the right shape and width and to cut it into length using a small saw. Here, an X-Acto saw is being used to cut this strip of balsa.

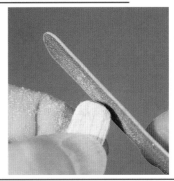

Step 2 – An easy way to shape balsa is to use a coarse, then fine emery board to sand and shape the sides of the bug body to the shape desired.

SLOTTING AND PREPARING CORK AND BALSA
BODIES – Cork and balsa bodies must be slotted for the hook. Use a fine-tooth hacksaw blade. With the bug in one hand and the blade in the other, make a straight cut into the center of the bug belly. If the hook shank, or wrapped hook shank, is too thick for this slot, use two or more hacksaw blades wrapped together, with the teeth angles alternating direction. If you have previously cut the belly of the bug flat to preserve maximum hook gap of the finished bug, make sure that you only cut deep enough for the wrapped hook shank. If you have not done this, try the bug on the hook, then cut the belly flat. Check and adjust the belly slot if required.

Step 1 – To slot bass bugs and balsa bodies, use a hacksaw blade to make a cut through the belly axis of the bug as shown here. Fine tooth blades are best for this.

Step 2 – Example of slotted body, ready for a prepared hook.

PREPARING FOAM BODIES FOR ADDING TO THE
HOOK – The standard method of adding the hook to the bug body is totally different from the slot-and-insert method used with cork and balsa. For this, use a thick bodkin to make a hole, front to back, through the belly of the bug. Make sure that you have first prepared the bug and flattened the underside of the belly if desired. Make sure that the hole through which the hook shank will be inserted is as close as possible to the surface of the bug belly to preserve the hook gap.

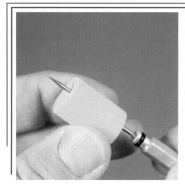

Step 1 – To make a pilot hole in a foam body for a foam bug, first run through the bug body with a large bodkin or thin awl. As shown, make this as close as possible to the belly area so that the bug rides right and has maximum hook gap clearance.

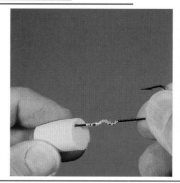

Step 2 – Check the pilot hole with a wrapped hook as shown. Once the hole is checked and will accept the wrapped hook, add CA glue (cyanoacrylate cement) to the hook shank and the hole and slide the hook rapidly in place. Hold and make sure the hook alignment is proper before the glue cures.

GLUING FOAM BODIES ONTO THE HOOK
– To glue a hook into a foam body, you can use either epoxy or CA (super glue) adhesives. The CA glues will work on almost all foams, with the exception of the lightweight closed-cell Ethafoam materials. Use the liquid type of CA glues, not the gel. After adding the tail and other materials to the hook shank, spiral wrapping the body with coarse thread, and making a bodkin hole through the foam body, check the fit by inserting the hook, eye-first, into the tail end of the body. Then remove the hook, add the CA glue to the hook shank and reinsert the hook. Do not glue your fingers to the bug, hook or tail! Immediately check the alignment of the hook in the body and set aside to cure for a few minutes. Add a small drop of glue to the tail end of the bug where the hook is inserted and it will wick along the inserted hook shank.

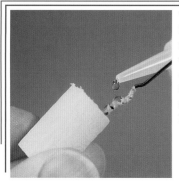

To glue hooks into prepared foam bodies, make a pilot hole through the bug belly and then coat the hook with a drop or two or CA (cyanoacrylate) glue before rapidly inserting the hook through the bug and checking the hook and bug body for proper alignment.

WRAPPING AND OTHERWISE PREPARING THE HOOK SHANK FOR THE BUG BODY – For the best glue bond of a hook into a bug body, it should be wrapped with coarse thread. In the case of balsa or cork bodies, this can be further improved with a wrap of chenille or yarn. Spiral-wrap the part of the shank inserted into the cork or balsa body and tie off where the whip finish will be hidden in the body.

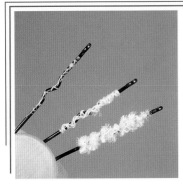

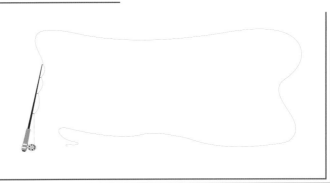

Examples of wrapped hooks that will improve the grip of the glue when glued into a cork or balsa body. Top to bottom, wrapped with thin thread, wrapped with thick thread, and wrapped with chenille. The least effective is the hook wrapped with light thread; the most effective is the one wrapped with chenille. This does require a larger slot cut into the bug belly.

GLUING CORK AND BALSA BODIES IN PLACE ON THE HOOK – Five-minute epoxy is fine, although the 24-hour glue will be slightly stronger. Add the glue to the slot and hook shank and insert it into the slot. Check to make sure that the hook is aligned properly with the body. Use a bodkin or toothpick to remove glue that has oozed out the end, taking care to keep any from filling the hook eye or from coating the hook shank in back of the body. Finish by making sure that you have a slightly raised area of glue on the belly and place the bug on its back to cure. (The glue will shrink slightly upon curing, thus the necessity of the slightly raised puddle of glue on the belly.) Once the glue is cured, use a file or emery board to remove any cured excess glue and to flatten the belly.

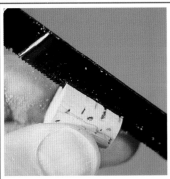

Step 1 – One easy way to make a larger, sided slot in a bug belly is to use two or three hacksaw blades, bound together, to make the cut in the belly. Reverse the teeth on adjoining saw blades to make this easy.

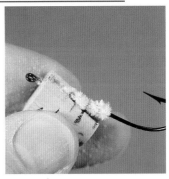

Step 2 – Chenille wrapped hook shank on kink shank hook checked for size in a cork body with a wide slot cut into the belly.

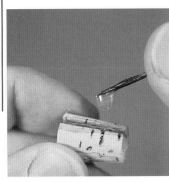

Step 3 – To properly glue a prepared hook into the slot in a cork or balsa body, add a drop of prepared mixed epoxy glue into the slot as shown. Spread the cement evenly throughout the slot.

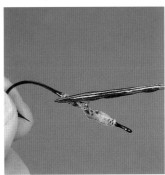

Step 4 – Use the same puddle of glue to evenly coat the prepared wrapped kink shank hook for adding to the slot in the cork or balsa body.

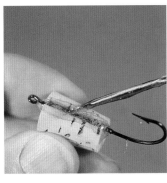

Step 5 – Once the hook has been inserted into the bug body, use your bodkin to remove any excess glue from each end of the exposed hook shank and spread glue into a slightly raised puddle on the slot as shown here. The cement will shrink somewhat upon curing.

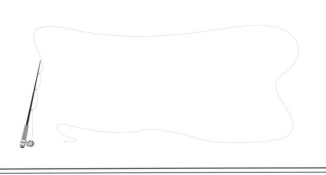

PREPARATION FOR PAINTING CORK AND BALSA BUG BODIES – Before painting, fill in any pockets or holes with a mix of glue and cork dust blended to a thick paste. Fill all pits to a slight bulge and sand smooth and level once the mix cures. Begin with several coats of primer or white paint, then coat with the finishing coat of paint. For balsa, sand the bug smooth, then give the bug body a coat of primer. This will cause wood fibers to rise up, which then requires light sanding and a second coat of primer. Then finish with the desired colors.

SHAPING FOAM BODIES – Soft foam bodies can't be easily sanded, since they will bend and twist from the pressure of the sandpaper. They can be cut, using razor blades or coarse scissors.

METHODS OF PAINTING BUGS – Spray painting – Mask those parts of the bug that you do not want painted. Use pliers or wear plastic disposable gloves to hold the bug. Spray, turning the bug evenly to completely coat all sides.

Spray painting a scale finish – Apply the base color under the scales. Then use scale-finish netting (sold in tackle, fly and catalog shops; also in sewing/fabric shops as tulle), wrap it around the bug and spray the outer coat. Carefully remove the netting material. A white base coat with a green overcoat will produce a green bug with white scale markings. A black base coat with a yellow overcoat will produce a yellow bug with black scale markings.

Brushing – Brushing is best for an overall even coat. It avoids the sags and clogged eyes of dipping and the waste of paint and necessity of masking the hook when spraying. For this, use a small disposable hobby brush and try to make each brush stroke only once to avoid brush marks in the finished bug. You can also brush two colors, such as a white body and red head. For this, brush the entire bug white first; allow the paint to cure, and then finish with a second brushed coat of the head with red paint. Take care to get an even border.

Dipping – Dipping has advantages and disadvantages. It creates an even coat, and allows making a banded body. But the paint tends to drip when the bug is hung to cure, and the paint will fill the hook eye. Use thinned paint (several coats may be necessary) to prevent sagging and drips and use a toothpick to remove the wet paint from the hook eye. Hang on a fly hanger to cure. You can run a scrap hackle feather through the hook eye, butt end first, so that the feather clears the eye and absorbs much of the paint.

To spray a bug body, mask the hook area with a fold of cardboard or paper as shown and wear disposable latex gloves or hold the bug with pliers. Spray from a distance. This bug has been given a base coat of yellow and a sprayed top coat of green.

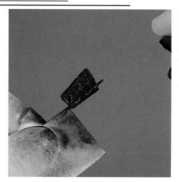

Example of spraying bug with masked hook and wearing gloves for protection. (Note: Spray can held close for photo illustration only. Use distance as recommended by the paint manufacturer.)

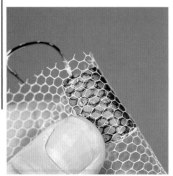

To get a scale appearance on a bug, spray paint a base color, allow to cure, and then wrap the bug body with tulle or netting that when sprayed again with contrasting paint will create a scale finish. Here a bug is wrapped with netting and ready to be sprayed.

Examples of two scale-finish bugs and the tulle or netting used for this process. The left bug has a light coat of paint over a dark base coat while the right bug has a dark coat of paint over a light under coat.

To brush paint a bug, use a disposable brush and coat the prepared glued bug with several coats of paint, allowing the paint to cure between each coat. Use an assembly line for this to avoid waste of brushes and paint.

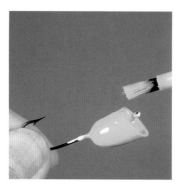

Bug with a finished coat of brushed paint.

To dip a bug, first dip in a wide mouth container, and dip several times to establish a base coat. Here, yellow was the base coat. A second dip in red paint gave this bug a nice two-tone red head/yellow body paint job.

ADDING RUBBER LEGS TO CORK, BALSA, AND FOAM BODIES – The most common way to add legs is to run them through the bug body. To do this, you will need a long, coarse needle. Tools are available for this, but you can make your own with a long doll-making needle available from sewing shops, and use a grinder or file to cut a small opening in one side of the eye. This allows adding legs to the threading needle without having to use a needle threader. Add the legs to the needle or threading tool, and then run the needle straight through the bug body at any angle you wish. Run legs through painted cork or balsa bodies shortly after the paint cures. If you wait too long, the paint may harden and crack where the needle enters and exits. Keep the legs long. You can always cut them short when fishing. One easy way is to tie the legs into the tail of the bug, rather than adding them to the body. You can also tie legs into the sides of the body, as when making some hopper and stonefly patterns, where the tie-down for the legs is the same as the tie-down for a wing.

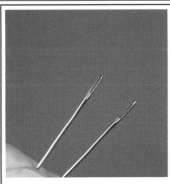

Step 1 – To add rubber legs to cork, balsa, and foam bugs, first prepare a tool that will hold the rubber legs and allow you to pierce the bug body. Here a doll needle (left) has been cut (right) with a file (a grindstone can also be used) to make a notch in the eye for adding legs before running the needle through the body.

Step 2 – Here, the needle has been run through the painted cork body of a bug with the rubber legs easily added to the notch in the needle eye. This makes it easy to add legs and run them through the body.

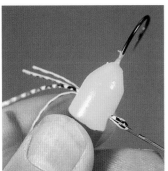

Step 3 – Here the needle has been run through the body of the bug then used to pull the legs through. Use care in this to avoid tearing or cutting the legs from too much force.

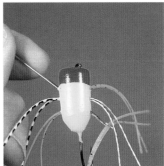

Step 4 – Legs can be run through at different angles to make a more leggy effect as with this bug. Here, three sets of legs are being used – one mottled black/white set straight through the body, and a second and third of green and mottled black through the body at angles.

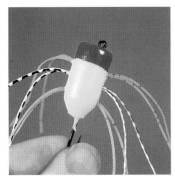

Example of the previous bug with the legs through the body at angles.

ADDING CARAPACE TO CRAYFISH AND LARGE NYMPH PATTERNS – Crayfish have a hard shell, which can be imitated by means of a carapace, or top, of thin plastic, Bug Skin, Thin Skin, vinyl and other materials made and sold expressly for this purpose. To use this, prepare a rectangular shape of the carapace material, then hold it in place over the back of the fly and wrap down with separate ribbing or a thread ribbing. Do this by spiraling up or down the body to form the carapace, and then tie off. You may wish to modify the rectangular form of the carapace by tapering it at both ends, cutting "V" notches in the ends, etc., to make it more life-like. You can use the same technique for the shellback – exoskeleton – of nymph and hellgrammite imitations.

Step 1 – To add a carapace to a fly such as a crayfish or hellgrammite, first cut and prepare the carapace as shown here. Carapace can be cloth-style vinyl, Thin Skin, Bug Skin, and other sheet materials. Prepare the fly body (in this case cactus chenille) to receive the carapace.

Step 2 – Here a hole has been punched in the front of the carapace to fit over the hook eye to make the tail of the crayfish pattern. The rest of the carapace is spiral wrapped with two wraps of thread at each point on the fly body to make it look like a segmented crayfish body.

ADDING RUBBER LEGS TO FLIES – You can tie rubber legs in at just about any location on the fly. They can also be tied onto the hook shank with the tie-down point covered by body material (often foam) as when making ant, beetle, and hopper/cricket patterns.

MAKING INDESTRUCTIBLE PIKE FLIES – See the Invincible Pike Fly for details on this fly. One way to make indestructible flies is to tie in synthetic tail material, then tie in Body Fur at this point, then coat the tie-down point and the hook shank with epoxy after wrapping the thread forward. Continue by spiral wrapping or palmering the Body Fur along the hook shank, burying the central thread strand into the wet epoxy. Finish by tying off the Body Fur, wrapping a head and using the remainder of the epoxy to coat and protect the head of the fly. You can also do this with palmered hackle, cactus chenille or any similar body material.

Step 1 – To make indestructible flies for pike and muskie, first wrap on the tail of the fly and spiral wrap the hook shank with thread. Tie in the body material (Body Fur) and coat with properly mixed and prepared epoxy. Completely coat the tail wrap area and Body Fur wrap area. Coat the entire hook shank with epoxy as shown.

Step 2 – Turn the hook shank now and again (a rotating vise is handy for this, or use a bodkin to catch any glue that might drip) and begin to wind the Body Fur around the hook shank as shown, burying the central Body Fur thread in the epoxy.

Step 3 – Continue to wrap forward, burying the Body Fur in the epoxy as before.

Step 4 – Tie off the Body Fur at the head of the fly, clip the excess Body Fur, and wrap and finish the head with a whip finish. Do this rapidly so that you can coat the head of the fly with the remaining puddle of five-minute epoxy. Place the fly on a fly rotator so that the head epoxy will not sag and drip.

SEGMENTING FOAM EXTENDED BODIES – Segmented foam bodies are used on patterns imitating caterpillars, damselflies, dragonflies, and sometimes hoppers and crickets. If the foam body is tied to the hook shank, segmenting is easily done by spiral wrapping ribbing or thread over the foam body. If the body is extended, as with dragonfly and damselfly patterns, Bill Skilton developed an easy way to prepare the bodies before tying in place on the hook shank. Use a thin strip of foam that will be folded over to make the body. Tie in the thread at the center, and then fold the foam together. Place a long needle horizontally into your fly-tying vise. The needle is used as a support for this method and serves as a temporary skeleton to the segmented body. Begin by tying a knot with the tying thread around the middle of the foam strip. Then, place the foam over the needle (which is placed there only for support.) Run the thread between the two foam sections for one segment length, and make two wraps of thread around both lengths of the folded foam. Continue this way, hiding the advanced thread between the two body sections, and making two wraps to form the segment. When finished, remove the foam body from the needle, tie the thread and foam body onto the hook shank, and continue with the rest of the tying process for the fly.

Step 1 – To make a detached segmented body of foam that will be later attached to a fly hook, first insert a long needle into your fly-tying vise. Tie a knot in the center of a strip of foam and fold it over and bracket the needle. Begin by making two wraps of thread around the body and needle, then run the thread between the strips (as shown) to the next segmenting point where two more wraps will be made. This assures that the segments are even and straight, rather than spiraled as with a standard spiral wrap.

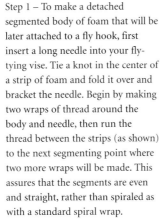

Step 2 – Continue to make the above segments with two wraps of thread and then running the thread between the two strips to complete the length of the segmented body desired. When complete, hold the segmented body and thread and slowly and carefully remove the body from the needle.

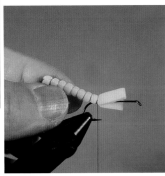

Step 3 – Move the segmented body and the thread (still attached) to the rear of the hook, now placed in the fly-tying vise. Hold the forward part of the segmented body in place over the rear of the hook and tie down by wrapping the thread twice around the body and the hook shank.

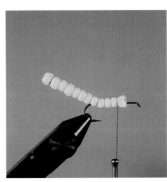

Step 4 – Continue to make thread segments by running the thread between the two foam strips and then wrapping around both foam strips and the hook shank to make the next segments as shown. Continue until reaching the head of the fly or at the point where the rest of the fly (legs, hackle, wings, etc.) are added.

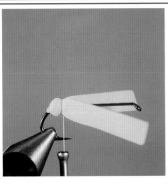

Step 1 – To make a segmented body on a fly hook, mount the fly hook in the vise and then tie down a strip of foam by the center at the rear of the hook shank. Fold the two parts of the foam strip forward and begin to wrap as above, bringing the thread between the strips and then wrapping around both the strips and the foam to make a segment.

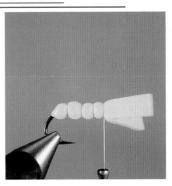

Step 2 – Continue the above as you work towards the head of the fly.

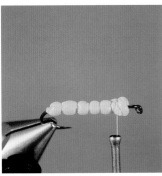

Step 3 – When complete, cut off any excess foam and then complete the rest of the fly (wings, legs, hackle, throat, etc.).

ADDING SIDE HACKLE TO CORK, BALSA, FOAM, AND HAIR-BODIED BUGS – Gerbubble bugs in cork or balsa were one of the first bugs to use strips of hackle along the side to imitate an injured baitfish laying on the surface. To do this, make a standard cork or balsa bug using a square-shaped body. Paint the bug and then use a hacksaw to cut a slot on each side of the body. Tie in the tail and collar. Prepare hackle, using two or more for each side. Add waterproof glue to the slits and gently force the hackle, butt ends forward, into the slots. Allow the glue to cure and cut off any excess along the front and rear of the bug.

Use marabou for more action, or Body Fur as a tough synthetic. To add hackle to a hair-bodied bug, first tie in the tail and then tie down the side hackle. Allow these side hackles to hang loose, and then complete the fly by spinning or stacking the body hair. Tie off the bug and then trim the bug to its final shape. Then re-attach the thread in back of the eye, pull the side hackle or materials forward, and tie in place. Cut any excess and tie off the head. Note that you cannot do this final step before trimming the bug, since that would make it impossible to trim the body hair without cutting the side hackle.

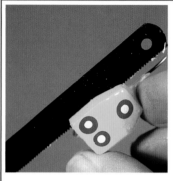

Step 1 – To add side hackle to a bug, as with a Gerbubble Bug, first use a hacksaw blade to cut a slot in each side of the bug.

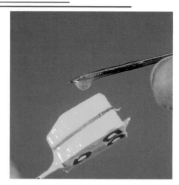

Step 2 – Once the slot is cut in each side and cleaned of sawdust, prepare and mix a puddle of five-minute epoxy. Add a drop or two of epoxy to each slot, but do one slot at a time as you add the hackle or side wing.

Step 3 – Prepare side hackle by using chicken or saddle hackle, pulling back on the fibers to flare them out at right angles to the central vane as shown here.

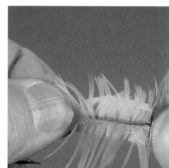

Step 4 – With the bug in a vise to hold it, use both hands to hold the ends of the hackle feather and force the central vane into the glued slot. This will fold the fibers over to make for a thicker side wing.

MAKING FLIES WEEDLESS – Mono loop – A length of 20- to 30-pound test mono is tied into the hook shank and wrapped around the bend of the hook before adding any materials. To help secure the mono and to lessen its bulk, squeeze the ends between pliers to flatten and roughen the mono portion that is tied down.

Tie the fly with the mono in place tied to the rear of the hook shank. Before tying off, bring the strand of mono forward and tie it in place on the underside of the head. Keep the loop long enough to protect the hook point until a fish hits. For best results, use two mono loops, one on each side of the hook. This allows a fly to be worked slowly through weeds or snaked over the top of limbs and brush without fear of snagging. To prevent the forward end of the mono from pulling out, use a flame to form a small ball on the end of each strand, and then tie down. The ball will prevent the mono from pulling out of the head wrap. Take care to not burn the thread or tying materials when balling the mono this way.

Prong method, mono – This involves tying the fly, then adding a short length of heavy mono when tying the head. First, fold the mono into an "L" shape to form a foot, then tie the mono down under the head of the fly so that the prong projects down in front of the hook point to protect it. Usually, 30- or 40-pound mono is used for this.

Prong method, single strand wire – For this, use 0.014 inch-diameter #5 size, single-strand wire and fold into an "L." Run the wire through the hook eye and tie down with the short folded end on top of the fly head after completing the fly. Then, fold the rest of the wire under the head, tie again and when complete, fold the rest of the wire down to project in front of the hook point. Just under the hook point, fold again so that the end of the wire forms a "skid" to protect the hook point.

Prong method, braided wire – This is really twisted fishing wire. 30-pound test is best for flies size 2 and under, and 40-pound test is best for those size 1 and larger. Tie the fly first, but do not finish it. Cut a length of wire several inches long, fold about 1/4 inch of the end to make a foot and tie it down to the underside of the head of the fly. Fold the end down to just in front of the hook point, and cut the excess just below the hook point.

Step 1 – To make a weedless fly using a single mono loop, first crimp the end of the mono used with serrated pliers to roughen and flatten the end of the mono. (Note – Shown with yellow, not clear, mono for photo clarity, and without tying the fly before finishing the weedless attachment at the hook eye.)

Step 2 – Begin by securing the crimped end of the mono with the tying thread as shown. Make sure that the mono curves down as shown here.

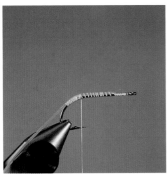

Step 3 – Wrap the thread evenly and tightly over the mono and partway down the hook bend. Then reverse the wrap to wind the thread back up the bend to the rear of the hook shank. At this point, begin tying the rest of the fly.

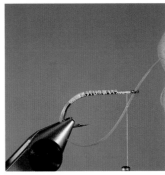

Step 4 – AFTER COMPLETING THE FLY, bring the mono loop forward between the vise jaws and through the eye of the hook. Position the mono loop so that it will protect the hook point.

Step 5 – Begin wrapping the thread around the mono and the hook shank as shown to capture the end of the mono.

Step 6 – Clip the end of the mono and use a flame as shown to make a ball on the end of the mono so that the mono will not slip out from under the tying threads.

Step 7 – Pull the mono back slightly so that the ball is no longer in the eye of the hook, but under the fly and in front of the tying thread as shown. Complete the fly by finishing the head with a whip finish.

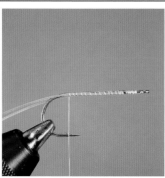

Double Loop Step 1 – To tie a weed guard with a double mono loop, follow the above instructions as to crimping the mono and tying it down, just use two lengths of mono as shown here, instead of one.

Step 2 – As above, wrap the thread part way down the hook bend and then back up again to the rear of the hook shank.

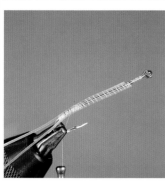

Step 3 – Here, a top view shows the two lengths of mono tied on each side of the hook shank.

Step 4 – As above, bring the two lengths of mono forward and under the fly AFTER TYING THE FLY. Make sure that the two loops are equal in size and adequately protect the hook point. Clip the ends and burn a ball on each with the flame as before.

Step 5 – Pull the mono loop slightly back to position the balled end of the mono loops and continue to wrap with thread to complete the fly. Tie off with a whip finish.

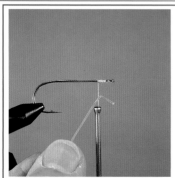

Prong Type Step 1 – To make a prong type of mono weed guard, first use pliers to bend the heavy mono into an "L" shape like this, with one very short leg for tying down onto the fly. Note that this is all done AFTER the rest of the fly is tied and as a last step in the tying process.

Step 2 – Hold the short end of the prong mono weed guard under the fly head and wrap in place with the tying thread.

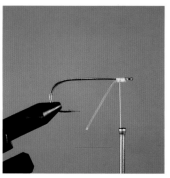

Step 3 – Once the prong weed guard is tied in place, clip it with wire cutters or heavy scissors to length as shown here. This can be done before (as shown) or after completing the head with a whip finish.

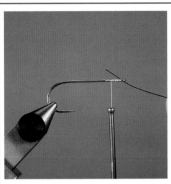

Mono Wire Step 1 – To make a mono wire weed guard, first get some wire (about 0.014 average – smaller or larger diameter as needed for fly size). AFTER THE REST OF THE FLY HAS BEEN TIED AND IS COMPLETE, insert the end of the wire through the hook eye as shown.

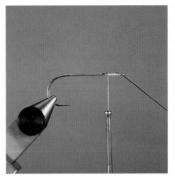

Step 2 – Use the working thread to tie down the end of the wire on top of the fly head as shown here.

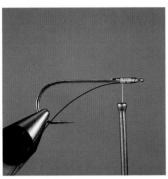

Step 3 – Fold the wire back parallel with the hook shank and tie again to secure the wire to the head of the fly.

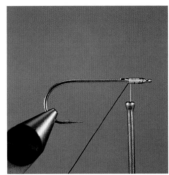

Step 4 – At the rear end of this tie-down point, bend the wire down as shown to form the weed guard that will protect the hook point.

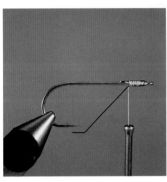

Step 5 – Clip the end of the wire and make a slight bend as shown to form a "sled" or step to protect the hook point. Complete the fly with a whip finish.

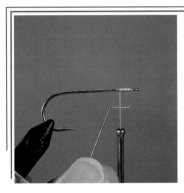

Braided Wire Step 1 – To make a braided wire prong weed guard, use braided (really twisted) wire and bend to a 60-degree angle as shown.

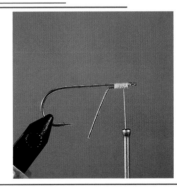

Step 2 – ONCE THE FLY IS COMPLETE, tie in the prong braided wire weed guard by the short leg under the head of the fly as shown here. The prong must extend in front of and below the hook point. Clip the end of the wire and complete the fly with a whip finish.

MAKING FLOATING BUGS WEEDLESS – You can use the same methods described above to tie in a weed guard of mono or wire to make a bug weedless. You can also take a shortcut by punching a hole in the belly of the bug body to insert the wire or the mono. For a single strand, you will have to place the hole just to the side of the hook shank. For double weed guards, you can place one prong on each side of the hook shank. Roughen the end of the mono or wire and glue it into the punched hole.

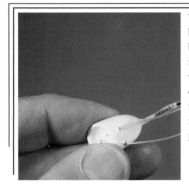

You can make weed guards in cork, balsa, or foam bugs the same way, but a handy tip is to bury the forward end or ends of the mono weed guards into the bug body. To do this, make a hole with an awl, cut the mono to length, crimp to roughen it, and glue into the prepared hole.

EXTENDING HOOKS FOR MAKING PENCIL POPPERS AND OTHER LONG-BODIED BUGS – If you need a very long hook you can extend the hook shank by adding a fishing connector link to the end of the hook. You could also cut off the bend of an identical hook (use care and eye protection) and then bend the cut shank end into a "U" shape. In some cases, you may have to heat the shank to soften the metal. Then loop the extension onto the hook and wrap the connection to prevent the hooks from disconnecting. In both cases, you must use ball eyehooks. Use a folded wire to pull this extended hook through the hole in a foam bug body, or enlarge the necessary slot area to hold the extension connection and hook eye on cork and balsa bodies.

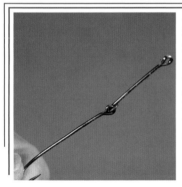

Step 1 – Of the several ways to lengthen a hook shank, one method is to make a wire form or use a hook with the bend cut off (careful – use safety goggles!) and attach this with a loop in the wire/hook to a ball eye long shank hook as shown. This will then extend the hook shank length for making pencil poppers.

Step 2 – Here, a hook with an extended shank has been placed in the belly of a balsa pencil popper. Note that the slot had to be widened for the eye of the hook to fit into the bug body. This will be glued in place, using standard methods previously described.

MAKING BUCKTAIL/SYNTHETIC LEGS FOR GLUING INTO FOAM/CORK/BALSA BODIES

Legs for some surface bugs are not tied on, but rather glued into the cork or foam body. First, use a small drill bit (handheld in a pin vise or carefully used in an electric drill) to drill a small hole or holes into the cork, balsa, or foam body. As a guide, holes are best when about 1/8-inch wide and about ?-inch deep, but can be varied as required. Cut a bundle (or two bundles as required for the bug) of bucktail, comb, and stack/even it. Cut it just slightly longer than desired for the bug being tied. Hold the bundle with the left hand close to the butt ends which are exposed and facing right. Hold the tag end of the working thread with the fingers and thumb of the left hand and begin to wind thread around the leg bundle. Wind the thread around the bundle where you want it to be glued into the bug body. Make a wrap that is about 1/8 inch to 3/16 inch wide. Tie off with a whip finish and clip the excess thread. Carefully cut the exposed fibers of bucktail so the wrap is at the very end of the bundle. When appropriate (often after finishing the rest of the bug), add epoxy glue or gel type CA (cyanoacrylate) adhesive into the hole in the bug and on the wrapped butt end of the leg or tail. Insert the bundle into the hole and use a toothpick to remove any excess sagging glue. Make sure the leg/tail is oriented properly before the glue sets.

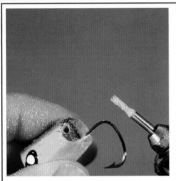

Step 1 – To glue frog legs into the body of a cork, balsa, or foam bug without tying to the hook shank, first drill holes in each side of the rear of the bug body as shown. Here a hobby router with a small cutting bit has been used to make the two holes.

Step 2 – To make the legs for such bugs, prepare (clip, comb, and stack/even) bundles of bucktail. Hold the bucktail at the position for the end of the leg and begin to wrap with tying thread, holding the tag end of the thread and the leg with the left hand. Wrap the thread around the bundle of bucktail with the right hand as shown.

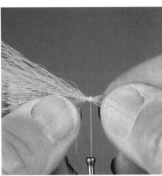

Step 3 – One way to speed the wrapping process is to use both hands to hold the leg – one on each side of the thread wrap, and spin (rotate) the bobbin around the leg. Use a short length of thread to avoid hitting yourself.

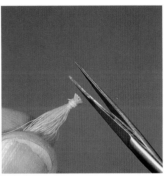

Step 4 – Once the leg is completely wrapped, tie off with a whip finish and then clip the butt end of the bucktail as shown here.

Step 5 – Prepare the bug body by mixing a puddle of five-minute epoxy glue, smearing some on the wrapped end of the leg and also inserting some in the previously drilled hole in the bug body.

Step 6 – Take each leg bundle in turn and carefully insert into the drilled and glued socket as shown to finish the bug. Hang or hold the bug in position until the glue cures to assure that the legs stay in proper position.

MAKING KICKER LEGS FOR FOAM AND CORK/BALSA FROGS – Legs for frog-style surface bugs can be tied onto or glued into bug bodies and fished with the legs straight, or made into bent "kicker" legs that resemble the bent hind legs of frogs. Do this after tying on legs or after the leg butt end is wrapped but before being glued into the bug body with separate legs. Hold the leg with your left hand where you will make the bend. Bury a stainless steel or nickel-plated pin or one-inch length of wire in the middle of the bundle. Begin to make the wrap by holding the tag end of the thread with the fingers of your left hand, and wind the thread around the bundle at this point. Continue to wind the thread around the bundle, making a smooth wrap that is about 1/4 inch to 3/8 inch wide. (You will need this width to make the bend in the wire and bundle and have the bend hold position.) Complete the wrap with a

whip finish and clip the excess thread. Fold the hair bundle so that the wire is sticking out and use wire cutters to clip the excess wire on both sides of the thread wrap. Use pliers or hemostats to hold the wrapped band, with one end of the pliers/hemostats at the point of the bend. Bend the legs at this point. The wire in the center of the bundle will hold the desired bend. Once you have the leg bent to the desired shape, seal and coat the thread wrap with several coats of head cement. When making legs with two colors or tails with flash, make sure that you make the bend in the proper orientation for the leg colors and tail flash. You can bend the knee anytime, but to make for easy tying, tie this after tying the end of the leg and before gluing it into the cork/balsa body. This will allow you to make the whip finish much easier.

Step 1 – To prepare "kicker" legs that have a knee bend, first prepare legs as above. Then hold the leg at the knee position and use a nickel-plated brass pin as a joint.

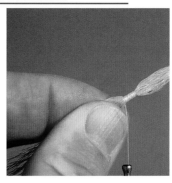

Step 2 - Wrap with tying thread as above with the pin in the center of the bucktail leg. Make a slightly longer wrap than above so that the bend to the knee is easily made later.

Step 3 – Complete the wrap with a whip finish and clip the excess thread. Wear safety goggles and use wire cutters to clip the excess wire on each end of the leg joint.

Step 4 – Use pliers to bend the wire in the center of the knee joint, bending in the center of the wrap to form the kicker leg.

Step 5 – Completed kicker leg, ready to be glued into a bug body or tied onto a hook shank. Seal the knee joint with head cement, nail polish, or other waterproof sealer.

Chapter 4

One Hundred Top Warmwater Flies

GENERAL NOTES ON THE PATTERNS, RECIPES AND TYING METHODS

The following list of 100 top warmwater flies is bound to provoke arguments. There are many reasons for these selections. We wanted to include the best possible flies for all species in the "warmwater" category, through all seasons, on any waters, in any part of the country. Obviously, no fly will do it all for a single species, much less the range of fish we are covering. Hard-bodied bass-bugs will not work on carp. Smallmouth nymphs will not take pike, and pike flies are entirely too big for any sunfish. Then too, there are patterns designed for just one part of the water column, such as bottom-fished (mostly) Clouser Deep Minnows, or top-water cork Sliders.

In addition, there are no exact patterns for each fly, even though the inventor might have had only one design and choice of materials in mind. One example is the original Gerbubble Bug for bass, which was originally made with a balsa body and hackle wings, but has recently been modified by some to a bug with a hollow hair body, a balsa body and synthetic body fur wings or a balsa body with marabou wings. Flies developed, promoted and sold by a particular company, may also promote the use of their brands of materials. Obviously, other similar brands can be used, provided that the end result is the same or what you want in your fly. Also, new hooks, materials, thread strengths and sizes, synthetics and hackle improvements have caused evolutions of fly patterns over the years.

Some thoughts on all this are as follows:

HOOKS – Suggested sizes are just that – suggestions. Assuming the materials are available, you can obviously tie flies larger or smaller than those listed. In most cases, you can get by with your favorite general-purpose fly hook, with standard lengths; a long-shank hook and a hump or kink-shank hook for hard bodied bugs are all that you will need. For streamers and some baitfish imitations, choose something between a 2X- and 4X- long-shank hook. You can also switch between standard fly hooks and the wide-gap stinger hooks. If trying to get a close match to a particular hook, check out *Hooks For The Fly*, by William E. Schmidt.

THREAD – Color of thread is particularly important not only in determining the color of the head of the fly, but also in the body color of some flies. This is less important with warmwater flies than with trout flies. Thread size is not listed since the thread size will vary with the fly or hook size, and most patterns can be tied in a wide range of sizes. Since warmwater flies vary widely in size, consider using 1/0 thread for flies larger than 2/0, size 3/0 thread for hook sizes from size 2 through 1/0 and size 6/0 for flies size 4 and smaller.

For more information on the many materials available, consult Modern Fly-Tying Materials, by Dick Talleur; Fly-Tying Materials, by Eric Leiser; and Fly-Dressing Materials, by John Veniard.

WEED GUARDS – Many warmwater flies are fished in slop, around snags and through weeds. Thus, directions for making several types of weedguards for flies and bugs are included in the Methods sections. Almost any fly described here can be tied with or without a weed guard.

The fly patterns listed show a variety of tying styles. In some cases, several patterns are included to show the ways in which a single material can be used (Messinger bugs, Chocklett bugs, Nix and Shimmer patterns). In other cases, patterns illustrate a single theme by using different materials and concepts (Gerbubble bugs, foam and cork/balsa poppers and sliders). Realize that with all of these flies and bugs, you can tie them in different colors and also often mix materials or use different materials, provided that it will give you the same general results.

Topwater Flies

GERBUBBLE BUG, ORIGINAL

This is a classic fly from the 1920s and perhaps one of the first with a side hackles and a big-bait silhouette that can still be cast with a fly rod.

When Tom Loving, a fly fisherman in the Chesapeake Bay region, fished the Susquehanna River below Conowingo Dam, he often noticed bass taking injured crappies that had come through the dam turbines and were flipping about on their sides on the surface. This surface bug, with a flat profile and hackle on both sides, matched the crappie shape and fins perfectly. The dimensions given here are those from the 1947 Joe Brooks book, *Bass Bug Fishing*. Joe, the seminal writer about fly-fishing at the time, fished with Tom Loving, so that the dimensions and descriptions are probably the most accurate available. Subsequent examples, located by tackle and lure collectors, have slightly varying dimensions, colors and spotting patterns. When originally designed, hump and kink shank hooks were not available, so all bugs – including this one, were modified with a metal clip soldered upright to the center hook shank to prevent hook rotation in the bug.

Tied by the author

Hook – Long hump shank hook, size 2/0

Thread – White, or to match the bug color

Body – Cork, squared dimensions of 9/16th inch high, 11/16th inch wide and 7/8th inch long, tapered on the back end. (Balsa is easier to work with today)

Tail – Two or three pairs of white saddle hackle, tied short

Collar – Rear of the collar white, **with** the front of the collar to match the color of the bug body

Side hackle – To match the bug body color

Paint finish – Brown, yellow or white, with three to five evenly spaced color spots top and bottom. Paint eyes on the flat front of the bug

Tying sequence:

1. Use cork or balsa, cut and shaped to the above dimensions. Slot the center belly to hold the hook shank.
2. Tie the thread on the hook and spiral wrap thread up and down the hook shank to give bonding surface to the glue bond of the bug on the hook. Finish with the working thread just in front of the hook bend.
3. Tie in the tail of paired white saddle hackles, with the hackles of each side flared out for more action in the water. Trim any excess forward hackle.
4. Tie in a white saddle hackle for the collar, followed by a saddle hackle that will match the color chosen for the bug body.
5. Wind the white saddle hackle around the hook shank, tie off with the working thread and then clip any excess hackle.
6. Repeat the above with the forward saddle that will match the Gerbubble Bug body color. Tie off and clip any excess hackle.
7. Wrap the working thread slightly forward and complete with a whip finish. Clip the excess thread.
8. Use five-minute epoxy to glue the body onto the hook shank, covering the thread wrappings, but with clearance for the tail and collar. Allow to cure over night.
9. Use an emery board to sand the belly smooth, and remove any excess glue.
10. Pull the hackle back to allow painting the body with two base coats of white paint. Allow to cure between each coat of paint.
11. Repeat the above, with two coats of the finish color.
12. Use two sizes of nail heads to make concentric rings of color – three to five on the belly and back and two on the front face to simulate eyes. Make the large spot first, allow to cure and then follow with the smaller center spot.
13. Carefully cut a slit with a razor blade or hacksaw blade along each side of the bug, equidistant from the top and bottom and parallel to the hook shank.
14. Open the slit slightly, add a small bead of glue and then insert a folded saddle hackle, butt end forward, that matches the bug color. Do this on both sides and allow to cure overnight.
15. Use a razor blade to trim the front and rear side hackle.

GERBUBBLE BUG, HAIR-BODIED

This variation of the original Gerbubble Bug is attributed to Dave Whitlock, who uses a body of deer hair in place of the cork or balsa body of the original.

One of the problems of tying the original Gerbubble Bug is in the sequence of tying and painting (or painting and tying) and the later addition of the side hackle. Some modern paints are very hard and make it difficult to slice the side with the razor or hacksaw blade, which can also sometimes cause the paint to crack. One solution is this all hair-and-hackle design, in which the bug can be completed in one step, without the delay or separate steps of shaping, painting and tying. It is an excellent bug, but as with any deer or hollow hair bug, will not float as high and long as will the original. In some cases, this can be an advantage, as the low-floating body hair bugs will "wake" more, and can attract more fish. This was designed as a largemouth and smallmouth bass bug, but can be used for any species that takes bait off of the surface.

Tied by Umpqua Feather Merchants

Materials Needed

Hook – Wide gap straight eye hook or stinger hook, long shank sizes 4 to 3/0

Thread – Tan or brown, or to match the bug if other colors are tied

Tail – A pair of yellow grizzly saddle hackles

Collar – Yellow dyed grizzly hackle

Body – Yellow deer body hair, spun and trimmed flat on the sides, top and bottom

Side hackle – Yellow dyed grizzly hackle on each side of the bug

Head – Black, then yellow deer hair, spun and trimmed to match the rest of the body

Tying sequence:

1. Tie in the working thread at the bend of the hook, and clip any excess thread.
2. Tie in the tail first of the yellow grizzly saddle hackles. Flare the hackle out for maximum action.
3. Tie in the collar of yellow grizzly hackle and trim the butt ends.
4. Wrap the collar hackle around the hook shank and tie off. Trim the excess hackle.
5. Tie in pairs of yellow dyed grizzly hackle by the tips, to be pulled forward to make the side hackle once the bug is complete.
6. Tie in the first bundle of clipped and combed deer hair, and spin it around the hook shank. Repeat the above until filling about half of the hook shank with yellow deer hair. Secure with a few half hitches.

7. Use scissors and then a double-edge blade razor to shape and trim the body. Make sure that the body is trimmed close on the belly for maximum hook gap clearance. Take care to not cut the collar or the loose side hackles.
8. Bring the side hackles forward and into the clipped deer hair and tie off on the hook shank immediately in front of the spun and trimmed deer hair. Clip any excess hackle.
9. Add a bundle of clipped and combed black deer hair.
10. Repeat the above with yellow deer hair again until filling the hook shank to the hook eye.
11. When reaching the hook eye, make a small head of the thread, and then tie off with a whip finish. Clip the excess and seal the head with head cement.
12. Trim the remainder of the deer hair (the orange deer hair head) to match the shape of the previously trimmed body hair. Take care to avoid cutting the side hackle.

GERBUBBLE BUG, MARABOU WINGS

This Gerbubble Bug modification is a great largemouth bug for still water, since the marabou side hackle has far better action and movement in the water than any other hackle or synthetic material.

Captain Norm Bartlett, an expert bass and saltwater fly fisherman and angler, first showed me his variation of the Gerbubble Bug some 40 years ago, long before he had his captain's license. The soft marabou in the cork or balsa body makes for a Gerbubble Bug that has far more movement of the side hackles than anything else available. As a result, it is a great bug for slow, stillwater fishing for largemouth. Norm likes it on wire-weedguard hooks for structure and weed fishing. Try it carefully around lily pads, other surface weeds and any surface structure. Fish it as slowly as you dare. Explosive strikes are often the result.

Tied by Capt. Norm Bartlett

Materials Needed

Hook – Size 3/0 wire weedguard hook	**Tail** – Yellow marabou	**Side hackle** – Yellow marabou with 1/2 to 3/4 inch long plumes
Thread – Yellow	**Collar** – Black marabou	
	Body – Balsa, painted yellow	

Tying sequence:

1. Use cork or balsa, cut and shaped to the original dimensions. Slot the center belly to hold the hook shank.
2. Tie the thread on the hook and spiral wrap thread up and down the hook shank for bonding surface on the hook shank. Tie off with a whip finish and clip the excess thread.
3. Use five-minute epoxy to glue the body onto the hook shank, covering the thread wrappings. Allow to cure overnight.
4. Use an emery board to sand the belly smooth.
5. Paint the body with two base coats of white paint. (Norm likes to seal balsa bodies first with a mixture of acetone and airplane glue. Other sealers will work also.) Allow to cure between coats of sealer.
6. Paint with two coats of yellow paint. (Other colors are also effective.)
7. Tie in the tail of yellow marabou plumes. Trim any excess forward marabou. Note that with this wire weed guard hook, you will have to bend the weed guard at right angles to the hook to allow for thread clearance while tying.

8. Tie in black marabou fibers for the collar. This can be tied in place or a small plume wound around the hook shank and tied off, then excess marabou stem clipped.
9. Wrap the working thread slightly forward and complete with a whip finish. Clip the excess thread.
10. Optional, but traditional with original Gerbubble bugs. Norm does not include this step in his version – use two sizes of nail heads to make concentric rings of color – three to five on the belly and back and two on the front face to simulate eyes. Make the large spot first, allow to cure and then follow with the smaller center spot.
11. Carefully cut a slit with a hack saw blade along each side of the bug, equidistant from the top and bottom and parallel to the hook shank.
12. Open the slit slightly, add a small bead of glue and then insert the folded marabou so that about 1/2 to 3/4-inch of plumes extend from each side. Do on both sides and allow to cure overnight.
13. Use a razor blade to trim the front and rear marabou.

GERBUBBLE BUG, BODY FUR WINGS

This is the author's variation of the Gerbubble Bug. It is quick and easy to make using the hard bodies, and allows using synthetic side hackles which can be trimmed to any shape if desired.

Body Fur is like a carpet fringe without the carpet. Or you can think of it as a synthetic hackle feather in which fibers only grow from one side of the main stem. It is a great material for selective purposes and allows easy and quick attachment of the side hackle on prepared and painted balsa bodies. This bug makes it easy to construct and tie Gerbubble Bugs quickly and to add the side "hackle" in one step, running the Body Fur around the bug from one side to the other.

Tied by the author

Materials Needed

Hook – Any long, hump shank bug hook, sizes 4 through 2/0.

Thread – To match the Gerbubble Bug color.

Tail – Synthetic tail material such as Super Hair, Ultra Hair or Poly Bear, to match the bug body color.

Tail Flash – Several strands of Krystal Flash on each side of the tail.

Body – Balsa, shaped to the rough "sugar cube" proportions of the original as above. Size based on hook size.

Side hackle – Synthetic Body Fur

Paint finish – Solid colors such as white, yellow, light green, dark green, black, orange, brown and tan, painted with the two concentric spots three times on the back and belly and with two spots for eyes on the flat front face. Painted white on this example.

Tying sequence:

1. Shape and sand balsa bodies. One easy way to do this is to buy balsa strips 36 inches X1/2 inch X1/4 inch, cut them into 3/4 inch long bodies, slot with a hacksaw blade and shape. Other sizes are appropriate for smaller and larger hooks.

2. Place a hook in the vise, then spiral wrap the full length with thread and tie off with a whip finish. Clip the excess thread.

3. If using the above size Gerbubble Bug, glue onto a long shank size 2 hump-shank hook.

4. Allow to cure overnight, and then use an emery board to file smooth any excess glue.

5. Paint the bug body, using two coats of white or primer, then two coats of the finish color (white). Add the concentric dots of contrasting color on the back, belly and face, as per above.

6. Use a hacksaw blade to cut (or to reopen and clear paint, if already cut) a groove around both sides and the rear of the bug body. This must be one continuous cut. An alternate to this is to use a fine rotary cutter or cutting disc in a hobby tool to form a slot in the side and rear of the bug.

7. Place the hook in a vise, and then tie on the thread immediately in back of the bug body. Clip any excess thread.

8. Tie in a tail of Super Hair, followed by some Poly Bear. (Other synthetics are also fine for this.)

9. Tie in several strands of Krystal Flash on each side of the tail.

10. Tie off the thread using a whip finish.

11. Seal the thread whip finish with several coats of head cement or Sally Hansen Hard as Nails fingernail polish.

12. Place a small bead of waterproof glue in the continuous side/rear slot.

13. Run a strand of Body Fur around the slot, pinning it at each end (the front) or using a spring clamp to hold the Body Fur taut until the glue cures.

14. Cut any excess Body Fur in front of the Gerbubble Bug face.

(Optional – trim the body fur to wing or other shapes, if desired.)

MESSINGER BUCKTAIL FROG

This classic frog imitation is a beauty to behold, aerodynamically correct and a joy to fish.

Joe Messinger Jr. notes that in all his research on early flies, to the best of his knowledge, his father was the first to develop the method of stacking. "I'm pretty sure that Dad was the first one to separate colors of deer hair laterally," Joe told me recently. His father never spun deer hair – only stacked it. This was prior to the beginning of World War I in 1914, when Joe Sr. went to fight in France. Later, in the 1920s he began to sell his creations. His stacking was not developed from a desire to make something different so much as it was a result of his method of tying by clamping the hook vertically and tying a bundle of hair on each side of the hook using knots, instead of the spinning/stacking method used by tyers today. The result of the two-sided tying was that it was easy to make a frog with a light belly and darker back. Joe, Jr. continues this tradition and the method of tying today (which many tyers consider more durable than standard methods of stacking) although standard tying and stacking procedures shown here will accomplish the same result.

Tied by Joe Messinger Jr.

Hook – Regular bass hook, straight ringed eye, wide gap TMC 8089 #6 and 10, Mustad 3366 #1 and 1/0 or other regular hook or stinger hook.

Thread – Cotton-covered polyester "button and carpet" thread for original Messinger method; size A rod winding thread for standard spinning and stacking.

Legs – Green on top of yellow bucktail, with a pin for the knee and heavy thread to bunch the thigh

Body – Green hollow deer hair back stacked over a white deer hair belly, with a yellow belly patch of hair at the rear to match the yellow on the legs. Trimmed with a round belly

Eyes – Plastic eyes, cemented into sockets burned into the trimmed deer hair head, or softened plastic melted in acetone (Messinger's original method) applied to the sockets.

Tying sequence:

1. Tie in the size A thread at the rear of the hook shank (directly above the hook point) and clip the excess thread.
2. Wind a small bundle or bump of thread in this area.
3. Wind the thread up to the hook eye and then back down to the raised bump to provide a no-slip surface for stacking the deer hair.
4. Coat the wraps with head cement and allow to dry.
5. Prepare (clip, comb and stack/even) a bundle of yellow bucktail from near the rump of the deer for the legs.
6. Repeat the above by preparing a bundle of green bucktail on top, placed on top of the yellow. With the two colors combined, this bundle should be about the diameter of a pencil and about twice the length of the hook shank.
7. Place this bundle on top of the hook shank and use a single length of button and carpet thread to tie the bundle down, tips forward, slightly in front of the thread bump. Use a square knot. (You may have to use your teeth to hold one end of the thread while one hand holds the bucktail bundle in place and the other forms and pulls the knots tight.)
8. Tie down the bundle of hair tips forward, with the yellow on the bottom and the green on top. (The tips forward assure that the final legs have enough spring in them when fished.)
9. Trim the butt ends. Use a bodkin to place a drop of medium viscosity cyanoacrylate glue on the thread bump. Slide the hair back into the glue and allow glue to cure.
10. Separate the combined bundle (top green and bottom yellow) with a bodkin into two identical bundles, each with a strand of heavy thread in the center of the bundle.
11. Divide the two bundles of legs with thread and make sure that the divided legs are roughly parallel to each other as they extend from the hook shank.
12. Tie the leg bundles temporarily with thread to hold them out of the way.
13. Prepare (clip, comb and stack/even) a bundle of green deer hair and tie onto the top of the hook shank, using the stacking method.
14. Push the deer hair to the rear and move the thread to just forward of this stacked bundle.

15. Repeat the above with yellow, then white deer hair on the underside of the hook after reversing the hook position 180 degrees, or tying the bundle in on the underside of the hook if held in a standard point-down position.
16. Repeat the above two steps, reversing back and forth on the hook shank as you tie forward along the hook.
17. Continue until reaching the hook eye, making the body white on the bottom and green on the top.
18. Tie off using a whip finish and clip the excess thread.
19. Seal the wraps with head cement.
20. Trim the bug body to an egg shape, making a rounded belly and back, and finish the shaping with a single edge razor blade.
21. Form knees in each leg by inserting a #17 nickel-stainless steel pin or wire into each leg bundle near the frog body. Wrap the bundle at this point with a 3/8-inch wide winding of separate tying thread. Begin this wrap about 3/8-inch from the body and wrap towards the end of the leg. Tie off with a whip finish.
22. Use pliers (if necessary) to bend the legs at a right angle and about 15 degrees up so that the lower part of the leg is facing forward and slightly angled up. Use non-serrated jaw pliers to avoid cutting or harming the thread wraps.
23. Hold the leg by the knee and pull on the heavy thread to bunch the forward part of the leg. Clip the excess thread.
24. Use wire cutters (wear safety goggles) to cut the excess wire extending beyond the wrap on each leg.
25. Seal the leg wrap with several coats of black lacquer or head cement.
26. If desired, burn or cut sockets into the position for the two eyes on each side of the body. Use epoxy or a flexible cement to glue plastic or doll eyes into the sockets or onto the surface of the trimmed deer hair.

Alternately, you can use Joe's method of making eyes, by melting plastic hook boxes in acetone to make a thick jelly. Dip a bodkin into this and remove a small ball, shaping this with the fingers to make a round eye. Then apply this to a socket cut or burned into the bug body to make a raised eye. Joe paints his eyes gold with a black pupil, thinking it is most like a live frog.

MESSINGER BUCKTAIL POPPER FROG

This popping version of the Bucktail Frog is another classic design from Joe Messinger Sr. and today also tied expertly by Joe Messinger Jr. The Messinger Bucktail Frog is more of a slider style while this is definitely a popper.

This is an obvious offshoot of the original Bucktail Frog, above, and involves almost the same techniques except for the difference in trimming and the heavily cemented cupped popping face. This was another of the many creative deer-hair styles developed by Messinger, an underrated, creative and inventive West Virginia coal miner who tied and sold flies and bugs to supplement the family income. Use it as you would a regular popper, casting it around lily pads and other weeds. As with any of the Messinger bugs, it can be tied weedless with a single or double mono weed guard, or left plain as in this example. It can be tied in any color. Note that in this example by the originator, it is all brown and tan. According to Joe Jr., Joe Sr. never tied any of his frogs in green, despite the popularity of that color today.

Tied by Joe Messinger Sr. supplied by Joe Messinger Jr.

Materials Needed

Hook – Regular bass hook, straight ringed eye, wide gap TMC 8089 #6 and 10, Mustad 3366 #1 and 1/0 or other regular hook or stinger hook.

Thread – Cotton-covered polyester "button and carpet" thread for original Messinger method; size A rod-winding thread for standard spinning and stacking.

Legs – Tan or light brown on top of yellow bucktail, with a pin for the knee and heavy thread to bunch the thigh

Body – Tan or light brown hollow deer hair stacked over white deer hair, trimmed with a round belly

Eyes – Plastic eyes, cemented into sockets burned into the trimmed deer hair head, or softened plastic melted in acetone (Messinger's original method) applied to the sockets.

Tying sequence:

1. Tie in the size A thread at the rear of the hook shank (directly above the hook point) and clip the excess thread.
2. Wind a small bundle or bump of thread in this area.
3. Wind the thread up to the hook eye and then back down to the raised bump to provide a no-slip surface for stacking the deer hair.
4. Coat the wraps with head cement and allow to dry.
5. Prepare (clip, comb and stack/even) a bundle of yellow bucktail from near the rump of the deer for the legs.
6. Repeat the above by preparing and tying down a bundle of brown bucktail on top of the yellow. Combined, this bundle should be about the diameter of a pencil and twice the length of the hook shank.
7. Place this bundle on top of the hook shank and use a single length of button and carpet thread to tie down the bundle, tips forward, slight in front of the thread bump. (You may have to use your teeth to hold one end of the thread while one hand holds the bucktail in place and the other forms and pulls the knots tight.)
8. Tie down the bundle of hair tips forward, with the yellow on the bottom and the brown on top. (The tips forward assure that the final legs have enough spring in them when fished.)
9. Trim the butt ends. Use a bodkin to place a drop of medium viscosity cyanoacrylate glue on the thread bump. Slide the hair bundle back into the glue and allow the glue to cure.
10. Separate the combined bundle (top brown and bottom yellow) with a bodkin into two identical bundles, each with a strand of heavy thread in the center of the bundle.
11. Separate and divide each bundle to make the legs. Make sure that the legs are angled back (almost parallel). Trim the butt ends of the hair.
12. Tie the leg bundles temporarily with thread to hold them out of the way.
13. Prepare (clip, comb and stack/even) a bundle of brown deer hair and tie onto the top of the hook shank, using the stacking method.
14. Push the deer hair to the rear and move the thread to just forward of this stacked bundle.
15. Repeat the above with yellow, then white deer hair on the underside of the hook after reversing the hook position 180 degrees or tying on the underside of the point-down hook, or tying by adding bundles to the under part of the bug.
16. Repeat the above two steps, reversing back and forth on the hook shank as you tie forward along the hook.
17. Continue until reaching the hook eye, making the body white on the bottom and brown on the top.
18. Tie off using a whip finish and clip the excess thread.
19. Seal the wraps with head cement.
20. Trim the back part of the bug body to an egg shape, making a rounded belly and back, and finish the shaping with a single-edge razor blade.
21. Trim the forward part of the body that is facing forward so that you have a rounded cupped popper face.
22. Use Duco or plastic cement to coat this front body hair cupped face. The top of the cup should angle forward of the bottom to make it easier to pick the bug up at the end of a retrieve. Make any final trimming necessary after the cement has cured.
23. Form knees in each leg by inserting a #17 nickel plated brass pin or wire into each leg bundle close to the body and wrapping the bundle at this point with a 3/8-inch wide winding of separate tying thread. Begin this wrap about 3/8-inch from the body and wrap towards the end of the leg. Tie off with a whip finish and clip the excess thread.
24. Use pliers (if necessary – non-serrated jaws to avoid damage to the thread windings) to bend the legs at a right angle and an up angle of about 15 degrees so that the lower part of the leg is facing forward and slightly angled up.
25. Hold the knee area and pull on the heavy thread to bunch the forward part of the leg and clip the excess thread.
26. Use wire cutters (wear safety goggles) to cut the excess wire extending beyond the wrap on each leg.
27. Seal the leg wrap with several coats of black lacquer or head cement.
28. If desired, burn or cut sockets into the position for the two eyes on each side of the body. Use epoxy or a flexible cement to glue plastic or doll eyes into the sockets or onto the surface of the trimmed deer hair.

Alternately, you can use Joe's method of making eyes, by melting plastic hook boxes in acetone to make a thick jelly. Dip a bodkin into this and remove a small ball, shaping this with the fingers to make a round eye. Then apply this to a socket cut or burned into the bug body to make a raised eye. Joe paints his eyes gold with a black pupil.

MESSINGER BASS KICKER DIVING FROG

This is another spin-off of the original Messinger frog designs that incorporates stacked body hair, a foam collar and rubber/plastic legs.

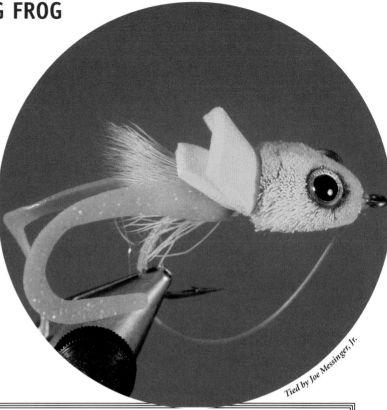

Think of this as a Messinger modification of a Dahlberg diving bug. It is available in kit form from Rocky Mountain Dubbing. This is a Joe Messinger Jr. design, and a variation of his father's original Bucktail Frog. It also incorporates some new materials that were not available when Joe Sr. was first tying the original frogs some 80 years ago. It uses curly rubber legs that come on a paper sheet and are easily pulled off by stretching the rubber to separate it from the paper. It is also possible to use other legs, such as bundles of silicone or rubber strands, cut chamois or Ultra Suede, or other materials that occur to you. Once tying down the rubber legs and the foam collar, the rest of the bug is tied and trimmed, as is any Messinger pattern. As with the Messinger Frogs, try this around lily pads and other waterweeds, and also around structures such as stumps, duck blinds, piers and such.

Tied by Joe Messinger, Jr.

Materials Needed

Hook – T.M.C. 8089 in sizes 6 or 10, or equivalent bass hook or stinger hook

Thread – Green, size E rod building thread

Tail/legs – Two yellow Flexi-Tail legs

Skirt – Yellow deer hair

Collar – Yellow foam triangular shaped collar

Body – Stacked deer hair, white on the bottom and yellow on top or back

Weed guard – 20-pound mono, single loop

Eyes – Plastic, glued in place to the trimmed body

Tying sequence:

1. Tie in the working thread at the rear of the hook shank above the hook point and clip the excess thread.
2. Tie in a length of monofilament for a weed guard and wrap partway around the hook bend to secure it. Return to a spot above the hook point.
3. Prepare (clip, comb, and stack) yellow deer hair and tie down at the thread point with the tips pointing towards the rear.
4. Tie in the two yellow legs on top of and at a 45-degree angle to the hook shank at the same point as the bundle of deer hair. Make sure that the legs are pointed down.
5. Tie in the triangular shaped foam collar in the middle, with the narrow end pointed towards the rear. Tie this in at the same point as the bundle of deer hair and the legs.
6. After several wraps of thread around the foam collar at this point, fold the collar back towards the bend of the hook and take several more wraps of thread in front of this fold to secure the hair bundle, legs and collar.
7. Prepare (clip, comb and stack/even) a bundle of yellow deer hair and tie down on top of the hook shank at this point, using the stacking method to keep the deer hair on top of the hook shank.
8. Repeat the above with white deer hair, tying it down to the hook shank on the underside of the body (turn the hook over 180 degrees) and stack as above.
9. Repeat the above two steps as you work your way to the hook eye.
10. At the hook eye, bring the mono loop forward and tie down with the thread, making sure that the loop is positioned to protect the hook eye. Clip the excess mono.
11. Make several final wraps and tie off the thread with a whip finish. Clip the excess thread.
12. Seal the wraps with head cement.
13. Trim the body, using scissors and a razor blade to make the butt flat on the bottom and rounded and tapered back to the collar on top.
14. Clip or burn eye sockets on each side of the top of the body.
15. Clip off the stems of plastic eyes or use doll eyes, add some glue (Duco, Goop, etc.) to the socket and add the eyes.

MESSINGER NITEHUMMER

Many writers have commented on smallmouth and largemouth bass taking moths from the surface. This is an ideal pattern for those situations.

Moths are obviously out more at night, when white bugs like this are ideal for largemouth. In some sections of the country, white mayflies, called white millers, are a frequent forage food of river smallmouth bass. Any of this fishing is best in the late afternoon or early evening, when mayflies and moths are more prevalent and found drifting or fluttering on the surface. Joe Messinger Sr. developed this Nite Hummer as a surface bug to imitate moths for this specialized fishing. While it can be tied in different colors for different fishing, this pattern color is best for the fishing for which it was designed. As with all of Messinger's patterns, it features the stacking technique if you want to make it like the original.

Tied by Joe Messinger Jr.

Materials Needed

Hook – Regular hook, wide gap, straight eye, sizes 10 to 1/0

Thread – Cotton covered polyester

carpet and button thread

Tail – Black body deer hair

Body – Stacked body deer hair,

white on the bottom and yellow on top

Collar – Black deer hair

Tying sequence:

1. Tie in the working thread at the rear of the hook shank. Clip the excess thread.
2. Prepare (clip, comb and stack/even) a bundle of black body deer hair for the tail of the bug.
3. Tie down the tail, making it short, and in line with the hook shank.
4. Clip the excess tail material.
5. Prepare (clip, comb and stack/even) a small bundle of white deer hair and tie this in on the belly of the bug, on the underside of the hook shank at the rear, using the stacking method.
6. Prepare (clip, comb and stack/even) a small bundle of yellow deer hair.
7. Tie this bundle in on the top of the hook shank using the stacking method after reversing the hook shank 180 degrees.
8. Repeat the above two steps, reversing the hook 180 degrees each time.
9. Continue as above, covering about 2/3 of the hook shank with the stacked deer hair. Leave the forward 1/3 of the hook shank for the wings and beard.
10. Tie off with a whip finish and clip the excess.
11. Trim the body of the bug to a rounded egg-shape body, using scissors first followed by a razor blade.
12. Retie the thread to the front of the hook shank, and clip the excess.
13. Prepare a bundle of black body deer hair (clip, comb and stack/even) and tie down on top of the hook shank, spinning the deer hair so that it surrounds the hook shank to make a uniform collar around the body. Tie this down by the butts so that the tips only form the collar. Trim the excess butts and wrap to make a large thread head.
14. Tie off with a whip finish and clip the excess.
15. Seal the head with head cement.

LEFTY'S POTOMAC RIVER POPPER

This bug was developed on the Potomac River for smallmouth bass, but is ideal for river fishing for any species.

Lefty Kreh developed this bug while guiding on the Potomac River in his early years, long before the world discovered him. His thought on this design was simplicity. The basic bug is nothing more than half a bottle cork with a simple squirrel tail. Recent improvements by Lefty include the cactus chenille collar, shown here. The lack of a traditional, heavily hackled collar makes this a streamlined bug for casting. It also makes it far easier pick up off the water for fast casting to get back to a glide in the current. Fish it fast, with a skipping action that is aided by the sloping face of the bug. The fish seem to care little that it lacks the hackle collar standard in bugs up to the time 50 years ago when this bug was first thought of and fished.

Tied by Lefty Kreh

Materials Needed

Hook – Any long shank popper hump shank hook, sizes 6 through 1/0

Thread – Yellow or brown, to match the tail or bug color

Tail – Yellow dyed squirrel tail

Collar – Gold cactus chenille, wrapped around the rear of the hook shank between the tail and the body

Body – A bottle cork, cut in half lengthwise, with a slight popping slope cut into the face, slotted and glued onto the thread-wrapped hook and painted yellow

Tying sequence:

1. Tie on the thread anywhere on the hook shank, and spiral wrap it up and down for a better glue bond. Clip off any excess thread and finish the wrap with the thread just in front of the hook bend.
2. Prepare a 1/2 bottle cork, slot the flat belly, and glue to the hook using epoxy glue.
3. If desired, use cork and glue filler to fill in any pits in the cork body.
4. Paint the cork with two coats of primer or white paint, then two coats of the finish paint. The traditional color for this is yellow, but other colors can be tried also.

5. Re-tie in the thread in back of the cork body and clip the excess thread.
6. Wind the thread to the rear of the hook shank.
7. Tie in a small bundle of squirrel tail for the tail of the bug. Clip any excess squirrel tail.
8. Tie in a length of gold cactus chenille.
9. Wind the thread forward to the bug body.
10. Wrap the chenille forward and tie off with the thread. Clip the excess chenille.
11. Tie off the bug with a whip finish. Clip the excess thread.
12. Seal the thread wrap with head cement.

CHOCKLETT'S DISC SLIDER

This unusual design allows making foam poppers without the hassle of cutting or shaping foam cylinders.

Tied by Blane Chocklett

Blane Chocklett, a James River guide and with his wife Dru, owner of Blue Ridge Fly Fishers, developed this fly from foam discs that are now available in several sizes and many colors from all fly shops. If you can't find these discs in the 1/4-inch, 3/8-inch and 1/2-inch sizes, you can punch out your own with a length of sharpened brass tubing from thin (2 mm) foam available in many colors from craft stores. The bug is a build-up of these discs, tying them in as you work forward on the fly after tying down any tail materials. To tie this fly easily, use a vise in which the jaws can be placed horizontal to easily switch the fly position for tying on back or belly discs. It is a little more complicated, but you can also reverse the disc direction to make a similar disc popper, tied the same way. This disc slider is designed for moving water. It was first fished on the James for smallmouth, but is ideal for any top water application. It is more a design than a pattern. This one in chartreuse is a favorite of Blane, but it can be tied in many colors, including contrasting colors on the belly and back. Fish it fast for maximum popping action.

Materials Needed

Hook – Tiemco 8089 wide gap hook, or similar wide gap hook, size 6 and 10. (The wide gap is suggested to allow for the space taken up by the belly discs.)

Thread – Chartreuse, or to match the color of the discs and fly.

Tail – Chartreuse marabou flanked with chartreuse Krystal Flash.

Skirt – Two chartreuse or yellow saddle hackles

Legs – Yellow or chartreuse rubber legs.

Body – Chartreuse foam discs, 1/2-inch top and 3/8-inch belly for the size 6 hook, and 3/8-inch top and 1/4-inch belly for the size 10 hook.

Eyes – Doll or prism eyes, glued to the face of the first disc.

Tying sequence:

1. Tie in the thread at the bend of the hook and clip off any excess thread.
2. Clip and tie in a bundle of chartreuse marabou.
3. Cut and tie in a few strands of chartreuse Krystal Flash on each side of the marabou tail. Clip the excess.
4. Tie in two chartreuse saddle hackles and clip the butt ends.
5. Wind the hackle around the hook shank and tie off with the thread. Clip the tip ends.
6. Tie in a bundle of yellow or chartreuse rubber legs just forward of the tail.
7. Rotate the fly vise to position the hook point up and tie in the first of the belly discs. Do this by wrapping the edge of the disc just enough to hold it. Note that for the slider, the free edge of the disc must be facing back.
8. Rotate the vise back to the hook point down position, and repeat the above with the larger back disc, again with the free edge of the disc facing back.
9. After tying down two discs each top and bottom, tie in another set of rubber legs.
10. Continue this top/bottom disc tying with two more discs top and bottom, until there are four discs top and bottom, with the top disc the last one tied in place.
11. Make a small neat head and tie off with a whip finish. Clip the excess thread and seal with head cement.
12. Use cyanoacrylate or epoxy glue to add the eyes to the front disc.

CORK POPPER

Cork poppers are a staple of any surface fly rod fishing. Depending upon size, color and dressing, they are ideal for everything from bluegill to big pike.

There are lots of ways to make cork poppers. This is a shaped cork popper with a cork bullet-head that is glued onto the hook and painted. Only after this is the bug actually tied, placing the hook in a vise and adding any tail, frog legs, collar or other additions along with a weed guard, if desired. Many shapes and designs are available, and finished bug bodies (both glued on the hook and also glued and painted and ready for tying) make constructing and tying bugs even simpler and faster. These, available from many fly shops and catalogs, allow tying without any of the shaping, sanding, cutting, gluing or painting. Many colors are possible, most in which the bug body and tail/collar are the same or complementary.

Tied by the author

Materials Needed

Hook – Long-shank kinked or hump shank bass bug hook, size 12 through 1/0

Thread – Yellow (or color of the bug tail and collar)

Tail – Yellow bucktail

Flash – Strands of yellow or green Krystal Flash

Collar – Yellow saddle hackle and grizzly saddle hackle, mixed

Body – Bullet shape cork body, glued onto hook shank

Finish – Body painted yellow with black spots

Tying sequence:

1. For bodies not available already prepared, cut and sand a cork cylinder into a bullet shape, using a rasp and then successively finer grades of sandpaper. Mix glue and cork dust to fill in any pits. Sand to final shape after the fill cures.

2. Once the cork is prepared, slot the belly with a hacksaw blade, just deep enough to hold the hook shank.

3. Prepare a long-shank kinked or hump shank hook that has a gap similar to the diameter of the cork body face. Do this by tying coarse thread onto the hook shank and spiral wrapping up and down the hook shank in the area to be covered by the body.

4. Tie off the thread with a whip finish and clip the excess.

5. Mix five-minute epoxy and with a bodkin add some to the slot and some to the hook shank.

6. Insert the hook into the slot, remove any excess glue from each end of the hook shank and make sure that the hook plane is at right angles to the bug belly. Add a small puddle of glue to the belly, since some glue shrinkage will occur.

7. Allow to cure.

8. Once cured, use an emery board to file and smooth the belly and remove excess glue.

9. Paint the bug body using one of the several techniques described in the Methods section. Add one or two coats of primer first, followed by final coats and any additional spots, stripes or decorations desired.

10. Once the final coat of paint is cured, place the hook in a vise and tie on the thread directly in back of the cork body. Clip any excess thread.

11. Prepare a bundle of yellow bucktail (clip, comb and stack to even the ends) and measure for length. (Generally about 1½ times the shank length.)

12. Place on the rear of the hook shank and tie down. Clip any forward excess. Add two sparse bundles of Krystal Flash to each side of the tail, the Krystal Flash extending a little beyond the tail feathers.

13. Tie in yellow and grizzly saddle hackles by the butt ends and wind the thread forward to directly in back of the bug body.

14. Use hackle pliers to wind the two hackles (individually or together) around the hook shank several times to build up a collar.

15. Tie off and clip any excess hackle.

16. Pull the hackle forward and wind the thread several turns, finishing with a whip finish.

17. Clip any excess thread and seal the thread wraps with head cement while holding the hackle collar back and out of the way.

CORK SLIDER

Cork sliders are basically cork poppers with the cork body turned around so that the body will not pop, but will make a "wake" like a surface-stranded moving baitfish or insect.

Tied by the author

Cork sliders are ideal skinny water bugs when the noise of poppers can scare fish. They involve basically the same construction and tying as do cork poppers, but are completely different even though using a bullet cork head. In these, the cork head is turned bullet end first, so that they do not pop, but do create a wake with an action like a swimming, fluttering insect, baitfish or small animal. Since these are worked more slowly and deliberately than poppers, one way to add more action to the bug is to thread rubber legs through the body. This version is a copy of a long popular feathered minnow or Wilder-Dilg Minnow from the 1920s, designed by B. F. Wilder and Will H. Dilg, the latter the founder of the Izaak Walton League of America. While this one is not tied with a weed guard, it is possible to add a weed guard using methods previously described. This cork slider is tied with a saddle hackle tail for maximum action, but it could also be tied with a bucktail, marabou or synthetic tail as desired. Many colors are possible.

Materials Needed

Hook – Long-shank kinked or hump shank hook, sizes 12 through 1/0

Thread – White (or color of tail and collar used)

Tail – Two pair (sometimes more with larger bugs) of yellow saddle hackle, flanked with a pair of grizzly saddle hackle

Flash – Silver Flashabou

Collar – White and red saddle hackle, mixed

Body – White bullet-shaped cork, painted white or pearlescent and with a red head, painted white and black eyes

Legs – White rubber legs or silicone legs, threaded through the body

Tying sequence:

1. Assume using a commercially prepared slider body, already painted and glued to the hook. If not, repeat steps one through nine described in making poppers.
2. Place the hook in a vise and tie on the thread directly in back of the bug body. Clip any excess thread.
3. Prepare two pair of yellow saddle hackle, with each pair flared out for more action.
4. Trim the butt ends and tie down on the hook shank.
5. Repeat the above with a single pair of grizzly hackles, one on each side of the yellow saddle hackle tail. Trim any excess hackle forward of the thread.
6. Add a few strands of silver Flashabou to each side of the tail.
7. Tie in a red and a white saddle hackle for use as a collar, and clip any excess butt stems of hackle forward of the tie down point.
8. Wind the hackle around the hook shank (together or individually) and tie off with the working thread. Clip any excess hackle tips.
9. Complete the tying by making several more turns of thread, then pulling the collar fibers back and tying off with a whip finish. Clip the excess thread.
10. Seal the thread wraps with head cement while holding the collar hackle back and out of the way.
11. Add rubber legs by threading the legs onto a needle tool.
12. Run the needle through the center of the cork body, at right angles to the hook (straight through) and at right angles to the plane of the hook.
13. Pull the legs out and leave them long. They can be trimmed if necessary while fishing.

HENSHALL HAIR BASS BUG

This hair-bodied bug is named for Dr. James Henshall, once considered the father of bass fishing, with his popularization of fishing for both largemouth and smallmouth bass in his 1881 treatise, The Book Of The Black Bass.

Fly-fishing for bass was pretty much in its infancy in the mid- to late-1800s. In the early through mid-1800s, fly-fishing with large flies and bugs such as this Henshall Hair Bodied Bug, was barely considered fly-fishing. This probably came from easterners primarily enthused over the trout fishing available then through much of the New England and Mid-Atlantic areas. However, the "bob" of early bass fishing (skittering a hair-bodied fly or lure was described by one 1839 magazine writer as "fly-fishing on a larger scale") did prevail. The Henshall Bug was not mentioned in the first edition (1881) of Henshall's book, and it is unclear today just when and how he developed it. He is generally credited with creating the prototype of the modern trimmed-hair bass bug, and his bugs were carried in later commercial catalogs, even after his death in 1925. This bug is seldom found today, but will still take its share of bass. It is also neat to tie some and know that you are fishing with a design that is over 100 years old. It can be tied in many other colors than the original described here.

Tied by the author

Materials Needed

Hook – Long shank bass hook, sizes 4 to 2/0
Thread – Black
Tail – Four yellow saddle hackles, two splayed to each side
Body – Dyed deer body hair, yellow roughly trimmed, then a band of black, then a band of yellow
Wings – Yellow bucktail, tied in spent wing fashion

Tying sequence:

1. Tie in the thread at the rear of the hook shank and clip the excess thread.
2. Tie in four yellow saddle hackles, flared out to the side.
3. Tie in a small bundle of prepared (clipped, combed and stacked) yellow deer body hair and spin it around the hook shank.
4. Push the spun deer hair to the rear and wrap the thread to just forward of this bundle.
5. Repeat as above, filling in about 1/4 of the hook shank.
6. Repeat as above with black deer hair, filling in a second 1/4 of the hook shank.
7. Repeat as above with yellow deer hair, filling in a third 1/4 of the hook shank.
8. Prepare a bundle of yellow bucktail (clip, comb, stack) and tie it down in the remaining 1/4 of the hook shank.
9. Use a bodkin to separate this bundle of bucktail into two equal parts and use thread to crisscross between the two bundles to separate and divide them.
10. Continue to wrap this way, crisscrossing and figure-eighting the thread around the hook shank and bundles.
11. Separately, wrap a few turns of thread around each of the wing bundles, with each of the bundles angled slightly up. This will make the bug land hook down in most cases.
12. Move the thread to the front of the fly, and wind around the hook shank to make a neat head.
13. Tie off the head with a whip finish and clip the excess thread.
14. Trim the deer hair (NOT the bucktail wings!) using scissors first, followed by a razor blade for final shaping. Leave the rear yellow deer hair band slightly roughly trimmed.
15. Seal the thread wraps with head cement.

TAP'S BUG

This is another classic and basic bug of deer hair that has proven the test of time and accounted for a lot of fun and largemouth bass.

H. G. "Tap" Tapply, the author of many books as well as his columns in *Field and Stream*, perfected this bug sometime in the 1940s. It has a simple tail of bucktail and body of two colors (usually) of hollow deer body hair. As his son, William G. Tapply notes in his book, *Bass Bug Fishing*, this simple bug offers much for fly rod bassers. While not singling out his father's bug, he feels that deer hair offers the advantages of feel, longer "hold" time, more alluring action, more natural presentation on the water, and more variety of action. William Tapply notes that when tied properly, this bug should look like a half circle when viewed from head on, and looks like an equilateral triangle when viewed from the top. He also notes that while it can be tied in any color or combinations of colors (one or two bands of color are typical and popular), natural deer hair "works at least as well as anything." He also likes white and yellow, more for fishermen to see it than for the bass to find it. This is a basic white with a green head.

Tied by the H. G. Tapply, supplied by son Wm. G. Tapply

Hook – Standard bass hook, long shank in sizes 6 through 1/0
Thread – White, or to match bug body color

Tail – White bucktail
Body – White spun deer hair with a head (about 1/2 the body length) of green spun deer hair

Tying sequence:

1. Tie in the working thread at the end of the hook shank, and clip the excess thread.
2. Prepare (clip, comb, and stack/even) a generous bundle of white bucktail.
3. Tie this bundle of bucktail onto the hook shank.
4. Prepare (clip, comb and stack if necessary) a small bundle of white body deer hair.
5. Tie the bundle onto the rear of the hook shank and spin it around the hook shank with several soft loops, followed by a tight wrap.
6. Push the deer hair to the rear, and move the thread in front of this bundle.
7. Repeat the above with more bundles of white deer hair until reaching the middle of the hook shank.
8. Repeat the above with bundles of green deer hair until reaching the hook eye.
9. Make a small neat head, complete with a whip finish and clip the excess thread.
10. Seal the thread wraps with head cement.
11. Trim the bug, making it flat on the bottom for gap clearance, and tapered from front to back to make a half of a cone shape.

CALL-MAC BUG

This is an old way of tying a bug, that while seemingly cruder looking than some more modern designs, is an effective design developed in the 1920s by Call McCarthy.

This design by Call McCarthy utilizes a cork body and wraps of thread around the cork body to hold the wings in place. Call was a close friend to Will H. Dilg, named in the Wilder-Dilg Bug. Both did much through their writings to popularize bass bug fishing in the 1920s, according to Paul Schullery in his book, *American Fly Fishing*. South Bend picked up this design with their Call-Mac bugs in 1921, yet earlier (1917) C. C. Refer debuted his Ref's Bass Bugs of the same design with bucktail tail and turkey or other game bird wings tied flat on top. This is an easy bug to tie, and as with most bass bugs, can be tied in any color or combinations of colors. It can be tied in one step, by preparing, gluing and painting the bug body on the hook, and then tying on the tail and the wings, which are wrapped on the body. As with most bass bugs, this can be tied plain or weedless. This is an original "Chadwick's Sunbeam" finish from the early 1930s, but another popular color was a brown bug with yellow bucktail and yellow game bird feathers on top. Some early bugs also had painted striped bands around the body.

Original, early 1930s example supplied by Vern Kirby from South Bend.

Hook – Long kinked or hump-shank hook, sizes 12 to 1/0

Thread – Black, or to match bug color (Alternatively, red to wrap the flat wings and simulate gills)

Tail – Red and orange bucktail

Body – Cork, painted orange

Wings – Mix of orange and blue bucktail on both sides, over that is tied a trimmed peacock eye

Tying sequence:

1. Prepare a long, bullet-shaped bass bug cork body by shaping (if necessary) and slotting for gluing onto the cork.
2. Prepare the hook by tying on coarse thread and spiral winding it up and down the hook shank area that will be covered with the body.
3. Tie off with a whip finish.
4. Force glue into the slot in the cork and over the thread wrapped hook shank.
5. Insert the hook into the slot and remove any excess glue on the belly and at both ends of the hook. Fill any pits in the cork body.
6. Allow to cure overnight, and then sand the body and belly with an emery board to smooth and provide maximum hook gap.
7. Paint with two coats of primer or base, then two finishing coats of brown. Allow to cure overnight.
8. Tie in the working thread immediately in back of the bug body and clip the excess thread.
9. Prepare (clip, comb, and stack/even) a tail bundle of orange bucktail.
10. Repeat the above with red bucktail.
11. Tie the prepared bundle (mixed red and orange) to the hook shank and clip any excess bucktail.

12. Make more wraps to secure the bundle and tie off with a whip finish.
13. Seal the thread wraps with head cement.
14. Tie on black thread by winding and securing around the cork body, about 1/4 the shank length in back of the hook eye. Clip any excess thread.
15. Prepare two small short bundles (clip, comb and stack/even) of blue bucktail.
16. Tie these bundles bucktail, one on each side of the cork body. Clip any excess bucktail.
17. Repeat steps 15 and 16 above with orange bucktail and tie these bundles in on top of (along the back) of the blue bucktail.
18. Tie in wing of a peacock eye, trimmed so that the eye will bracket the sides of the bucktail wings. This should be shorter than the bucktail wings. Clip any excess feathers forward of the thread.
19. Continue winding with the thread to completely cover the ends of the bucktail and feathers and make a smooth, even, narrow band of thread around the cork body.
20. Tie off the thread with a whip finish.
21. Seal the thread wraps with head cement or a clear sealer. (Make sure that the sealer or cement will not react adversely with the paint on the bug body.)

DIRTY DANCER

You can call this by any name, but it shows the variety of ways in which bugs can be made using readily available materials such as deer hair and rabbit strips.

Tied by Riverborn

Typical legs or tails on all types of bass bugs include bucktail, synthetics such as Super Hair, flash materials, deer hair, saddle hackle, marabou and mixes of all these. Rabbit strips are common for some diving bugs that are designed to imitate an eel, water snake or long baitfish, but this shows that they can also be used for long legs on a typical deer-hair frog-pattern. The benefit of legs like this in stillwater largemouth fishing is that they will have a lot more action in the water because of the soft fur, yet still remain as separate legs. Longer fibers of marabou can mat if used for the same purpose. If the rabbit strips are made thin enough to fit into a slot, or just glued to the surface, the same thing could be tried as the side "hackle" on a Gerbubble Bug. This bug also shows the color patterns possible by stacking separate bundles of deer hair on top of already-tied deer hair. Try this bug also in white, black, yellow, cream and tan.

Materials Needed

Hook – Regular hook, sizes 6 through 2/0
Thread – Light green, or to match the body color

Legs – Orange strips of rabbit fur
Body – Spun light green deer hair, with stacked spots of red and light green

Eyes – Plastic eyes, yellow with a black pupil
Weedguard – Single 20-pound mono Weed guard

Tying sequence:

1. Tie in the working thread at midpoint, and clip the excess thread.
2. Tie in one length of 20-pound mono weed guard and wind over it to part way around the bend of the hook.
3. Return the thread to the rear of the hook shank.
4. Prepare (clip, comb and stack/even) a small bundle of light green deer hair.
5. Tie onto the rear of the hook, and spin it, using the spinning technique described in Methods.
6. After the bundle is spun and secured, push the bundle to the rear and move the working thread in front of the bundle.
7. Repeat as above one or two more times.
8. Move the thread back through the deer hair and prepare a small bundle of red deer hair. Fold it over the working thread and use the working thread to pull it down onto the top of the already tied deer hair to make a red spot on top of the bug.
9. Repeat the above with a smaller bundle of light green again, pulling this bundle down into the center of the red spot.
10. Move the working thread forward again to the front of the spun deer hair.
11. Cut two one- to two-inch lengths of orange rabbit fur.

12. Tie in the two strips of rabbit fur as close as possible to the compacted deer hair with the fur on each side flowing to the rear.
13. On top of this wrap, repeat the above steps in preparing, tying down and spinning a bundle of light green deer hair.
14. Repeat and continue as above until reaching the hook eye.
15. Repeat the above steps in backing up the thread and stacking first a bundle of red followed by a bundle of light green on top of the red bundle. (When complete and trimmed, this will make for four streaks or two "V" shaped streaks of red on the back of the bug.)
16. Bring the mono loop forward and tie it under the hook eye on the shank, making sure that the loop is properly sized to protect the point.
17. Tie off with a whip finish and clip the excess thread.
18. Seal the thread wraps with head cement.
19. Careful trimming is a must to avoid damaging the weed guard and especially the rabbit legs. Pull the rabbit legs up to scissor and razor the flat belly of the bug, followed by moving the legs to the bottom, back and front to respectively trim the top, front and back.
20. Clip or burn holes in the trimmed body hair for eyes, and use flexible cement to glue plastic eyes into the sockets.

PFEIFFER'S PILL POPPER

This is a simple frog imitation that can be made easily from bottle corks or wine corks.

This little bug can be made to pop or can be retrieved as a slider. When it sits in the water with the legs down and the round body, it closely resembles a frog. I first came up with this idea about 40 years ago, fished it for a while, then abandoned it and am now fishing it again, with much success. The name comes from its resemblance to a Tums or Alka-Seltzer tablet. It has proven good on smallmouth and largemouth bass and in very small sizes on panfish. It is easy to make from bottle and wine corks, since it does not involve any special shaping. This bug is made by cutting wine corks into "slices" almost like slicing a loaf of bread. The same can be done with bottle corks, although this will give you corks of slightly different diameters due to the cork taper. I like a 3/4 inch diameter (that of most wine corks) although small bottle corks can be used to make very small ones for panfish. Light green seems best, although they can be painted any color. This one has the legs glued into the cork body, but you can also tie on a single tail, or a tail that is then separated to make two legs.

Tied by the author

Hook – Long shank popper hook, sizes 10 to 2/0	**Legs** – Light green bucktail	hook and painted light green with white and red eyes on the front of the bug
Thread – Light green	**Body** – Round, pill-shaped or coin shaped cork, glued to the	

Tying sequence:

1. Prepare the cork by cutting round slices from a wine cork or tapered bottle cork. Sand the cut surfaces smooth.
2. Slot one face of the cork with a hack saw blade.
3. Tie coarse thread onto the hook, spiral wrap up and down where the cork will be glued and tie off with a whip finish. Clip any excess thread.
4. Glue the hook into the cork body by adding a little prepared epoxy to the slot and also to the wrapped hook. Fill any pits in the cork (or holes from a wine corkscrew) with a mix of glue and cork dust.
5. Insert the hook into the cut slot and remove any excess glue at both ends of the hook. Make sure that a puddle of glue covers the slot. Allow to cure.
6. Sand the bug with an emery board, paying particular attention to the flat belly. Sand any filled pits or holes.
7. Paint with two coats of base white, followed by a coat or two of light green.
8. Use two sizes of nail heads or painting sticks to paint white with red pupil eyes on the front of the bug.
9. Use a pin vise and 1/8 inch diameter drill bit or a Dremel hobby tool with a 1/8 inch cutter to make two sockets, 1/4 inch deep in each side of the rear of the bug body. These should be at a slight angle so that the bug legs are angled out naturally.
10. Prepare two legs for gluing into the sockets. Begin by cutting, combing and stacking/evening two equal bundles of light green bucktail.
11. Hold each bundle with your left fingers, hold the working thread with the left fingers also and use the bobbin to wrap the thread around the bundle at the appropriate tie-down point.
12. After the thread grips the bundle, clip the excess thread.
13. Hold the leg bundle on both sides of the thread wrap and spin the bobbin around to make a tight wrap.
14. Tie off with a whip finish and clip any excess thread. Clip the excess bucktail on the butt side of the bundle.
15. Repeat to make an identical second leg.
16. Prepare some five-minute epoxy and with a bodkin add a small drop to each of the two sockets. Add epoxy also to the thread wrap of each leg.
17. Insert each of the bundles into the sockets and adjust any positioning. Ideally, the legs should be slightly angled out from the hook shank and slightly angled up so that the bug lands hook side down.

An alternative is to make the bug body as described, but without the sockets. Then tie thread on the hook shank and add any tail material which can be left straight or divided in two to make legs.

BALSA PENCIL POPPER

Pencil poppers, with a length that resembles baitfish, and noisy enough to resemble frantic baitfish, are ideal surface bugs when baitfish are in the shallows.

Some pencil poppers are just a slightly longer popper, but this one is very long for the hook size and thus more closely resembles an injured minnow when worked on the surface. It can be made in a number of sizes, provided that the diameter of the balsa cylinder is about the same as the hook gap. Some very long shank hooks (8X to 10X long) are available, but lacking that you can use any ball eye fly-tying hook with a wire extension that has an eye on one end (leader tie) and a "J" shaped hook on the other to hold the hook eye. To easily make the balsa cylinder, buy some blocks of balsa from a hobby shop and cut them into appropriate lengths for the pencil poppers being made. From the same hobby shop, buy several diameters of brass tubing, cut each into a six-inch length and sharpen one end with a file or grinder. (Use proper safety equipment when doing this!) Then hammer the tubing cutter through the long grain of the balsa. Use a wood dowel to punch out the balsa "blank" for the popper, and then sharpen it in an electric pencil sharpener. The result is an easy-to-make pencil popper that is very effective when minnows are prevalent.

Tied by the author

Materials Needed

Hook – Ball eye long shank hook (8X long) or long shank with a wire extension, sizes 8 through 2/0

Hook extension – Stiff wire, size 0014 inch or larger, formed into an eye on one end and a hook to hold the hook eye on the other

Size to make the necessary length that together with the hook will allow gluing into the long pencil popper body

Thread – White

Tail – White marabou (or color marabou to match the popper body)

Flash – Silver Krystal Flash

Body – Balsa dowel or cylinder, tapered at one end with pencil sharpener

Paint – White or cream, although other colors can be painted also

Eyes – Painted red with white and black pupils

Tying sequence:

1. Prepare a balsa body based on the above description and instructions in "Methods." Use a tubing cutter to punch out a balsa cylinder, remove it with a wood dowel and then taper one end in an electric pencil sharpener.
2. Slot the belly with a hack saw to hold the hook shank and any extension. Cut out a little in the center of the belly to accommodate the hook eye and extension attachment.
3. Prepare a wire hook extension that with the hook length will allow the wire eye to extend just in front of the popper face when attached to the fly hook.
4. Attach the thread by winding around the hook shank and over the thread wraps and clip any excess thread.
5. Wind down to the rear of the hook shank.
6. Prepare and tie in a bundle of white marabou to make a tail.
7. Prepare and tie in on each side a small bundle of a few strands of silver Krystal Flash.
8. Wind the thread forward to the hook eye, attach the "J"-shaped hook, and then wind the thread over this attachment back and forth several times to secure this hook/extension attachment.
9. Tie off with a whip finish and clip the excess thread.
10. Check the slot cut into the belly of the balsa body and make sure that there is sufficient room for the hook eye and wire extension attachment.
11. Apply five-minute epoxy to the slot and to the hook, and then insert the hook/wire into the slot in the belly of the balsa body.
12. Allow to cure overnight.
13. Use an emery board to file down any raised glue.
14. Use painting techniques (see Methods), dip, brush or spray the body with two coats of primer and then two coats of white paint. (An option here is to lightly sprinkle the final wet coat with silver glitter to simulate scales. The glitter will adhere to the wet paint.)
15. When the final coat of paint is dry, use two different size finishing nails or painting sticks to add first the eye color, and after curing, the pupil color to both sides of the front of the bug.

MIHULKA FOAM PANFISH POPPER

Small poppers like this are ideal for bluegills and most other sunfish. Foam poppers like this one are easy to make.

One of the joys of fly-fishing in midsummer is using a light outfit while casting to bluegills. This bug is an almost generic style for that fishing, and many fly tyers and fly companies have developed slight variations of this basic design. Often bedding bluegills in the spring will not take on the top as readily as underwater wet flies, but summer fishing brings out the best in these small fighting fish. A small popper such as this foam pattern, with plenty of hook gap clearance, worked rhythmically across the surface can produce good fishing all afternoon. Just make sure that the poppers are small, otherwise the popper will be hard to get out of the bluegill's mouth. They tend to inhale them like a cork stuck in a bottle. This red/white peppermint color is ideal, but obviously, foam bugs like this can be made in solid colors or any combinations of stripes and bands.

Tied by McKenzie

Hook – Size 8 through 12 long shank hooks or kink shank bug hooks

Thread – White or red

Tail – White marabou, surrounded red collar hackle followed by a white collar hackle

Body – Red and white banded foam popper cylinder

Tying sequence:

1. Tie the thread onto the hook at the midpoint of the hook shank, and clip any excess thread.
2. Spiral wrap the thread up to the eye of the hook and then back to the hook bend.
3. Tie in a small bundle of white marabou.
4. Then tie in the butt end of a small red saddle hackle.
5. Wind the red saddle hackle around the hook shank several turns and tie off with the thread. Clip the excess hackle.
6. Tie in the butt end of a white saddle hackle.
7. Wind the white saddle hackle around the hook shank several turns in front of the red hackle and tie off with the thread. Clip the excess hackle.
8. Tie off the thread with a whip finish and clip the excess thread.
9. Prepare a cylinder of red/white foam. The foam must be about 1/4 inch diameter for a size 10 hook.
10. Use a bodkin to make a hole through the foam body, close to the side that will be the belly of the bug. Slide the foam bug on the hook to check for size.
11. Add CA cement (cyanoacrylate glue) to the hook shank and rapidly slide the foam body onto the hook. Align the bug body on the hook so that the belly side is down.

MIHULKA SPITTIN' BUG

This bug floats well, has a split tail to give it a large profile and spits and skips along the surface as a result of the unique foam tie.

Popping, skipping and spitting bugs are not new. This fly is a variation of a Jack Gartside Gurgler, a striper fly for salt water, but also excellent for warmwater species. The difference is that the Gartside Gurgler utilized a foam body under the foam back, which is spiral wrapped and then palmered with a hackle to create "legs." Unlike a lot of bugs of foam or cork/balsa, this is made of sheet foam that does not require any gluing or other preparation. In short, it is a straight tying (no gluing) bug that works well in all colors and all sizes. Naturally, the foam sheet must be adjusted based on the size of the hook. The following is based on a size 1/0 hook and is tied in all white. Many other colors and combinations are possible and effective. Note that this bug floats almost horizontal to give the bug its spitting action. Work it in fits and twitches so that the long rubber legs interest fish after the spitting surface noise attracts fish to take a look.

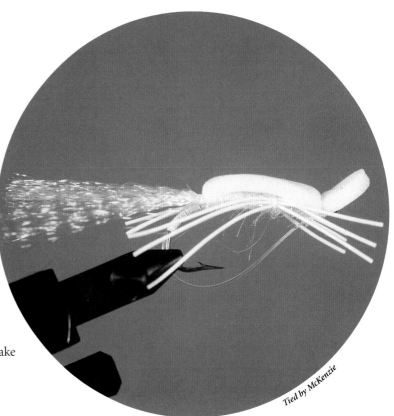

Tied by McKenzie

Hook – Standard hook or 1X or 2X long hook, sizes 10 to 2/0	**Tail** – White Super Hair	thick and cut to 3/8-inch wide and 2-3/4-inches long for a size 2/0 hook, proportionately smaller or larger for other hooks or different flotation characteristics
Thread – White (or color to match body and foam of bug)	**Body** – White or silver body braid material	
Weed guard – 20-pound mono Weed guard	**Legs** – White rubber legs	
	Foam – White sheet foam, measuring approximately 2 mm	

Tying sequence:

1. Tie in the thread at the midpoint of the hook shank. Clip the excess.
2. Tie in a length of monofilament for the weed guard and wind the thread evenly back to half way down the hook bend.
3. Reverse the thread direction and wind up to the rear of the hook shank.
4. Tie in a tail of white Super Hair.
5. Split the tail into two bundles and wrap each bundle separately with the thread, using crisscross and figure-8 wraps to separate the bundles into two tails or legs.
6. Tie in rectangle of foam sheet measuring 3/8-inch by 2-3/4-inch, slightly tapered at the rear end and rounded at the front end.
7. Tie in a length of white or silver braided body material.
8. Wind the thread up the hook shank half way and tie in two bundles of three each strands of white rubber legs. Tie each bundle in on the side of the hook.
9. Pull the legs back and continue to wrap the thread forward to the hook eye.
10. Pull the legs forward and wrap the body material up to the half way point, make one wrap around the leg tie down point, pull the legs back and continue to wrap the body material forward and tie off with the thread.
11. Clip the excess thread.
12. Fold the foam over the hook and tie down at the head, tying tightly enough to flare the forward part (about 3/8 inch) up over the hook eye.
13. Bring the mono weed guard forward and tie under the hook with the thread, positioning the loop of mono so that it protects the hook point.
14. Clip the excess mono and tie off the thread with a whip finish.
15. Seal the thread wraps with head cement.

FROGGIE

There are lots of ways of working with foam to make frogs and other floating bugs. This is a simple and effective method of making frogs of all shapes and sizes.

Tony Spezio of Arkansas began developing and tying this fly in 1991, and both it and he have been in demand ever since. This shows another way of working with closed cell foam to make a neat little frog that is easy to tie and effective to use. It involves tying on and folding over the foam in a horizontal plane to make a flat frog imitation. Tony has found this a great surface bug for smallmouth bass, largemouth bass and large bluegill. He often fishes it with 18 inches of mono tied to the bend and a small sinking fly as a trailer. It is a great bug in this light yellow color, but also good in white, green, gray, orange, red and black.

Tied by Tony Spezio

Materials Needed

Hook – Long shank hook, 3X or 4X, in sizes 2 through 14

Thread – Chartreuse flat waxed nylon

Tail – Chartreuse hen saddle hackle

Body – Strip of light yellow fly foam Use 1/8 inch thick by 3/16 inch wide for size 12 hook; adjust for other hook sizes

Eyes – Small plastic round head pins, available from craft stores, painted with fabric paint

Color – Painted with felt tip markers, fluorescent yellow on belly, green on back

Tying sequence:

1. Tie the working thread in at the head of the hook and clip the excess thread.
2. Wind the thread to the rear of the hook shank.
3. Tie in a tail of two dyed white or light green hen hackles with the hackles flared out for action.
4. Wind the thread to the eye of the hook.
5. Tie in the bundle of foam in the middle, using crisscrossing wraps to secure the foam at right angles to the hook shank and horizontal.
6. Wind the thread to the rear of the hook shank.
7. Take one of the foam strips and fold it over the hook shank and tie it in with several wraps of thread.
8. Repeat the above with the second part of the foam strip and tie down as above.
9. Cut the foam to leave about ⅛ inch of foam in back of the tie-down point.
10. Use scissors to split each of these legs to make four little legs.
11. Color the foam using permanent felt tip markers to tint the belly yellow and the back green. If desired, add black stripes to the top and black dots to the bottom, as Tony does.
12. Put on safety goggles and use wire cutters to carefully cut the pins so that they can be inserted into the foam head.
13. Add CA (cyanoacrylate) glue to the pins and stick them horizontally into the foam at the head to simulate eyes.
14. Use fabric paints of your choice to dot eyes with a light color, allow to dry and repeat with a smaller black pupil.
15. (To preserve the felt tip colors, Tony suggests dipping the bugs into Rain-X, a sheeting solution for wind shields.)

BILL'S WEEDLESS FROG

There are many ways to use sheet form to make bugs, with this one of the most unusual.

Bill Skilton, originator of this unusual design, admits that the hooking percentage goes down when using it, but that it is also one of the bugs that can be fished in the toughest of structure. (See also Pfeiffer's Sandwich Minnow for another highly weedless design.) The concept is different in that the foam body is made of a rectangular sheet of thin foam (like that used in some packaging) that is tied on with the foam facing forward after the foam is folded around the hook shank to make a circular tube. The rest of the bug is tied on, then the foam folded over and taped to make for a complete tube that protects the hook point.

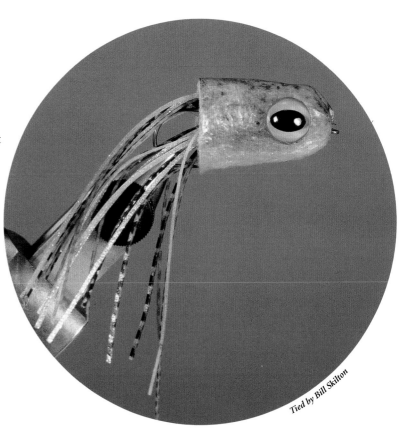

Tied by Bill Skilton

Hook – Eagle Claw 3214 UK or similar bass hook in sizes 2 to 3/0

Thread – Tan

Tail/legs – Mixed color (green and mottled) silicone or rubber legs

Body – USA-Flies 11/32 inch clear white or olive poly plastic foam, or similar closed cell foam, measuring about 1-1/2 times the length of the hook shank and 3 times the width of the hook gap

Eyes – Oversize plastic doll eyes

Coating – Magic Tape and Softex

Colors – Green or olive permanent felt tip marker

Tying sequence:

1. Tie the working thread onto the hook shank at midpoint, and clip the excess thread.
2. Wind the thread to a spot directly above the hook point.
3. Select 18 to 20 strands of rubber or silicone legs, twice the length of the hook shank and tie on the shank in directly above the hook point. Clip any excess leg material.
4. Return the thread to just in back of the hook eye.
5. Cut rectangular piece or sheet foam about 1½ the length of the hook shank and 3 times the width of the hook gap.
6. Fold the foam in half lengthwise (like a cylinder) and slip over the hook shank in back of the hook eye.
7. Hold the end of the foam with your left fingers, with the bulk of the foam extending in front of the hook shank.
8. Tie down with several soft loops to and pull gently to secure the foam to the hook shank. Tie down so that the edges of the foam sheet meet.
9. Trim any excess foam in back of the tie down point.
10. Whip finish and clip the excess thread.
11. Seal the wraps with head cement.
12. Gently fold the foam back over the hook shank and around the legs and the hook point.
13. Trim the foam so that it extends just in back of the hook point. Take care to not cut the skirt material.
14. Make sure that the edges of the foam meet and seal them with a strip of Magic Tape. Trim excess tape.
15. If desired, color the foam body with permanent felt tip markers.
16. Attach eyes with a drop of Softex or marine Goop.
17. Coat entire surface of the body with Softex.

WEEDLESS SKILTON SWIM & SKIM FROG

Another of Bill's innovative designs, that while decreasing hooking percentage, is one of those bugs that you can throw into the thickest cover.

Two-hook or double hook flies are common for some salmon fishing and as tandem rigs for salt water, but are not common in warmwater flies. This exception uses two hooks to slightly increase the hook rate, even through the design with the foam decreases hooking ability. This is one of those rare bugs that you can throw into thick algae, floating duckwort, into brush piles and the thickest patches of lily pads and spatterdock and other surface-pad weeds. Fish it as a frog, with pauses and short twitches as you swim it through the worst muck and weeds. Bass love muck and weeds though, so be prepared for some explosive strikes, and enjoy even those fish that miss the bug or that come unbuttoned. One big advantage of this bug is that the top and bottom are the same, so it won't make any difference how the bug lands.

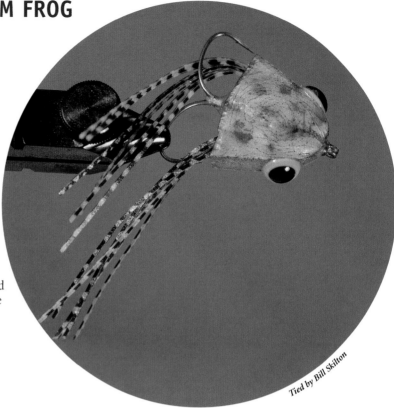

Tied by Bill Skilton

Materials Needed

Hook – Stinger hook in sizes 4 to 3/0	mottled Silicone or rubber skirting or USA-FLIES polymer skirting	ethafoam white plastic sheeting, colored with permanent felt tip pens
Thread – Light green		
Legs – Light green or green/black	**Body** – USA-FLIES or any similar	**Eyes** – Stemmed plastic eyes

Tying sequence:

1. Place hook in vise and place second hook on top of it, points at 180 degrees to each other. Tie on the wrapping thread and wrap both hook shanks along their entire length to secure them together. Make sure that the hook eyes match up exactly.
2. Whip finish and trim any excess thread.
3. Trim a piece of sheet foam (about 3/16 inch thick) to a rough triangle, making the triangle slightly longer than the distance from the hook points to the hook eyes.
4. Cut a "V" into the top point of the triangle.
5. Run a bodkin or needle through the center of the triangle from top point to bottom center.
6. Coat hook shanks with CA glue (regular foam) or epoxy glue (ethafoam) and slide the hook shanks into this opening. Clean up any excess glue.
7. Reattach the thread in back of the hook eyes and trim the excess thread.
8. Wind thread around the foam and the hook shanks to draw the foam "V" cut into a sharply tapered triangle.
9. Whip finish the thread and cut the excess.
10. Trim excess foam, trimming the base to be in line with the hook points and about 1/8 inch forward of the hook points.
11. Color the fly (yellow or light green) with felt tip pens and coat with Softex. Make holes in the forward part of the body and use CA or epoxy to glue in stemmed plastic eyes.
12. Use a curved needle (available from sewing/craft stores) to run legs through the body from one side to the other.

HOT LIPS

Greg Webster developed this neat little bug that makes use of folded foam in an innovative way to make a unique surface popper and gurgler.

Folding sheet foam is a way to make dragonfly tails (Bill Skilton), frogs (Tony Spezio), Gurglers (Jack Gartside) and surface Gerbubble-style minnows (the author), along with a lot of other ways to make flies and bugs. This one is different in that Greg Webster created a way in which half the folded foam is wrapped over with body material, while the top foam back keeps the bug floating. The two sheets form the lips to make for a different gurgler style of bug that is easy to tie. Webster credits Gartside and some friends in Florida for introducing him to the similar Gurglers, which lack the bottom lip of this popping, gurgling bug. Try it in small sizes for panfish, and in larger sizes for everything from bass to pike. You can obviously tie it using different materials, different colors for the tail and different body color and foam sheeting to create a family of such bugs. Greg's favorite colors are all black, black and chartreuse, orange and black and black and yellow. The directions are as Greg Webster ties it.

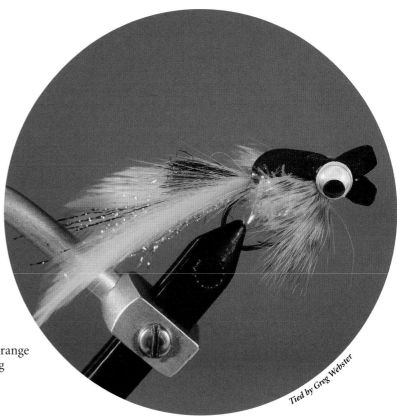

Tied by Greg Webster

Hook – Gamakatsu stinger hook or Partridge bass hook or similar hooks in sizes 6 to 2/0

Thread – Yellow

Tail – Mix of chartreuse and black Krystal Flash, black Angler's Choice Poly Bear and three pairs of yellow bass/saddle hackles

Body – Chartreuse Estaz or cactus chenille

Foam back – Black sheet foam, cut into a long rectangle twice the length of the hook and a width about 1/6 of the rectangle length

Throat – Brown or yellow dyed guinea hackle, tied throat or collar style

Eyes – Large white or yellow rattle eyes, glued on with Goop or super glue (CA glue)

Tying sequence:

1. Tie in the working thread at the mid-point of the fly, and clip the excess.
2. Wind the thread to the bend of the hook and tie in the first part of the tail of mixed black and chartreuse Krystal Flash. This should be about 1½ times the hook length.
3. Next, tie in a short length of black Poly Bear.
4. Prepare and tie in three pairs of yellow saddle hackles, with the three feathers on each side of the previously tied tail and splayed outward. Clip any excess of the above materials.
5. Cut foam into a long rectangle about two times the length of the hook and slightly round the two ends with scissors.
6. Double the foam on itself and punch a hole at the fold with scissors or a bodkin.
7. Push the hook through the hole in the foam and slide the foam back to the tail of the fly.
8. Tie in a length of chartreuse cactus chenille.
9. Tie over the bottom piece of foam and wind the thread over the foam and hook shank to within ⅛-inch of the hook eye.
10. Wrap the cactus chenille around the hook shank up to the thread and tie off. Clip any excess chenille.
11. Tie in a brown or yellow dyed guinea hackle by the butt and clip the excess. Wind the hackle around the hook shank several turns and tie off with the thread.
12. Clip the excess.
13. Fold the foam over the back of the fly and tie down at the front about ⅛-inch from the hook eye.
14. Tie off with a whip finish and clip the excess thread.
15. Seal the thread with head cement.
16. Glue rattle eyes onto the sides of the foam using CA glue (super glue) or Goop.

CLOUSER FLOATING MINNOW

Floating minnows imitate baitfish that are injured or have their swim bladder on the fritz and thus float and swim on the surface. This is an easy and effective tie.

Bob Clouser, known for his deep-fished Clouser Deep Minnow, stuck to the top in developing this surface floater that has a minnow shape formed by two sponge cricket bodies glued together as a sandwich. Basic colors for these sponge bugs are white, yellow and black, and these make up the basic colors for this surface minnow imitation. You can also make the tail of any length, color or shape to simulate minnows on your local waters. Work a fly like this in small short twitches to suggest an injured minnow, or in fast short jerks to simulate a minnow trying to avoid becoming a meal.

Tied by Bob Clouser

Materials Needed

Hook – Regular length bass hook, sizes 4 to 1/0

Thread – White

Tail – Yellow bucktail over white bucktail

Flash – Pearlescent Flashabou on each side

Gills – Short red Krystal Flash

Body – Pair of white foam spider/cricket bodies

Tying sequence:

1. Tie the thread onto the midpoint of the hook, and clip any excess.
2. Wind the thread to just in front of the bend of the hook and tie in the gills of a short bundle of red Krystal Flash.
3. Next, tie in a tail of white bucktail, followed by a bundle of yellow bucktail on top.
4. Tie in a few strands of pearlescent Flashabou on each side of the tail.
5. Wrap forward with the thread and tie off at the midpoint of the hook using a whip finish.
6. Prepare two sponge spider/cricket bodies, and coat with CA glue.
7. Hold one of the sponge bodies against the side of the hook, with the tapered tail end covering the wrapped tail of the hook.
8. Place the other sponge cricket body against the first to make a "sandwich" with the hook in the center. Hold until the glue cures in a few minutes and the bug is ready to use. (Alternately, use five-minute epoxy glue or contact cement, following directions for use.)
9. Add prism or plastic eyes and coat the bug body with a clear coating. Optionally, you can also add or sprinkle some fine glitter to the clear coat.

BILL'S FLOATING/DIVING THIN MINNOW

Foam can be used in a variety of ways to make floating bugs, such as this floating minnow from Bill Skilton.

Bill Skilton uses a lot of foam to tie everything from terrestrials for trout to foam frogs, minnows and all sorts of underwater insect larva and nymphal forms. This is a foam pattern that is easy to tie and effective to use when the bass or other game fish are schooling or targeting minnows just under the surface. As with Clouser's Floating Minnow, this can be worked in a number of ways, including short twitches and fast "escaping" retrieves. This fly uses very thin strips of foam, cut into 1/16-inch widths to form the back and belly of the fly. Bill also ties a variation of this in a floating model that lacks the clear plastic diving lip that is glued into the bottom piece of foam. In fishing the version here, just be careful when picking up the fly, since the lip will have a tendency to dive the fly. Pick it up smartly when the fly is floating.

Tied by Bill Skilton

Hook – Long shank hook, 2X or 3X, sizes 10 to 4	**Body** – USA-Flies gray or white dry fly foam strip, or other 1/16 inch wide closed cell foam; two strips, three inches long each	cut from a lure or hook box, glued into the bottom foam body
Thread – White		
Tail – Olive marabou, topped with an equal bundle of brown marabou	**Eyes** – Flat prism eyes	**Color** – Permanent felt tip markers, as desired, light on the belly, dark on the back
	Lip – Small piece of clear plastic, as	

Tying sequence:

1. Tie in the working thread at the midpoint of the hook shank and clip the excess thread.
2. Wind the thread to a spot above the hook point in back of the barb and tie in a bundle of olive marabou.
3. Repeat the above with a bundle of brown marabou.
4. Prepare two strips of foam, three inches long and cut 1/16-inch wide.
5. Cut a point on the end of each strip for tying to the hook shank.
6. Tie one strip on top of the hook shank on top of the marabou tie down point, with the foam pointing to the rear.
7. Tie the second piece of foam on the bottom of the hook shank at the same spot, with the foam pointing towards the rear.
8. Wind the thread to the eye of the hook.
9. Fold the bottom and top pieces of foam forward over the hook shank. Pull to get the shape desired.
10. Wrap both pieces of foam with the thread, making sure that the foams stay in position on the top and bottom of

the hook shank.
11. Closely trim the excess foam.
12. Tie off with a whip finish and clip the excess thread.
13. Cover each side of the minnow with a piece of Magic Tape, covering each side of the minnow with the tape.
14. Trim the excess tape.
15. Color the minnow with permanent felt tip markers, using light colors on the belly and working up to darker colors on the back of the minnow.
16. Glue prism eyes to each side using Goop or Softex.
17. Add the diving lip cut from clear plastic (such as a lure or hook container).
18. Cut a small opening in the bottom foam and slide the end of the lip into this opening. Glue with a heavy coat of Softex.
19. Trim the lip to about 1/4 to 1/2 inch long – Bill says that short is better than long.
20. Coat entire body with Softex. Take care to prevent getting Softex on the tail.

DEVIL BUG

Sometimes called a Doodle Bug, Cooper Bug, or Tuttle Devil Bug, this is an old design deer-hair bug that is easy to make and that produces a lot of fish.

One of the ways of making a deer-hair bug does not involve spinning or stacking the hair around the hook shank. Instead, it involves tying and folding the deer hair to make a rounded body that is tied down at both ends. This is an example of an early way of tying that was also used in the Tuttle Devil Bug that was developed in the 1920s. It floats low in the water, but this can be an advantage, since most of the heavier insects, small mammals or birds that fall into the water usually struggle in or below the surface film, rather than floating on top of it. This is a simple version of these bugs that can be also tied with tails or legs and with a variety of body materials including yarn, clipped deer hair, peacock herl and dubbing. Many colors and color combinations of deer hair and body material are also possible. Try this for panfish in small sizes and largemouth and smallmouth bass in the larger sizes.

Tied by the author

Hook – Long shank (2X) hook, sizes 8 to 1/0

Thread – Black

Tail – Tips of brown deer hair or longer moose hair

Body – Black chenille

Back – Deer hair, folded over and tied down front and rear (the rear makes up the tail)

Front – Deer hair (from the folded deer hair for the back) clipped in front of the hook eye

Tying sequence:

1. Tie in the working thread at the rear of the hook shank and clip the excess thread.
2. Tie down a length of black chenille.
3. Move the thread to just in back of the chenille tie down point.
4. Prepare (clip, comb and stack) a bundle of brown natural deer hair and tie in place with the working thread. Tie down with the tips facing to the rear and about half the hook shank length. Make sure that the deer hair bundle stays on top of the hook shank and does not spin around the shank.
5. Wind the thread forward to a spot about 1/8-inch in back of the hook eye.
6. Wind the chenille forward to the thread and tie down. Clip any excess chenille.
7. Fold the deer hair over the body and tie down with the working thread, making soft loops to keep the deer hair bundle on top of the hook shank.
8. Wind the thread around the hook shank under the forward bundle of deer hair and tie off with a whip finish. Clip the excess thread.
9. Clip the forward bundle of deer hair straight across and about 1/8 to 1/4 inch in front of the hook eye.
10. Seal the thread wraps with head cement.

Alternatively, you can make this with legs or a tail, or make the body with a palmered hackle to make it more "buggy" looking. A small bundle of rubber legs, tied into the middle of the hook shank, is also a possibility.

SCRUBBER BUG

Sponge cricket bodies can be used in many ways for making bugs rather than the one for which it was originally designed. This is another way to make a diving floater to achieve a swimming frog look.

Sponge bug bodies were designed and shaped to be tied onto a hook with a few hackles or rubber legs to make a simple-to-tie and easy-to-fish surface bug, primarily for panfish. This is a variation in using these bug bodies, which are available from any fly shop or catalog. (Another variation is with the Clouser Floating Minnow that uses two sponge bodies.) This bug also has long rubber legs and thick cactus chenille bodies to give it a different look for a floater/diver. Try it also in the black, white and yellow colors in which these sponge bugs are available. In green, as shown here, it has a definite froggy look and will swim like a fleeing frog.

Tied by Riverborn

Materials Needed

Hook – Regular bass stinger hook, sizes 6 through 1/0

Thread – Green or to match bug body color

Tail – Two to three pairs of green dyed grizzly hackle

Collar – One or two dyed green grizzly hackle

Body – Green or dark green cactus chenille

Back – Dyed or painted green sponge bug body (size based on hook size used)

Legs – Variegated black/green rubber or silicone legs

Eyes – Plastic, orange with black pupil

Tying sequence:

1. Tie in the working thread at a point 2/3 back on the hook shank and clip any excess thread.
2. Prepare (remove, strip the butts and arrange in pairs) three pairs of green dyed grizzly hackle. Tie to the hook with the feathers splayed out for action. Clip any excess hackle.
3. Tie in one or two green-dyed grizzly hackles for a collar.
4. Wind the hackles (individually or together) around the hook shank.
5. Tie off the hackle and clip the excess.
6. Tie in a length of dark green cactus chenille at this point.
7. Prepare a sponge rubber bug body by painting or staining it green. Permanent felt tip markers are ideal for this.
8. Tie in the sponge spider bug body by the long tapered end.
9. Wind the thread forward to a point 1/4 the shank length in back of the hook eye.
10. Wind the cactus chenille forward and tie off with the thread. Do not clip the chenille now.
11. Tie in long green/black variegated legs at this point, with the legs equal on both sides of the body. These legs should be about two- to three-times the length of the hook shank.
12. Wind the cactus chenille over this leg wrap and tie off with the thread.
13. Tie off with a whip finish and clip the excess thread.
14. Use an awl to punch a hole through the nose of the sponge bug body about 1/4 inch from the end. (This is approximate – the position of tying down the bug body must allow stretching the bug body so that the hook eye will go through the punched hole.)
15. Coat the top of the cactus chenille and the bottom of the sponge body (up to the punched hole) with clear waterproof flexible glue.
16. Stretch the bug body forward and force over the hook eye and onto the hook shank.
17. Use waterproof cement to glue eyes onto the top of the bug body, in back of the hook eye.

WATER SNAKE/RABBIT STRIP DIVER

*This follows a design of Larry Dahlberg, who designed his
Dahlberg Diver as a hair-bodied fly that will dive on retrieve,
to effectively allow fishing both the surface and slightly under
the surface.*

Water snakes are commonly taken by largemouth bass,
pike and any other fish big enough to get one into their
mouth. This is one style of making imitations of these
snakes, which are commonly seen swimming along the
surface of any of the waterways we fish. They seem most
common in rivers, but are certainly not unknown in
ponds and lakes. This is a simple fly to tie once you have
mastered spinning deer hair and also allows for a different
method of trimming to make the bug dive on retrieve.
This bug with the natural brown tail of rabbit fur and
body of dyed yellow natural hair makes for an ideal water
snake imitation. Try this also in white, black, yellow,
chartreuse and two-tone combinations of red head/white tail,
black/yellow, black/tan and red/chartreuse. Note that as
photographed, this fly also has a horizontal loop to keep the tail
from wrapping around the hook bend when casting.

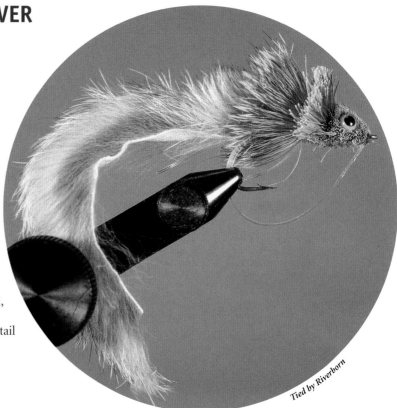

Tied by Riverborn

Hook – Regular hook, wide gap if preferred, sizes 4 through 2/0

Collar – Tips of spun dyed natural deer hair

Body – Spun and clipped natural deer hair

Eyes – Plastic prism eyes, yellow with black pupils

Weedguard – Single length of 20-pound mono

Tail guard – Single length of 20-pound mono, tied horizontally at rear

Tying sequence:

1. Tie in the working thread at the midpoint of the hook shank, and then tie in one length of 20-pound mono.
2. Wind over this strand and the hook shank to the rear.
3. Tie in a short loop of mono, and clip any excess mono.
4. Continue to wind the thread evenly forward until at the midpoint of the hook shank.
5. Prepare and tie in a three-inch length of natural rabbit fur, with the fur flowing to the rear.
6. Prepare (clip, comb and stack/even) a bundle of natural deer hair in which the tips have been dyed yellow.
7. Tie this bundle to the hook shank with the long tips facing to the rear, and spin the bundle around the hook shank.
8. Make several turns between the rear-facing tip ends and the butt ends to slightly separate them.
9. Push this bundle to the rear to compact it while holding the hook to prevent the bundle from sliding.
10. Wind the working thread to the front of bundle and repeat as above, tying and spinning more deer hair around the hook shank.
11. Repeat as above, continuing to wrap and spin deer hair around the hook shank until reaching the end of the hook shank.
12. Bring the mono weed guard forward and tie under the hook eye, with the loop protecting the hook point. Clip any excess mono.
13. Tie off with a whip finish and clip any excess thread.
14. Carefully trim the fly, starting on the belly with scissors and then a razor blade, trimming this area flat.
15. Trim around the body to make a bullet-shaped tapered head. When doing this, take care to leave untrimmed all of the tips of the hair (the collar) that are facing to the rear from the first wrap of hair onto the hook shank. Also, slightly trim the area between the head and the tips facing to the rear that form the collar so that the bug will dive. In short, you will have a flat belly, long untrimmed tips to the rear, trimmed long collar, and a tightly trimmed tapered head.
16. Cut or burn sockets for the eyes.
17. Use cement to glue plastic eyes into the sockets.

PFEIFFER'S SANDWICH MINNOW

This design uses simple saddle hackle feathers and a sandwich of thin sheet foam as take-off of the Gerbubble Bug, which has hackle sticking out from the sides to simulate an injured crappie or minnow.

Baitfish that are dying or injured lie on their sides on the surface with their head and tail curved down into the water. This simple foam pattern suggests that and has accounted for some great bass fishing for the author. With the double mono weed-guard and the pointed shape that slides through weeds, it is a bug that can be thrown back into lily pads and spatterdock and snaked out – or twitched along until a bass decides to bust it. It is also ideal for open water (where it does not have to be weedless) and as a weedless model when fished along the edges of weeds or through brush piles, log jams and other structures. White is a good basic color, but it can be tied in other colors as well, with yellow, tan, black and chartreuse also good choices.

Tied by the author

Materials Needed

Hook – Long shank hook, sizes 6 through 2/0

Thread – White

Weedguard – Two loops of 20 –pound monofilament

Tail/wing – Four to six white saddle hackles

Body – Thin white sheet foam, cut in a slim hourglass shape, or like two arrowheads point-to-point

Eyes – Single large prism eye, silver with black pupil

Gill – Red, painted with fine tip permanent felt tip marker

Tying sequence:

1. Tie the thread to the hook directly in back of the hook eye. Clip any excess thread.
2. Wind halfway down the shank, then tie in two strands of 20-pound monofilament for loop weedguards. Continue wrapping over the mono and hook shank until part way around the hook bend.
3. Return the thread up the hook shank to just in back of the hook eye.
4. Prepare (cut the butts) four to six white saddle hackles so that they are about two to three times the length of the hook shank.
5. Tie these saddle hackles down on the hook shank, with all of the feathers curved downward.
6. Tie off with a whip finish and clip any excess.
7. Prepare a sheet foam body by making a rectangle about 1-1/16 times the hook shank length, and a width about 1/6 of this length. Taper both sides towards the middle so that the result looks like two arrowheads point-to-point. Make sure that there is enough of a connection to allow punching a hole and sliding over the hook eye.
8. Use a bodkin or an awl to punch a hole through the center connection, and then slide the hook eye into this hole.
9. Flare out the hackle fibers from the saddle hackle so that they will stick out from the side of the foam body (when completed) to resemble dorsal and ventral fins.
10. Coat the center of the hackle feathers (both top and bottom) and the adjoining sides of the foam body with contact cement. Wait until dried (about 15 minutes) and then carefully sandwich the hook and feathers between the top and bottom foam sheets. (A quicker alternative is to use CA super glue, but take extreme care that you do not glue your fingers to the feathers or foam.)
11. Reattach the thread to the hook just behind the end and in front of the pointed body and clip any excess thread.
12. Bring the two loops of mono forward and tie down under the hook shank with the thread. Make sure that the two loops are equal and sufficient to protect the hook point. Clip any excess mono.
13. Tie off with a whip finish and clip any excess thread.
14. Use a red permanent felt tip marker to draw a gill on the underside of the body.
15. Use five-minute epoxy to add one prism eye to the belly of the bug, and coat the eye and thread wraps with the remainder of the epoxy.

MOUSE RAT DEER-HAIR BUG

Mouse-rats, or similar shaggy hair bugs, are ideal for fishing stillwater ponds for largemouth and pike.

Mouse-rats are deer-hair bugs that are left shaggy when tied, except for the belly where they are trimmed to create optimal hook gap. By not trimming the body (other than the belly) they look and act like a swimming mammal and are ideal for fishing around structure and shorelines for largemouth bass. These shaggy surface bugs are all tied similarly, although different tyers will vary the type of deer hair and tail material and also with eyes and ears optional. These surface swimming bugs can imitate mice, small rats, meadow voles, shrews, and even moles (if they got lost and fell out of a hole into the water) and any other small mammal that might have the misfortune to fall in. For best results, work them with an uneven swimming motion; strips and pauses with an occasional twitch or two.

(Note – Steps 15 through 20 are optional. If not adding eyes and whiskers finish after step 13 by sealing the head with head cement. If not adding ears, continue.)

Tied by Spirit River

Hook – Any regular to 2X long-shank hook, sizes 6 through 3/0	**Tail** – Thin strip of brown leather, Ultra Chenille or Ultra Suede	**Eyes** – Black beads, glued in place or black prism or plastic eyes (optional)
Thread – Brown	**Body** – Hollow natural brown or grayish deer hair	**Whiskers** – A few strands of black hackle fibers or short black body calf fur
Weedguard – Two strands of 20-pound monofilament	**Ears** – Brown Ultra Suede or thin leather (optional)	

Tying sequence:

1. Tie in the thread at the midpoint of the hook and clip any excess thread.
2. Tie in two strands of monofilament on each side of the hook shank and wind the thread over the mono evenly to a point about half way around the hook bend.
3. Reverse the thread direction and bring the thread back to the rear of the hook shank.
4. Tie in a tail or a long thin strip (up to two inches) of leather, Ultra Chenille or Ultra Suede.
5. Prepare (clip, comb and stack) a small bundle (pencil size) of deer hair. Clip this so that the length of the hair is about 1/8-inch to 1/4-inch longer than the length of fur that will be left untrimmed once tied in place.
6. Tie in this bundle of deer hair, slightly spinning it around the hook shank. The method of tying for this particular bug is to tie so that the thread is as close as possible to the butt ends (not in the middle as with trimmed hair bugs) so that the clipped ends are hidden beneath the shaggy hair ends.
7. Push the bundle back with your fingers and wind the thread just forward of the spun bundle.
8. Repeat as above, adding more and more bundles until filling about 3/4 of the hook shank.
9. Prepare ears by cutting Ultra Suede or thin leather into teardrop shapes.
10. Tie the ears onto the hook shank by the teardrop point, flared back on either side of the spun body.
11. Tie in another bundle and continue to spin and add short bundles (only one or two bundles will be needed) until filling the hook shank. (Short bundles are a must for the ears to show.)
12. Tie off in back of the hook eye with a whip finish and clip the excess thread.
13. Trim the head area of the bug with scissors and then a double-edge razor blade, leaving a small flared portion of deer hair in front of the ears.
14. Trim the belly of the bug with a razor blade to preserve the hook gap.
15. Reattach the thread at the whip finish, and clip the excess thread.
16. Bring the loops of mono forward, make them even and protective of the hook point on both sides and tie down with the working thread.
17. Tie in a bundle of hackle fibers or small sparse bundle of calf body fur, then figure-eight the wraps so that the fibers stick out to each side like whiskers.
18. Tie off with a second whip finish and clip the excess thread.
19. Seal the head with head cement.
20. Add a tiny drop of glue to each side of the trimmed head and add black beads or eyes.

BILL'S 3D FOAM MOUSE

Even though it is not as shaggy as a hair-bodied mouse or rat, this foam mouse is also an effective imitation when bass or pike are feeding on the surface and looking for a big, easy meal.

Most bugs use one piece of foam (as with typical poppers and sliders) or two pieces of foam (as Bill's Floating Thin Minnow or Clouser's Floating Minnow). This bug uses three pieces of foam to make for a fat, durable body. The technique of folding over the foam and sealing it with a soft, clear liquid sealer makes this a unique bug to try when fish are taking large baits. Since this is designed to imitate a mouse, vole or shrew, fish it with a slow but constant retrieve that will simulate a mouse swimming across a pond or pool after falling in the water.

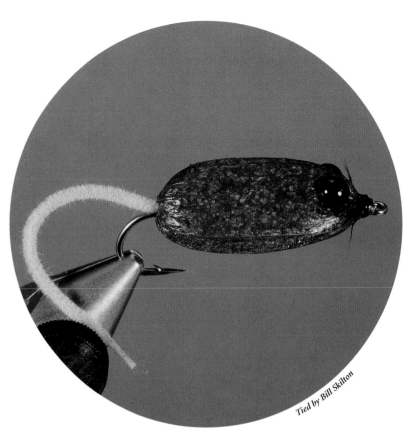

Tied by Bill Skilton

Materials Needed

Hook – Long shank, 2X or 3X, bass hook, weedless or plain, sizes 6 to 2/0
Thread – Black
Tail – Black-colored chamois or

Bug Skin (Ultra Suede is also a possibility)
Body – Three pieces of black USA – Hard Shell foam strips or other closed cell foam

Whiskers – Black bucktail
Eyes – Prism or doll eyes
Colors – Black or dark gray permanent felt tip markers, if necessary

Tying sequence:

1. Tie in the working thread at midpoint on the shank and clip any excess thread.
2. Wind the thread to the rear of the hook shank, above the barb.
3. Prepare (cut, color, etc.) a strip of Bug Skin, chamois or Ultra Suede. This tail should be about twice the hook length.
4. Tie in the tail on the hook shank and clip any forward excess material.
5. Prepare (cut to width – about gap size for the hook – and point one end) three strips of black foam.
6. Tie in each strip of foam by the point at the tail, tying one on the underside of the hook shank and two on either side of the top of the hook shank. All three pieces should point to the rear.
7. Wind the thread forward to slightly in back of the hook eye.
8. Fold the bottom strip under the hook shank and tie down with the thread.
9. Fold the two top pieces of foam over the hook shank (like a tent) and tie down with the thread.
10. Clip any excess foam close to the thread.
11. Prepare (clip, comb and stack/even) a short bundle of black bucktail.
12. Tie this bundle of bucktail on the eye to extend horizontally as whiskers.
13. Apply prism or glue on doll eyes.
14. Coat the entire foam body with Softex or other soft flexible clear sealer.

PFEIFFER'S SWINGING POPPER

Of the many ways to make weedless bugs, this is one of the most unusual that also does not incorporate any wire or mono over the hook. It is very effective over most surface weeds.

I first developed or invented this pattern in the 1990s and only a few years later discovered that the same idea was published some 50 years prior in a leading outdoor magazine. Such is true with a lot of "new" flies, lures and designs in fishing tackle and other things in life. Had I paid more attention and more thoroughly read (or remembered) ideas from *Fly-Tying and Fly Fishing for Bass and Panfish*, by Tom Nixon, I would have found the basis for the idea, albeit without the weedless slant. The original idea was for a long bullet-shaped or torpedo-head bug, with a wire through the center that in turn is attached to a free-swinging hook. The difference in this – and it is an important distinction – is that the wire through the body is not through the center, but through one edge to make this the belly of the bug. With the hook in the bug properly, this means that it hangs down and swings up out of the way when dragged over weeds rather than catching on them. Any color or color combination can be tied and tried.

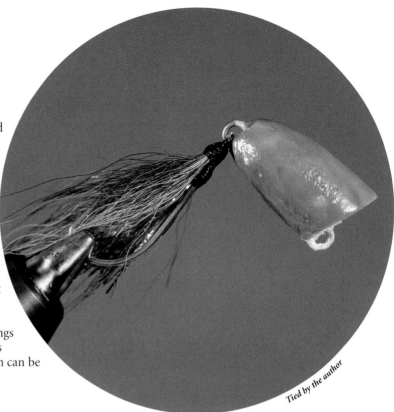

Tied by the author

Materials Needed

Hook – Regular length bass hook, sizes 6 to 1/0

Thread – Green, or to match the color of the tail used

Body wire – 0024 inch spinnerbait wire or similar stiff wire

Body – Bullet-shaped cork, diameter equal to the hook gap, painted green

Tail – mix of bucktail or synthetics in colors of your choice, along with a little Krystal Flash. Tie to cover hook point.

Collar – Green saddle hackle

Eye – Single prism or doll eyes, glued to the belly (which is the only side the fish will see)

Tying sequence:

1. Prepare a bullet-shaped cork by slotting the cork bug for the belly wire.
2. Prepare a wire for the cork body by forming an eye in one end using tapered round nose pliers, or buying short, closed-eye spinnerbait shafts.
3. Bend the wire into a series of zigzag bends to keep the wire from turning in the cork body.
4. Glue the wire into the slot in the cork body using epoxy glue. Note – this wire must be as close as possible to the outer skin of the cork bug.
5. Allow the glue to cure overnight and use an emery board to file smooth the belly area.
6. Fill in any pits using a cork and glue mix, allow to cure, and then file smooth with an emery board.
7. Paint the cork body, first with two coats of primer or base coat, then with two coats of green paint. If desired, add yellow, dark green and black "frog spots" to the body.
8. Add a prism or doll eyes, glued to the belly of the bug.
9. Place the hook in the fly-tying vise and tie on the working thread just in back of the hook eye. Clip the excess thread.
10. Tie in a small bundle of bucktail or synthetics, along with a little Krystal Flash. Clip an excess material.
11. Make a small neat head and tie off with a whip finish. Clip the excess thread.
12. Seal the head with head cement.
13. Use your tapered round-nose pliers to begin to make an eye in the tail wire (bullet end). Add the hook once the eye has been formed. Make sure that the point of the hook is up when the bug floats on the surface (belly down).
14. Complete the eye with one or more wraps of wire around the main stem.
15. Wear safety goggles and clip the excess wire with wire cutters.

Note – This same design can be used to make Pfeiffer's Swing Slider by just reversing the hook in the body so that the hook is at the flat face instead of the tapered end as with this popper version.

BUBBLER/BABBLER

As a result of the round body, this bug rocks back and forth with the slightest twitch, and thus is good when you want to keep a bug in the strike zone when casting to fish that will be spooked by other surface bugs that make noise.

In the later editions of George Leonard Herter's *Professional Fly-Tying, Spinning and Tackle Making Manual and Manufacturers' Guide* he credits this bug to his son Jacques. John and Jim Muma, in their book *Old Flyrod Lures*, credit the same design as a Bugeyed Babbler to the Tropical Bait Company, but dates on both claims are unknown. Basic round bugs have been done before, but this one differs in that it has a large cut out "mouth" that makes the gurgle and bubbles that are the secret of this bug. It is a simple bug to tie. A large eye glued to the bottom completes this simple bug. The Bugeyed Babbler lacks the front rubber legs and substitutes bug eyes on the top of the bug for the single large eye underneath. White is a good color, but any color can be tied. This one is made of a plastic foam ball instead of cork.

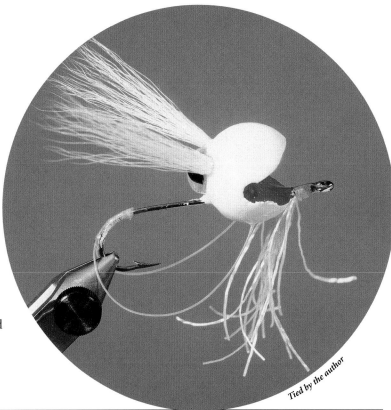

Tied by the author

Materials Needed

Hook – Hump shank hook, sizes 6 through 1/0
Thread – White
Weed guard – Double mono loops

Body – Round cork ball, although plastic foam balls available from craft shops are also possible
Tail/legs – Two white bucktail legs,

inserted into the cork body
Front hackle – White rubber legs
Eye – Single, large on bottom of bug

Tying sequence:

1. Obtain a small (3/4 inch to one inch) cork ball (available from most tackle shops and craft stores) or a foam plastic ball (available from craft shops). Make a 60 to 90 degree cut to the center of the cork bass to open up a "mouth" on the bug.

2. Use a hacksaw blade to cut a slot into the bottom of the ball and into the center of the lower cut face for inserting the hook.

3. Use a drill or small router bit to cut two small holes for legs in the back of the ball. Cut these on the side of the ball directly opposite the lower cut face.

4. Prepare the hook (wrap it with coarse thread) and glue the hook into the slot in the bottom of the round ball. Leave a short length of the hook shank extending in front of the ball body for tying down the front legs.

5. Paint the bug with two coats of primer and two coats of white paint. A neat option here is to paint the bug white and paint the cut open face red to look like an open mouth.

6. Tie in two lengths of 20-pound mono and wrap over the hook shank and mono to half way down the hook bend.

7. Wind the thread back up the hook shank in back of the eye and tie off.

8. Bring the two lengths of mono weed guard forward and glue into small holes made on either side of the hook

shank in the bottom of the bug body. Make sure that both mono strands are equal length and protecting the hook point.

9. Tie in the thread in front of the bug body and clip and excess thread.

10. Tie in a bundle (about ten to twenty strands) of plastic, rubber or silicone legs to the hook shank.

11. Tie off with a whip finish and clip the excess thread.

12. Seal the thread wrap with head cement or nail polish.

13. Separately, prepare (clip, comb and stack/even) two equal bundles of bucktail. Hold a bundle close to the butts, with the butts extended and wrap with thread. To do this, hold the tag end of the thread with the fingers of your left hand, and wrap the thread around the butt ends to make an even, smooth wrap. Tie off with a whip finish.

14. Insert five-minute epoxy into the two holes drilled in the back of the bug, add epoxy to the two bucktail bundles and insert them into the hole.

15. Glue a large rattle eye (doll eye) or solid plastic eye onto the bottom of the cork ball between the two legs and the hook shank.

An option to the above is to make kicker legs by wrapping the middle of each leg with a 3/8-inch band of thread with a stainless steel pin in the center. Complete with a whip finish, and then clip the ends of the stainless steel pin. Use pliers to make a 90-degree bend in the wrapped leg and seal the wrap with head cement.

BILL'S FLOATING SEGMENTED LIZARD

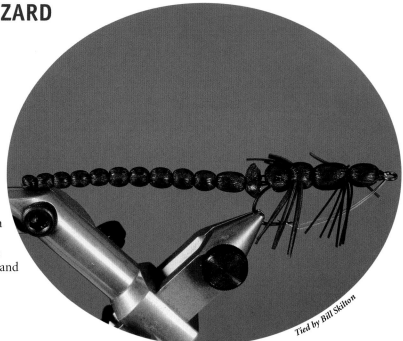

Lizards, salamanders and efts (immature salamanders) often swim along the surface when accidentally ending up in deep water and are relished by bass. This is a great imitation of this favorite bass food.

Bill Skilton uses his unique segmenting technique to make this two-part floating fly, which is not a bug in the traditional sense. The segments make this into a life-like imitation and the legs make for a lot of action in this segmented fly. They are easy to make once you have perfected the segmenting technique described in the Methods chapter. Fish this on a heavy rod to cope with the mass /air resistance ratio that can make this, in larger sizes, a more difficult fly to cast. Fish it with a slow swimming retrieve to simulate the real thing. The weedless hook makes this a fly that you can fish through almost any muck, weeds and brush without fear.

Tied by Bill Skilton

Hook - Weedless wire Weed guard bass hook, sizes 6 to 3/0

Thread – Black

Tail section – Segmented black USA-FLIES hard shell foam strips or similar closed cell

foam strips

Connection – Loop of 12 to 20 pound mono wrapped on the hook connecting to a hook eye in the rear section in which the bend and point have been cut off

Body – Segmented black USA-FLIES hard shell foam strips or similar closed cell foam strips

Legs – Black rubber, silicone or USA-FLIES polymer leg material

Tying sequence:

1. Place a long needle into your fly-tying vise.
2. Take a long piece of strips foam, and wrap around the center with your tying thread or tie a knot in the center with the tying thread. Clip the excess thread.
3. Fold the foam over at the knot and place on the needle for support.
4. Bring the thread between the two parts of the foam and then wrap the thread twice around both foam lengths and the needle.
5. Continue as above to build a segmented foam body.
6. Clip (carefully – use wire cutters and wear safety glasses) the bend from a hook.
7. Close to the end of the foam body, add the shank of the clipped hook and continue making thread-wrapped segments.
8. At the trimmed hook eye, tie off with a whip finish and clip the excess thread.
9. Trim the end of the foam lengths and carefully remove (pull straight off) the segmented body from the needle.
10. Remove the needle from the vise and replace with the hook. Bend the wire weed guard straight down for easy tying.
11. Tie in the working thread, clip the excess thread and tie down a length of 12-to 20-pound mono.
12. Wind the thread to the rear of the hook shank and run the mono through the eye of the hook of the segmented rear body.
13. Fold over the mono and wrap securely with the tying thread.
14. Just forward of the hook bend, tie down six three-inch rubber/silicone legs, using figure eight wraps to secure the wraps and the legs.
15. Repeat the above with another set of legs about 1/4 inch in back of the hook eye.
16. Return the thread to the rear of the hook shank and tie down a length of black foam by the middle.
17. Wrap the thread forward one segments and then fold the foam – top and bottom – over the hook.
18. Tie down this segment by wrapping thread twice around the foam and hook shank.
19. Repeat the above, working toward the eye of the hook and taking care that the segments are even and regular and that the legs stick out from the sides of the body.
20. At the hook eye, trim the foam and wrap the end of the foam to make a neat head to the fly.
21. Whip-finish the thread, clip the excess and seal with head cement.

LETORT HOPPER

Grasshoppers are common along meadow streams throughout the east and west, and as imitations make great flies for almost all surface feeding warmwater fish.

There are hundreds of grasshopper species, details of which the fish and angler care little. The important thing is that they are a large and protein-rich fish food that can be easily imitated by a number of different patterns. Ernie Schwiebert developed the Letort Hopper, as a modified fly from earlier patterns of these large fun-to-fish flies. It originated as a trout fly, named for the Letort, a Pennsylvania limestone stream. This isn't the only pattern for hoppers, and many can be found in books on terrestrial fishing. A hopper like this, or others, should be in the fly box of any warmwater fishermen trying for panfish, sunfish, smallmouth and even largemouth.

Tied by Umpqua Feather Merchants

Hook – Dry fly hook 2X long, sizes 6 through 12

Thread – Yellow

Body – Yellow fur dubbing or synthetic yellow dubbing

Wing – Brown mottled turkey feather, lacquered

Collar (or legs) – Tips of brown deer hair

Head – Trimmed deer hair

Tying sequence:

1. Tie in the thread at mid-point on the hook shank. Clip the excess thread and wind it to the bend of the hook.
2. Tie in the synthetic dubbing or secure dubbing (natural or synthetic) to the waxed tying thread. Wrap the thread forward to a point about 1/3 the shank length in back of the hook eye.
3. Wrap the dubbing forward to build up a body and tie off at the tying thread position. Clip or remove excess dubbing.
4. Cut a section of turkey tail or wing that has been previously lacquered or sprayed with clear sealer. Round off the free end with scissors. Position it tent-like over the wing so that the wing extends just beyond the hook.
5. Tie down the wing at the head of the fly. Clip any excess turkey.

6. Prepare (clip, comb and stack/even) a bundle of natural deer hair.
7. Position it so that it extends just beyond the wing.
8. Tie down with two snug loops (not tight) of thread to hold the bundle on top of the wing, where it will flare up. Allow a little of the hair to spin around the fly to simulate legs. (This last is optional.)
9. If necessary, pick another bundle of prepared deer hair and add it to the first to make a tighter bundle. Clip the deer hair to a tight bundled head, leaving the long fibers to surround the fly and cover the wing. (Alternatively, to prevent cutting the working thread, finish the fly first and then trim. This is the method I prefer.)
10. Tie off with a whip finish in front of the hair bundle.
11. Seal the head and whip finish with head cement. Trim the fly if this has not yet been done.

LETORT CRICKET

This simple, but effective, pattern is one of several cricket patterns, all of which will take actively surface feeding fish. Pennsylvanian Ed Shenk developed it as a companion to the Letort Hopper.

While both the Letort Hopper and Letort Cricket were developed on a Pennsylvania limestone stream, both will work anywhere that fish take hoppers or crickets. This, as with the hopper, offers a large meal to any surface feeding bass or panfish. It works best in the fall, when crickets are more prevalent and active as the cooler weather begins. Fish this on still water such as ponds and lakes using a slight twitching retrieve that is more designed to move the fly in place, than to retrieve across the water. In running water, fish it with a dead drift or with slight twitches as it floats downstream. Be prepared for hard, fast strikes.

Tied by Umpqua Feather Merchants

Hook – Standard dry fly, sizes 8 to 12	**Body** – Black fur or black synthetic dubbing	**Collar** – Tips of black deer hair
Thread – Black	**Wing** – Black wing quill section	**Head** – Black deer hair, trimmed

Tying sequence:

1. Tie in the working thread about 1/3 the shank length in back of the hook eye. Clip any excess thread.
2. Tie in a synthetic dubbing or yarn, or add black fur dubbing to the waxed tying thread.
3. Wrap the dubbing or body material to the bend of the hook and back up to the tie-down point again. Tie off and clip the excess or remove any excess dubbing.
4. Tie down a black wing quill, using a soft loop to control the wing position. Trim any excess in front of the thread.
5. Prepare (clip, comb and stack/even) a bundle of black deer hair, and tie it down with the tips to the rear to form the collar in the completed fly. Tie with a soft loop to keep most of the hair on top of the hook.
6. Weave the thread through the head, and then tie off in front of the head with a whip finish. Clip any excess thread.
7. Seal the head with head cement.

SPONGE SPIDER

Panfish won't care whether these are spiders, craneflies, mayflies, crickets or hoppers. All they will care about is that this is a meaty morsel with wiggly legs struggling on the surface.

Sponge bug bodies in spider and beetle shapes are available from every fly shop. They are cheap and easy to use and can be tied down straight as shown here, or tied and folded as with some other styles of bugs and tying. Basic colors that are available include white, cream, yellow and black. Try them when panfish and bluegills are splatting the surface in the summer, or around lily pads and other surface weeds under which panfish hide in the summer for shade. The photo shows a size 10 bug, but they can be tied with readily available sponge spider bodies in any size. Bugs for panfish, sunfish and perch can't be made much simpler than this.

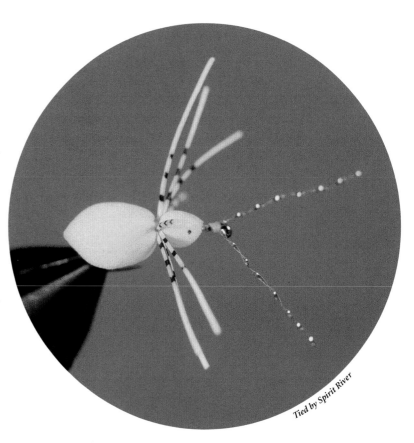

Tied by Spirit River

Materials Needed

Hook – Regular shank length, sizes 12 to 6	**Body** – Yellow sponge bug, eyes marked with permanent felt tip pen	legs, marked with permanent felt tip marker or mottled legs
Thread – Yellow	**Legs** – Yellow rubber or Silicone	**Antennae** – Two strands of Crystal Splash or Krystal Flash

Tying sequence:

1. Tie in the working thread at the midpoint of the shank and clip any excess.
2. Tie down a foam spider sponge body in the middle so that the head or one end just reaches the hook eye. Tie so that the foam body partly wraps around the hook shank.
3. Tie in two mottled or solid color yellow legs on each side at the same point.
4. Fold the forward part of the body up and wind the thread forward around the hook shank to the hook eye.
5. Tie in two lengths of Crystal Splash or Krystal Flash to serve as antennae.
6. Fold the forward part of the foam down, fold around the hook shank and secure the end with the tying thread.
7. Tie off with a whip finish and clip the excess thread.
8. Seal the head with head cement.

DAMSELFLY

Damselfly and dragonfly imitations are very effective for both largemouth and smallmouth bass. They can be tied using parachute hackle, or with cut wings as with this pattern. The photo is slightly angled for the best view.

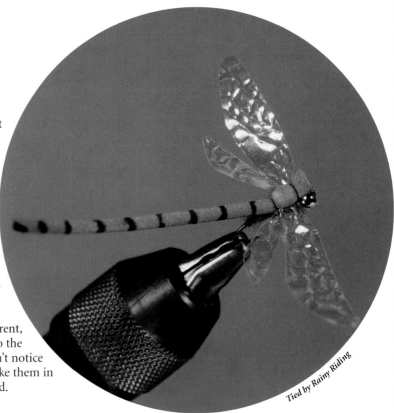

Tied by Rainy Riding

Damselflies are not standard dry flies or surface bugs, but they do float and do deserve a place in most warmwater fly boxes. They are best when fishing lakes, ponds, or slow moving waters where both damselflies and dragonflies are prevalent and taken by surface feeding smallmouth and largemouth. Some panfish will also take small size damselflies. Damselflies offer a large chunk of meat for a surface feeding smallmouth and are often taken with enthusiasm when presented in quiet pools and glides. There are a number of ways to tie damselfly adults, including making bodies from deer hair, yarn, and other materials, but one of the best and simplest ways is to use long thin cylinders of foam, as per this Rainy Riding pattern. While this pattern uses cut wings tied spent-wing style, an alternative is to use parachute hackle or poly wing material to imitate the transparent, gossamer wings of the naturals. Note that the wings are out to the side as with the larger dragonflies, but the trout probably won't notice or care. While this pattern is for a blue damselfly, you can make them in any of the bright colors in which natural damselflies are found.

Materials Needed

Hook – Standard dry fly hook in sizes 8 to 14

Thread – Blue

Tail – 3/64- or 1/16- inch diameter blue foam

Body – 1/8-inch diameter blue foam

Wings – Cut wings (parachute hackle is an alterative)

Eyes – Mono or Rainy's Bug Eyes

Tying sequence:

1. Tie in the thread at the mid-point of the hook and clip the excess.
2. Dub in some blue sparkle dubbing on the waxed tying thread and wrap this dubbing on the rear of the hook shank.
3. Prepare the length of tail foam by trimming the tail end to a point and cutting the tie-down end at an angle. Mark the foam with thin bands of black, using a fine tip permanent felt tip marker and rolling the foam on a paper towel as you make these concentric marks.
4. Tie the tail in front of the dubbed body and wrap over enough of the tail so that it will lie horizontal and parallel with the hook shank.
5. Cut the body foam cylinder in half lengthwise. Tie in front of the tail.
6. Tie in the cut wings by placing them centered on the hook shank and crisscross or figure-eighting the thread to hold securely and horizontally.
7. Tie in Bug Eyes on the front of the hook so that they will extend in front of the body once the fly is complete.
8. Fold the body foam over the wings and on top of the Bug Eyes, and tie down with the working thread.
9. Tie off with a whip finish and clip the excess thread.
10. Seal the wraps with head cement.

MC MURRAY ANT

Tying everything on at the mid-point in the hook shank is a characteristic of the McMurray Ant. It is quick and easy to produce and is very effective when fish are taking ants.

This started as a trout fly developed by tyer Ed Sutryn, but has proven to be equally effective for surface feeding panfish and bluegills. It is great for pond and reservoir fishing, along with drifting through a slow pool on a meandering sunfish stream. Ants will typically nest in rotten streamside logs or along the banks of ponds and are frequently washed into the water during rain or any disruption of their nest. The McMurray Ant pattern can be tied in any color, since ants come in many colors. Typical patterns are black, red and cinnamon, but white is also possible as a termite imitation. As it is tied with the balsa wood abdomen and thorax sections, they are high floaters. The component parts for making these flies are available through supply catalogs and fly shops.

Tied by Rod Yerger

Hook – Standard dry fly hook in sizes 12 through 20

Thread – Black to make a black ant as described here, thread color appropriate to the fly in making other color McMurray ants

Body – Two small cylinders of balsa, the forward one slightly shorter and smaller than the rear section, both connected by a length of monofilament threaded through them Painted appropriate to the ant pattern

(An alternative is two small cylinders of black foam, threaded on monofilament and glued in place with CA glue)

Hackle – Black, or a color appropriate to the pattern color

Tying sequence:

1. Tie in the thread at the center of the hook shank.
2. If not bought assembled, use a fine needle and fine monofilament to thread through short lengths of balsa cylinders, then paint them the desired color. See above for foam alternative.
3. Tie down the prepared section of thorax/abdomen, with the mono curving up to give the abdomen and thorax a curved up appearance.
4. Tie in a hackle tip and clip the excess butt ends.
5. Wind the hackle around the waist of the fly, between the two balsa cylinders.
6. Tie off the hackle with thread and clip the excess hackle.
7. Hold the hackle out of the way and tie off with a whip finish. Alternatively, wrap the thread forward under the forward balsa body and then tie off on the bare hook shank.
8. Seal with head cement.

DEER-HAIR INCH WORM

Inchworms vary in abundance throughout the country. Where they are abundant, they are excellent when shoreline fishing for panfish and perch.

This inchworm is tied with light green-dyed deer hair or antelope hair. Only one material is used, other than the hook and thread, but that material must be spiral wrapped back and forth to make it retain the inchworm body form. It is an ideal fly for small stream or pond fishing along the banks where inchworms occasionally fall into the water. Inchworms can be found in streamside trees and bushes from mid-spring through the summer. When they fall into streams or ponds, panfish eagerly gobble them up. There is never a "rise" or a "hatch" of inchworms, but when and where they are available, these offbeat flies are worth trying. Another easy way to make an arching (walking) inchworm is to use light green cylindrical foam slightly longer than the hook shank and tie down just the two ends of the foam to the two ends of the hook shank with an arc in the foam to make the inchworm appear to walk.

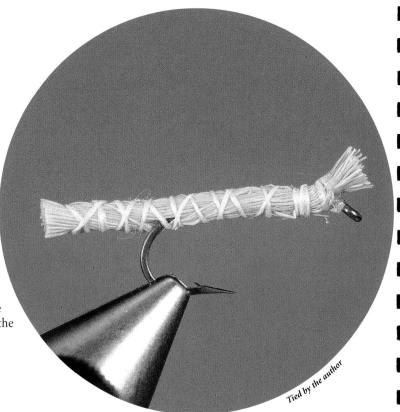

Tied by the author

Hook – Dry fly hook 2X long in sizes 6 to 10, turned-down eye

Thread – Light green or yellow
Body – Small bundle of light green or dark yellow deer hair

Tying sequence:

1. Tie down the thread in back of the hook eye. Clip any excess thread.
2. Wrap the thread evenly and neatly to the bend of the hook, then back up to the hook eye. (This additional wrap to camouflage the hook shank is optional.)
3. Clip a small (large finishing nail size) bundle of deer hair, and comb out any underfur. Place it in a hair evener to even the tips.
4. Position the deer hair bundle over the hook shank so that the bundle is about 1-1/2 times the length of the hook shank with about 1/3 of the bundle extending in back of the hook bend. Make a snug, but not tight, wrap to secure the bundle in back of the hook eye. (Since inchworms are blunt worms, you can clip the tip end of the hair bundle before doing this, then measure. Tapered or neat ends are not necessary for this fly.)
5. With the bundle in place, make a spiral wrap down the

hook shank, wrapping snugly (but not tightly) around the hook shank and the bundle.

6. At the hook bend, continue this spiral wrap around the bundle alone that extends in back of the hook bend. (You may wish to reverse the hook position in the vise for this.) At the end of the bundle, reverse this to spiral back over the bundle, then over and up the hook shank and bundle to in back of the hook eye.
7. At this point, continue the spiral wrap over the forward part of the bundle that extends in front of the hook eye, and then reverse this spiral wrap to return to the tie-down point.
8. Tie off with a whip finish, making snug (not tight) wraps. Clip any excess thread.
9. Seal the tie-down point with head cement. Alternatively, you can protect all of the thread with a coating of head cement over the whole fly.

FOAM JAPANESE BEETLE

Foam provides an easy way to make a wide variety of beetles, jassids, ladybugs, and other insect imitations by just tying down and folding over the foam to make a high floating body.

Closed-cell foam, available through most fly-tying shops and also in sheet form through craft stores, is an ideal material for many floating flies and fly designs for all types of fish. In cylinders and small "logs" it can be fashioned into McMurray Ants. Cylinder lengths of it can be used for dragonfly abdomens, and short plugs of it used for hopper and cricket bodies. This method of folding the foam over itself to make a beetle is one used by Bill Skilton and many others for terrestrial patterns of all types. This is a great fly for sipping river smallmouth and pond panfish and sunfish.

Tied by Spirit River

Materials Needed

Hook – Standard length to 2X long hook in sizes 6 to 16
Thread – Black

Body – Black foam, cut into rectangular shape
Legs – Black CDC or marabou
Side legs – Black biots

Antennae – Black Crystal Splash or Krystal Flash
Visibility marker – Yellow foam

Tying sequence:

1. Tie in the thread in back of the hook eye, and clip any excess.
2. Wrap the thread tightly to the bend of the hook. Prepare a rectangular section of sheet foam, the length of the foam about 1-1/4 times the shank length and the foam width about 1/2 the shank length. Tie in one end of the closed-cell foam, securing it tightly.
3. Wrap the thread back up to a point about 1/3 the shank length in back of the hook eye.
4. Tie in black CDC feathers or a very short length of black marabou.
5. Tie in two lengths of black Crystal Splash to serve as antennae.
6. Fold the foam over and wrap it tightly at the thread position, taking care to avoid matting the legs with the thread.
7. Tie in a black biot on each side at this same point to make "backswimmer" legs.
8. Tie in a short small length of yellow foam, directly on top of the foam body, to serve as a visibility marker.
9. Wrap the thread forward to just in back of the hook eye.
10. Tie off with a whip finish. Clip the excess thread.
11. Coat the head and the tie-down points with head cement.

MARABOU COTTONWOOD SEED CARP FLY

Carp in late spring and early summer often cruise the surface, sipping in cottonwood seeds that have blown onto the water and float there as a result of their light fluff.

This fly in any size can imitate cottonwood seedpods that carp relish when these light bits of fluff land on the water surface. This fly can also be tied using CDC feathers or rabbit fur in place of the marabou, but the marabou will float for a while and makes a simple fly to tie. Since these cottonwood seeds are small, these flies are best tied as small as possible, considering the size wire and hook necessary to handle a big carp. Realize that as a result of the light wire hook, you must play these fish lightly and carefully, even though you might be using a powerful rod that will allow for a tougher fight.

Tied by the author

Materials Needed

Hook – Standard dry fly hook, sizes 14 to 10

Thread – White

Wing – Short full wing of white marabou

Flotation – Tiny cylinder of white foam, tied McMurray style (optional)

Tying sequence:

1. Tie in the thread at the midpoint of the hook shank.
2. Tie in a small short bundle of white foam, pinching the foam in the middle with the thread. (Optional – provides additional flotation for longer fishing and use.)
3. Prepare a thick but very short bundle of white marabou. This bundle should be very fluffy and no longer than the length of the hook.
4. Slightly moisten the marabou bundle to handle it, and tie in the butt ends in the middle of the hook, on top of the tie down point for the white foam.
5. Make a few more wraps with the thread and tie off with a whip finish. Clip the excess thread.
6. Seal the wrap with head cement, taking care to avoid getting it on the marabou.

DEER HAIR MULBERRY CARP FLY

In midsummer, carp will often feed along the banks near mulberry trees where they wait for mulberries to ripen and fall into the water. This fly is another vegetarian imitation for carp.

Carp fishing can be great for the short period of time that mulberries ripen and fall into the water along rivers, streams, lakes and ponds. Carp take these berries – and flies – readily and provide great fishing during the months of July and August. There are lots of ways to tie these flies, including tying fat bodies of chenille, cactus chenille, dubbing, and yarn. These flies won't float and are best when the carp are taking berries under the surface. Most often, they are taking berries off the surface, particularly if they have competition from other carp. The deer hair used in this fly floats low in the water, but continues to keep the fly on the surface, making it an ideal carp offering. Tie all of these flies with red/purple materials and a green stem.

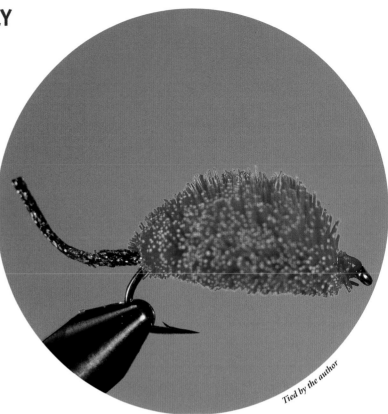

Tied by the author

Hook – Size 6 through 1 2X long shank hooks

Thread – Purple/red

Tail – "Stem" of green braid, such as Kreinik or gudebrod heavy braid

Body – Spun and trimmed body of dyed purple/red deer hair

Tying sequence:

1. Tie in the thread at the rear end of the hook shank.
2. Tie in a 1-inch length of stiff green braid material.
3. Dab the end of the green braid with a drop of head cement or other flexible glue to prevent it from unraveling.
4. Prepare a bundle (clip, comb and stack) of purplish-red dyed deer hair and tie onto the hook shank with two loose turns, then pull tight to spin the deer hair around the hook (see Methods for details.)
5. Push the deer hair back and wrap the thread just in front of this flared bundle.
6. Tie in another bundle of deer hair, and repeat as above.
7. Continue until covering the entire hook with deer hair.
8. Tie a small neat head and tie off with a whip finish. Clip the excess thread.
9. Seal the wraps with head cement.
10. Use scissors, then a double edge razor (broken in half with the break covered with tape) to clip and then shave the deer hair into a round ball to simulate a mulberry.

Underwater Flies

PFEIFFER'S INVINCIBLE

As the name indicates, the Invincible is an indestructible fly (almost) and ideal for pike, pickerel, muskie and even bowfin.

Tied by the author

When most flies for pike are hit, they become a bundle of fluff, whether or not you get the pike or muskie to the boat. The materials start to unwind from the hook as soon as you get a strike. This fly is different. I developed the idea before the material – Body Fur – was even available, and tried to get several companies to make it before Dan Bailey independently came out with their Body Fur. The basis for this design of fly is the use of tough synthetics, to prevent it from being chewed up too much and imbedding the material into a base of epoxy to keep the fly and working thread from being cut by teeth. It is not like some saltwater flies that use epoxy over the body material to protect them and thus create a hard body. It can be tied in any color, using the same color for tail and body (as with this yellow tail/yellow body example) or mixed colors, as with a yellow tail and red body. Good colors include all white, all black, all yellow, all chartreuse, all green, yellow/red, white/red, and white/black. This is also a good fly for any toothy fish such as bowfin or grinnel.

Materials Needed

Hook – Standard streamer hook or saltwater stainless steel hook, 4X long hook, size 4 (pickerel) to 3/0 (pike) 2/0 seems to be the best size for most big pike

Thread – Color of the Body Fur used, yellow for this example

Tail – Yellow Super Hair

Tail Flash – Silver, gold or red Krystal Flash (optional – will ultimately get cut off by pike

teeth)

Body – Yellow body fur

Head – Yellow thread, epoxied

Eyes – Prism eyes on large head, coated with epoxy for protection

Tying sequence:

1. Tie in the working thread at the middle of the hook shank. Wrap tightly and wrap the thread to the bend of the hook.
2. Cut a three- to five-inch length of yellow Super Hair and tie in at the bend of the hook.
3. Tie in the Krystal Flash material on each side of the tail.
4. Tie in a length of yellow Body Fur on top of the tail tie.
5. Spiral wrap the thread up and down the hook shank several times, ending up with the thread about 1/5 the shank length in back of the hook eye.
6. Thoroughly mix a puddle of five-minute epoxy and completely coat and cover the tail wrapping and the hook shank.
7. Palmer wrap the Body Fur forward, making sure that the central cord of the Body Fur is imbedded into the epoxy

and that the Body Fur flares back towards the tail of the fly. (You may wish to use a rotary vise or vise with horizontal jaws to allow rotating the hook to prevent sags and drips as you wind the Body Fur forward.)

8. Upon reaching the thread, tie down the Body Fur and clip any excess.
9. Continue to wrap around the tie down point and make a large tapered head with the working thread.
10. Tie off with a whip finish.
11. Add stick-on prism eyes or doll rattle eyes or glue on body fur. to the head at this point.
12. Use the remainder of the epoxy to completely coat the head and cover the eyes with epoxy.
13. Place the completed fly on a fly turner to rotate it and prevent the epoxy from dripping or sagging.

BARRY'S PIKE FLY

Tied by Umpqua Feather Merchants

This Barry Reynolds' Pike Fly is considered a basic for any pike fishing. When tied in a variety of colors, it can represent a number of baitfish and will take lots of strikes from big fish before becoming unusable.

Barry Reynolds and John Berryman wrote *Pike On The Fly*, an excellent treatise on the subject. Unfortunately, this pike fly did not get included in the book. It is an excellent fly, though not indestructible, as is the Invincible. It could be made this way by using Invincible tying methods of coating the tail tie down area with epoxy and then coating the shank with epoxy after winding the thread forward and before winding the rabbit strip body forward, then finishing with epoxy covering the thread head with plastic eyes. This fly does have more action in the water than the Invincible, and is thus ideal for those situations where pike might need a little encouragement to get them to hit. This one is a basic red/white, but other good pike colors include all black, all chartreuse, all white, black/yellow and red/tan. Dimensions here are based on a 3/0 hook size.

Hook – Tiemco 811s or long shank stainless steel hook, sizes 1 to 3/0

Thread – White

Tail – White rabbit (Zonker) strip over mixed red and gold Krystal Flash

Body – Red cross-cut rabbit strip

Head – White thread wrap, coated with epoxy after eyes are added

Flash – gold Krystal Flash over body

Eyes – Prism eyes, red with black pupil

Tying sequence:

1. Tie in the working thread in the middle of the hook shank and clip the excess thread.
2. Wind the thread back to the rear of the hook shank and tie in a three-inch length of mixed red and gold Krystal Flash.
3. Tie in a 3-inch length of white rabbit fur strip.
4. Tie in a length of red cross-cut rabbit strip. Tie down so that the fur will flow back when the strip is wound around the hook shank.
5. Wind the thread forward to about 1/4 the shank length distance in back of the hook eye.
6. Wind the red rabbit fur around the hook shank and tie off at the thread position. Clip the excess red rabbit fur.
7. Tie in a few strands of gold Krystal Flash on each side of the fur body. Clip any excess.
8. Make a neat head with the working thread and tie off with a whip finish. Clip the excess thread.
9. Add self-stick plastic or prism eyes to each side of the head.
10. Seal the head and protect the eyes with a coat of epoxy.
11. Place the fly on a fly turner to prevent the epoxy from sagging.

SCOTT SANCHEZ CARDIAC PIKE FLY

Bead flies are nothing new now, but this fly uses a large pony bead available from craft stores to make a large head on this large fly.

Scott Sanchez, the creative and inventive fly tyer with Dan Bailey, developed this fly as one of a series of flies that are made using large heart-shaped pony beads for the head. It is easy to cast, looks good in the water and is great for pike, pickerel and muskie. This shape perfectly simulates the shape of a fish head, and is ideal for big flies. These beads are plastic, and do add weight, yet are nowhere near as heavy as the lead dumbbell eyes in smaller sizes or the tungsten beads used primarily on trout nymphs. You can also use the same beads to make this fly in many other colors or to tie it using the Body Fur body and a bucktail or saddle hackle tail. Phil Camera creates a similar fly using large round pony beads, tied in a similar way to create the head of the fly.

Tied by Scott Sanchez

Materials Needed

Hook – Dai-Riki 899 loop eye long shank hook, sizes 1 to 3/0
Thread – White or yellow
Head – Red heart-shaped pony bead, slipped on fly after tying down the thread, and glued in place
Eyes – Stick-on prism or painted eye and pupil
Collar – Red Body Fur
Wing/tail – White rabbit strip (Zonker strip)

Tying sequence:

1. Tie in the working thread in back of the hook eye and clip any excess.
2. Make a smooth wrap until reaching the inner diameter of the hole in the hear pony bead. Tie off with a whip finish and clip the thread.
3. Remove the hook from the vise and slide a red heart shaped pony bead onto the hook and up to the eye.
4. Add some CA glue to the thread base and slide the bead in place, aligning it vertically in the hook plane.
5. Reattach the working thread to the hook in back of the bead and clip any excess thread.
6. Wind the thread to the rear of the hook shank.
7. Tie in a 3-inch length of white rabbit strip, with the fur flowing backwards.
8. Tie in a length of red Body Fur.
9. Wind the thread forward to just in back of the red pony bead.
10. Wind the Body Fur forward around the hook shank, making sure that the Body Fur angles to the rear.
11. Tie off the Body Fur in back of the bead and clip any excess.
12. Make a whip finish and clip the excess thread.
13. Seal the wraps with head cement.
14. Add a prism or self-stick eye to the red heart shaped bead.
15. Seal and protect the eye with head cement or very thin epoxy.

LEFTY'S DECEIVER

This basic design of streamer developed by Lefty Kreh has the advantage of a tail and wing that will not tangle or wrap around the hook, making it ideal for all fly-fishing.

Lefty Kreh developed this fly some 50 years ago for stripers after a fishing trip in the Chesapeake Bay area in which some of his flies got fouled when the long wing wrapped around the hook bend on a cast. This design prevents that, since it has a long saddle hackle tail and a veiling wing of bucktail. While developed for stripers and an excellent saltwater fly, it has proved over the ensuing decades to be equally excellent for everything in cold water (trout and salmon) to warmwater (the subject of this book) and salt water on all three coasts. It can be tied in any size and a number of variations and styles, with this basic white pattern a favorite of Lefty's for warmwater fishing for bass and pike. If you can have only one color, this is the fly to have.

Tied by the author

Hook – Long shank stainless steel hook, size 6 to 2/0

Thread – Gray or white

Tail – Also called the wing, this is tied at the bend of the hook, and consists of two or more pairs of white saddle hackles

Body – Silver tinsel or Mylar (This can be skipped, since the veiling of the collar/wing will hide the hook shank)

Forward wing or collar – White bucktail that will surround the hook shank and thus veil the body and blend with the white saddle hackle tail

Beard – Optional – Lefty prefers red Krystal Flash

Head – White (thread color)

Eyes – Painted yellow with black pupil or prism eyes, coated with head cement or epoxy

Tying sequence:

Variations of this are to add grizzly saddle hackle over the white for a barred appearance; to add a topping on the collar/wing of peacock herl; to tie a two-tone collar/wing that is light on the belly and dark on top to closely simulate a baitfish; and to vary all of the colors to match the local baitfish.

1. Tie in the thread at the bend of the hook, and clip any excess thread.
2. Tie in the tail or wing of saddle hackles, with the pairs of hackle flared out for more action.
3. Tie in the tinsel body material.
4. Wind the thread forward; making sure that the base for the tinsel is level and smooth.
5. Wind the tinsel forward and tie off with the working thread.

6. Prepare (clip, comb and stack/even) a bundle of bucktail. This should be just a little longer than the hook shank, and blend with the tail/wing. Tie down in back of the hook eye. Push down on the bundle to make it surround or veil the hook shank and blend with the saddle hackle tail.
7. Clip any excess material forward of the tie down point, and wrap a smooth tapered head.
8. Tie off with a whip finish.
9. Add painted or prism eyes. If adding painted eyes, use two different size nail heads to make the eye and pupil. Seal with head cement or epoxy. If using epoxy, place on a fly rotator.

MUDDLER MINNOW

This famous pattern is a great one for bass, and can be fished on the surface or down deep where it can imitate a sculpin or mad tom catfish.

The Muddler Minnow is one of those rare flies that, depending upon how it is tied and how it is fished, can be fished on the top, right on the bottom, or anyplace in the water column in between. Dressed with some fly dope, it is a great top-water fly, fishing in the surface film and twitching it along like an injured minnow. With its brownish coloration, it will also imitate bottom-living sculpins, and if weighted or fished with split shot on the leader, can be fished deep. Without weight to sink or fly dressing to float, it can be fished in mid-depths. While designed as a trout fly, it has proven excellent over the years for a number of warmwater species, and perhaps best for smallmouth bass. It is imitative of the one hundred-plus members of the sculpin family, most of which are smallmouth forage. The Muddler was developed about 1950 by Don Gapen, who designed it to imitate the plentiful sculpin found in the Nipigon River of Ontario. In warm waters, it has caught bass, pike, walleyes, crappies, and sunfish.

Tied by Umpqua Feather Merchants

Materials Needed

Hook – Standard streamer fly hook, 3X to 4X long, in sizes 2 – 12

Weight – Wrapped lead or non-lead wire, (no wire if fished on the surface)

Thread – Brown

Tail – Mottled turkey quill fibers

Underwing – Gray squirrel tail (wolf used in the original pattern)

Body – Oval, flat or embossed gold tinsel

Overwing – Mottled turkey quill section

Collar – Natural brown deer hair, spun

Head – Natural brown deer hair, spun and clipped

Tying sequence:

1. Tie the thread on in back of the hook eye and clip any excess.
2. Wrap the hook shank with wire to weight, or leave unweighted if fishing the surface. Spiral wrap the lead up and down the shank with the tying thread.
3. Tie in the tail, and then tie in the gold tinsel. Wrap the thread forward in tight even turns to a point about 1/3 the shank length back from the hook eye. This thread wrap forms an even base for the tinsel body, and is a must if wrapping over wire.
4. Wrap the tinsel forward evenly, and tie off at the thread. Clip the excess.
5. Tie down a small bundle of gray squirrel tail, after clipping closely and combing out any body fur.
6. Clip matching quill sections from matched turkey wing feathers and tie down so that the wings act as a tent over the underwing. Position so that the wing extends no farther than the end of the tail. Clip any excess forward of the tie down point.

7. Prepare (clip, comb and stack/even) a bundle of brown deer hair. Position it over the hook shank so that it is no longer than the bend of the hook. Hold the bundle in place and tie down with loose wraps of thread. The deer hair will flare as you pull the thread tight. Keep most of the deer hair on top of the hook shank, but allow some to spin around the hook.
8. If necessary, add another short bundle of natural deer hair to the first, taking two loops of thread around the bundle and hook shank and then pulling tight to flare the bundle. Make several wraps of the tying thread through the bundle to help secure and stabilize it.
9. Pull the hair back and wrap the thread around the hook shank, then complete with a whip finish and clip the excess thread.
10. Seal with head cement, then use scissors to trim the head into a bullet shape, leaving the deer hair tips flaring out and covering the wing.

MARABOU MUDDLER MINNOW

This looks and ties very similar to the Muddler Minnow, but with the marabou wing, has a lot more action, and is especially good for stillwater fishing.

The Marabou Muddler Minnow is one of many variations of the basic 1950-developed Muddler Minnow. It can be tied in any color of marabou wing, including white, black, chartreuse, red, etc. Yellow, as shown here, is perhaps the most popular color with white a close second. It can be tied weighted to sink, but usually has more and better action if tied unweighted and fishing with a sinking line or split shot on the leader to get the fly deep. This example varies slightly from most Marabou Muddlers in that it has a multi-colored head of natural, yellow and brown bands of deer hair.

Tied by Riverborn Fly Company

Hook – Long shank hook (4X to 6X) in sizes 12 through 2

Thread – Brown, or to match head color

Tail – Red Krystal Flash or red hackle fibers

Body – Embossed silver tinsel or Diamond Body Braid

Wing – Yellow marabou

Flash – Yellow Krystal Flash

Collar – Natural spun deer hair

Head – Natural deer hair in back of a band of yellow deer hair in back of brown deer hair, all spun and clipped

Tying sequence:

1. Tie in the working thread at the head of the hook shank and clip any excess thread.
2. Wind the thread to the rear of the hook shank.
3. Tie in a short tail of red Krystal Flash.
4. Tie down a length of embossed silver tinsel or silver Diamond Braid.
5. Wind the thread forward to a spot 1/4 the shank length in back of the hook eye.
6. Wind the body material forward around the hook shank and tie off with the thread. Clip any excess tinsel.
7. Tie down a bundle of yellow marabou and clip any excess forward marabou.
8. Tie in a sparse bundle of yellow Krystal Flash on top of the marabou. Clip any excess Krystal Flash.
9. Prepare (clip, comb and stack/even) a bundle of natural deer hair.
10. Tie it in place with the tips facing the rear of the fly and spin it around the hook shank.
11. Prepare as above a bundle of yellow deer hair and spin it onto the hook shank as above in front of the natural deer hair.
12. Prepare a bundle of dark brown deer hair as above and spin it on the hook shank in front of the yellow deer hair. Continue if necessary until filling the hook shank up to the hook eye.
13. Tie off the fly with a whip finish and clip any excess thread.
14. Seal with head cement.
15. Use scissors followed with a razor blade to trim the head, leaving the tip ends of the rear bundle intact and facing the rear of the fly. Trim the belly flat and the rest of the head to a tapered bullet shape.

DOUBLE BUNNY

Sometimes flies involve as much gluing as tying. This is one of those, but a very effective pattern for all large gamefish. As a result of the natural fur, it is a little hard to cast.

Rabbit strips have become increasing popular for fly-tying in this country since Dan Byford developed the first Zonker years ago. This fly utilizes two different color rabbit strips, tied and glued together so that the make a two-tone fly that will resemble the dark back and light belly of most baitfish, eels, and other forage and prey. It can be tied in any color or color combinations. It can even be tied in one solid color (both strips the same color) if you just want a thicker, meatier fly that does not have the color contrast. Other possibilities for this pattern of solid colors is to add a topping of dark (black, dark blue or dark green) synthetic material such as Poly Bear or Super Hair, or natural materials such as strands of peacock herl.

Tied by Riverborn Fly Company

Hook – Long shank hook (4X), sizes 2 to 2/0

Thread – Black

Tail and body – Two strips of rabbit fur, glued skin-to-skin, white and olive

Flash material – Yellow Krystal Flash

Eyes – Large plastic eyes, orange with black pupils

Tying sequence:

1. Tie in the working thread in back of the hook eye and clip any excess thread.
2. Wind the thread back on the hook about 1/4 inch.
3. Prepare two lengths of rabbit fur – one white and one olive – about two- to three-inches long.
4. Hold the white (bottom) strip against the hook to measure where to piece the skin to insert the hook.
5. Use a bodkin or awl to punch a hole through the skin at this point.
6. Remove the hook from the vise and run the point through the skin, with the fur side down. (Alternatively, you can save time by doing this step first, then placing the hook in the vise and adding the working thread.)
7. Tie down the front edge of the rabbit strip with the working thread, skin side up. If necessary, trim any excess rabbit fur.
8. Place the olive rabbit strip on top and tie down with the working thread, with the fur flowing back.
9. Prepare and tie down two sparse bundles of yellow Krystal Flash, one on each side.
10. Make a large, tapered head.
11. Complete the wrap with a whip finish and clip any excess thread.
12. Seal the head with head cement.
13. Glue large plastic eyes to each side of the rear of the head. Alternatively, use prism eyes on the head itself and coat with epoxy, then turn on a fly rotator.
14. Use a waterproof flexible glue (Weldwood Contact Cement, Marine Goop, AquaSeal, etc.) on the two skin sides and glue them together as per the glue manufacturers directions.

ROD'S RABBIT

There are lots of ways of using rabbit fur to make warmwater flies, with this one involving clipped rabbit fur in a dubbing loop that is later clipped for the streamlined minnow appearance.

Rod Yerger finds this a top smallmouth fly for fishing rivers in his area. He even refers to them as "smallmouth magnets", and the most productive smallmouth fly of the many patterns that he ties. This fly involves rabbit fur spun in a dubbing loop and wrapped onto the hook shank, then clipped on the bottom. It is a good minnow imitation, but with the red chenille head, it might also be taken as an egg-sucking leech. Rod suggests that while he ties these neat for his customers, he likes them as rough as possible for his personal fishing. Try these in colors other than the white shown here, with yellow and black particularly good.

Tied by Rod Yerger

Hook – Mustad 79580 or other long shank hook in sizes 8 and 6
Thread – White
Weight – Lead wire, .020-inch

diameter, wrapped on hook shank
Tail – White rabbit fur
Body – White rabbit fur, spun onto

dubbing loop and picked out for appearance, then clipped on bottom
Head – Red Chenille

Tying sequence:

1. Tie in the thread at the midpoint of the shank and clip any excess thread.
2. Wind the thread to the rear of the hook shank and tie in a bundle of white rabbit fur.
3. Prepare a dubbing loop and spin in some rabbit fur. Rod suggests that this is easiest when clipping fur from a Zonker strip.
4. Wind the thread forward to a point about 1/4 the shank length in back of the hook eye.
5. Wind the dubbing loop with rabbit fur forward to make

the body and tie off with the working thread. Clip any excess loop material.
6. Tie in a short length of red chenille.
7. Wind the chenille forward to the hook eye, then back over itself and tie off in between the head and body. Clip any excess chenille.
8. Make a whip finish and clip the excess thread.
9. Seal the thread wraps with head cement.
10. Use scissors to trim and rabbit fur on the sides and belly to allow for hook gap clearance.

FLASHTAIL WHISTLER

Long, big flies for pike and large bass are a must, and this variation of the basic saltwater Whistler fills the bill for size and flash.

Dan Blanton, an experienced West Coast saltwater fly fisherman, developed his Whistler as a fly that will "push" water to alert fish who can feel these waves through their lateral line. This is a variation of this, with a long trailing bucktail-and-flash tail. The bead chain eyes help it to sink without the weight or casting problems of heavy lead eyes. Fish this in short to long strips to get maximum action out of the bucktail and the Flashabou in the tail. While this red head and white tail pattern is excellent, try it also in all white, all yellow, red/yellow and black/white.

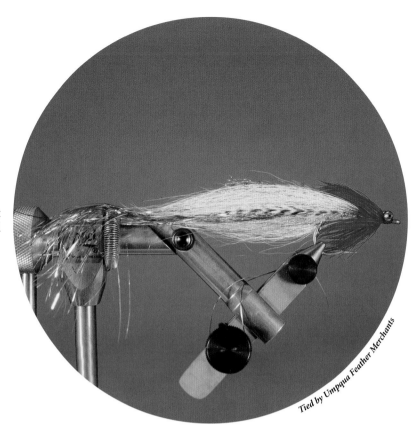

Tied by Umpqua Feather Merchants

Materials Needed

Hook – Tiemco 800S or regular stainless steel hook, sizes 2 to 3/0

Thread – Red, or to match the hackle color used

Tail/wing – Long white bucktail, mixed with long tail of silver Flashabou and flanked with short lengths of mixed color Krystal Flash and pair of grizzly saddle hackle

Body – Short wrap of red chenille

Collar/hackle – Red saddle hackles

Eyes – Silver bead chain

Tying sequence:

1. Tie in the working thread in back of the hook eye. Clip any excess thread.
2. Tie in a pair of silver medium size bead chain eyes, crisscrossing and figure-eighting to hold them in place.
3. Wind the working thread to the midpoint or slightly beyond on the hook shank.
4. Prepare and tie down a large, long bundle of silver Flashabou.
5. Prepare (clip, comb and stack/even) a length of white bucktail, shorter than the tail/wing of Flashabou.
6. Tie the bucktail in place over the Flashabou, pushing the bucktail down so that it surrounds or "veils" the Flashabou.
7. Tie in a shorter bundle of mixed color Krystal Flash; tying is so that it also surrounds the bucktail.
8. Tie in a length of red chenille.
9. Wind the thread forward to just in back of the hook eye.
10. Wind the red chenille forward and tie down with the working thread. Clip any excess chenille.
11. Tie in one or two red saddle hackles by the butts and wind the thread slightly forward. Clip any excess hackle butt.
12. Wind the hackles around the hook shank and tie off with the thread. Clip any excess hackle tips.
13. Finish the head by wrapping with the working thread and tie off with a whip finish. Clip the excess thread.
14. Seal the head with head cement.

MISSISSIPPI BUG

This old fly goes by many names and is a weedless variation of the more recent Hi-Tie method of tying multiple hair "wings" on a hook shank.

This underwater fly, also called the Ozark Weedless Bug and the Itasca Bucktail, uses bucktail or other furs of the wing to guard the hook. This makes it a weedless style without the necessity of using wire weed guards or mono loops. It is not a floating bug of the same name that closely resembles a CallMac bug. A floating version of this fly called a Whisker Bug is made with hollow deer body hair, but is trimmed around all the sides except the hook plane to make the bug weedless. The method of tying is a little different, since it utilizes the butt ends of the bucktail wing as a part of the design, rather than tying them down with thread as with most flies. The secret of tying this fly is to use many small bundles of fur for the wing. A good guide, even for a large fly on a 1/0 or 2/0 hooks, is to use bundles that are no larger in bulk than a wood household match. Note also that the thread becomes a part of the fly body, so that you can use thread colors that match or contrast with the wing colors. You can tie this in one color, or alternating colors to make a banded wing pattern. Popular colors include white, black, yellow, purple, black/white, yellow/brown, yellow/black, blue/white and similar combinations.

Tied by the author

Materials Needed

Hook – Long-shank hook in sizes 6 through 2/0

Thread – White
Tail – Yellow bucktail

Wing – Yellow bucktail, alternating with black bucktail

Tying sequence:

1. Tie in the thread at the eye of the hook and wind evenly back to the rear of the hook shank.
2. Prepare (clip, comb and stack/even) a small bundle of yellow bucktail. Make sure that this bundle is about half again longer than the tail.
3. Tie in the tail and wind the thread forward about ten to fifteen turns. (The number of turns you choose here should be followed with each subsequent bundle tied down.)
4. Once you have wound the thread forward, fold the butt end of the tail on top of the hook shank and wind back towards the tail. Use fewer turns than the forward wrap. This will assure that the butt ends will flare out at an angle.
5. Wind the thread forward again, equal to the turns initially used. Tie in a second bundle, this of black bucktail, equal in length to the first bundle. Wind forward ten to fifteen turns. The tips of the bucktail must face forward at this

step and be long enough to cover the hook point when folded over the hook shank.

6. Split the bundle into two parts, and fold around the hook shank so that it "guards" the hook point. Wind the thread back ten to fifteen turns as before to hold the wing in the position under the hook shank and over the hook point.
7. Wind the thread forward again and tie in another bundle of yellow bucktail, tips forward, as above.
8. Repeat the above steps, and add successive bundles, alternating with black and yellow bucktail.
9. Once reaching the head of the fly in back of the hook eye, complete the head and tie off with a whip finish. Clip the excess thread.
10. Seal the head with head cement and coat the thread windings along the body with head cement to protect them.
11. Trim the top butt ends of bucktail as shown.

MICKEY FINN

The bright sides of this old pattern make it an especially good attractor pattern for everything from panfish to pike, depending upon the size tied.

Most fly fishermen have heard of this basic trout streamer fly that has been around since 1932 when writer John Alden Knight discovered it and his fishing group had phenomenal success with it on trout. It has since proved great on all manner of game fish, including bass, pike, walleye and crappie. Knight, who did not invent, but did popularize this streamer that was made by Wm. Mills & Son, originally named it The Assassin. In 1936 it was renamed the Mickey Finn by Canadian war correspondent Gregory Clark, who named it for the knock-out drink that supposedly killed silent film star Rudolph Valentino. Even through considered a basic trout pattern, it is ideal for both bass species, in large sizes for pike and muskie, and in small sizes for both species of crappie. It is an excellent fly anytime warmwater species are feeding on baitfish, or as an explorer fly to search out fish throughout the year.

Tied by Umpqua Feather Merchants

Hook – Standard 4X to 6X long streamer hook in sizes 4 through 10 for crappie, 2 through 2/0 for bass and up to 4/0 for pike

Thread – Black

Body – Flat silver tinsel

Rib – Oval silver tinsel

Wing – Layers of yellow, red and yellow bucktail

Tying sequence:

1. Tie in the thread just in back of the eye, and wrap tightly down to the bend of the hook.
2. Tie in a length of oval tinsel, with the tag end extending up to the eye of hook.
3. Tie in a length of flat tinsel, the tag end tapered to a long point. Alternatively, tie in and make a smooth winding over the hook shank and tinsel tag end up to the eye of the hook.
4. Wrap the thread tightly and evenly over the hook shank to just in back of the hook eye. (If not already wound to that point, as above.)
5. Wrap the flat tinsel tightly and evenly up to just in back of the hook eye and tie off. Clip any excess tinsel.
6. Spiral wrap the oval tinsel up to the thread position in back of the hook eye and tie off. Clip any excess tinsel.
7. Cut a small bundle of yellow bucktail, remove any underfur and place it in a hair stacker/evener to align the tips. Measure the bundle to be about 1-1/4 the length of the hook shank and tie down on top of the hook shank. Clip any excess bucktail in front of the tie-down point.
8. Repeat the above with a same-size bundle of red bucktail.
9. Repeat the above again with a slightly thicker bundle of yellow bucktail. (Some tyers make all three bundles the same size, although the original pattern calls for the top yellow bundle to be about twice the bulk of either of the first two bundles.)
10. Finish by making a neat tapering head, and tie off with a whip finish.
11. Seal with head cement. Use a coating of epoxy in place of head cement for larger flies, or if tying for pike/muskie.

Optional-paint eyes on the lacquered block head.

WHITE MARABOU STREAMER

Marabou streamers, as a result of the soft marabou used in the wing, have a lot of action in the water. This color can imitate any baitfish and is a good basic attractor fly.

This is a simple, almost generic streamer fly. While white is described here, it is also extremely effective in yellow, with the same simple tinsel body. Black is also excellent, with a black chenille body, silver ribbing and red calf tail throat. Variations of this White Marabou can include ribbing the body with oval silver tinsel (as with the Mickey Finn), adding a tag end of red yarn, and not including the topping of peacock herl. It can also be weighted if desired, using metal dumbbell eyes, metal beads or lead/non-lead wire on the hook shank before wrapping with tinsel. Because of the action of this fly even when fished slowly and deep, it is an ideal early season big fish fly. Any color marabou can be tied with wrapped or parallel shank lead for added weight to get deep. The slim, minnow-like wavy action of the wing and the ability to keep it in the strike zone when weighted makes this a must for any early season fly box. In small sizes, it is ideal for panfish, perch and crappie, while in larger sizes is great for smallmouth and largemouth bass.

Tied by the author

Hook – Standard 2X to 6X long streamer hook in sizes 4 through 12 for perch, panfish and crappie	and sizes to 1/0 for bass **Thread** – Black **Body** – Flat silver tinsel	**Wing** – White marabou **Topping** – Peacock herl **Throat** – Red calf tail

Tying sequence:

1. Tie in the thread just in back of the hook eye
2. Tie in a length of flat tinsel, the tag end tapered to a long point.
3. Wrap the tinsel to the hook bend, then reverse direction to bring the tinsel back up to just in back of the hook eye. Tie off and clip and excess tinsel. (If tying this with an oval tinsel ribbing and/or red tag end, then follow the directions and tying sequence of the Mickey Finn.)
4. Clip a length of marabou from the central stem, bundle it together and slightly moisten it for easier handling. Measure the wing to be about 1½ times the length of the hook shank and tie down with several thread wraps. Clip any excess marabou forward of the tie.
5. Prepare a bundle of four to six peacock herl strands, measure them for length on top of the wing and tie down with thread. Clip any excess forward peacock herl.
6. Turn the hook over in the vise (point up) and prepare (clip, comb and stack/even) a throat of a small bundle of red calf tail. Position this against the fly. The throat should be about 1/3 to 1/2 the length of the hook shank. Tie in place with several thread wraps and clip any excess fur.
7. Turn the hook back over in the vise (point down) and make a neat tapered head with the tying thread. Tie off with a whip finish. Clip the excess thread.
8. Seal with head cement.

DIVE-IN MINNOW

Diving flies are tough to pick up off the water, but great to fish with as a result of their wiggling action that is more like a diving plug than a fly.

This simple fly with the foam body and marabou/Flashabou tail is simple to tie and easy to fish. While it is a floating fly, it is really designed to be fished underwater, just as would a floating/diving plug. The weedless hook makes it ideal to cast in almost any situation. Without the weedless hook, or with a different mono weed guard, it is also very simple to tie. The position of the hook shank and eye in this model makes this fly dive only a few inches below the surface, but this can be changed by inserting the hook through the foam so that more of the lip is below the hook eye. Realize that in doing this however; it will be much harder to pick up over the water. Tie this in any color, using tapered foam bodies or cut and shaped foam cylinders. A similar Wiggle Critter from EdgeWater differs only in that it has rubber legs through the body, and saddle hackle flanking the marabou tail. Fish both of these flies like a crankbait after making a long cast.

Tied by EdgeWater

Materials Needed

Hook – Bass hook, 2X long,
Thread – White
Weed guard – 45 pound test nylon covered twisted wire

leader material
Tail – White marabou
Flash – Silver Flashabou
Body – White tapered foam body,

cut at a sharp angle
Eyes – Stemmed eyes, inserted and glued to the sides

Tying sequence:

1. Tie in the working thread in front of the bend of the hook and clip the excess thread.
2. Prepare and tie in a bundle of white marabou.
3. Tie in a few strands of silver Flashabou along the sides of the marabou.
4. Complete with a whip finish and clip the excess thread.
5. Buy or prepare (shape, cut and taper) a foam body, sized for the hook. When in place at the butt end of the marabou, the hook should extend through the body, and exit the lip close to the forward edge. Make a pilot hole for the hook with a bodkin.
6. Glue the foam body in place on the hook shank. Make sure that the hook eye is clear of the foam body.
7. Prepare weed guard wire (fold in half) and make the hook point bend, then make a right angle bend in the two weed guard legs to fit the hook size used.
8. Make a hole with a bodkin on either side of the hook shank, just in back of the forward part of the lip.
9. Clip the ends of the wire to 1/2 inch long and glue into the preformed holes.
10. Bend the weed guard back to clip onto the hook point.

CLOUSER DEEP MINNOW

This minnow imitation can be tied as desired to imitate local lake and river minnows. The dumbbell eyes get it deep to where big fish are located.

The Clouser Deep Minnow, developed by smallmouth expert Bob Clouser, has become a fly-fishing classic in short order. It was developed as a smallmouth fly for the Susquehanna River in Pennsylvania, but has since caught dozens of species all over the world. Much of its success relies on the fact that with the heavy dumbbell eyes it gets to the bottom where many fish are cruising for meals. The slim profile imitates many baitfishes. It can be fished through riffles, in deep pools, in pocket water worked with short twitches or long even strips. Since it is tied with dumbbell eyes, it can be weighted, as the tyer desires using the smallest to the largest of the lead dumbbell eyes available. Casting the heavy versions can come close to requiring the steelheader's "chuck-and-duck" method of fishing. Here is one of the many color combinations possible for this fly and a favorite of Bob Clouser. Realize in tying this that the fly is fished with the point up, so that the throat/belly is tied on what would otherwise be the top of the hook shank and the wing on the "bottom" to fill up the gap of the hook.

Tied by Bob Clouser

Materials Needed

Hook – Mustad 3366 or standard length fly hook, sizes 2 to 6	**Throat or belly** – Chartreuse green bucktail	**Wing** – Fluorescent yellow bucktail
Thread – Light yellow, 6/0	**Center wing** – Gold Krystal Flash or gold Flashabou	**Eyes** – Lead dumbbell eyes, painted red with black pupil

Tying sequence:

1. Place the hook in the vise normally (point down). Tie on the thread in back of the hook eye, and clip the excess.
2. Tie on the dumbbell eyes about 1/4 the shank length in back of the hook eye.
3. Wrap down the hook shank past the dumbbell eyes and tie down a prepared (clipped, combed and stacked) small bundle of chartreuse green bucktail. Tie in front and back of the dumbbell eyes. Spiral wind the thread once, down and up the hook shank and over the bucktail. Trim the hair butt ends.
4. Turn the hook over in the vise so that the point is up. Tie in a small bunch of gold Krystal Flash or gold Flashabou. Clip any excess.
5. Tie in a length of fluorescent yellow bucktail and trim the excess butt ends.
6. Wrap the thread over this to form a head.
7. Complete the fly by making a whip finish, and then clip the excess thread.
8. Seal with head cement.
9. If needed, paint the eyes red with black pupils.

CLOUSER BABY SMALLMOUTH

This is another variation of the Clouser Deep Minnow in a baby smallmouth style and color that is generally tied longer than the standard Clouser Deep Minnow.

The Clouser Baby Smallmouth is one of the many variations of the Clouser Deep Minnow. In large sizes it will take pike, pickerel, drum, and inland stripers; and in small sizes will take large carp. The combination of flash material and natural bucktail makes for an attractive, active deep-fished streamer fly. It was developed by Bob for fishing his favorite Pennsylvania Susquehanna River, but will work well throughout the world. As with the Clouser Deep Minnow, it is tied with dumbbell eyes that make the fly ride point up. As with any of the Clouser series, you can weight it with the size eyes desired, but take care in casting those tied with the heavier eyes.

Tied by Bob Clouser

Materials Needed

Hook – Standard length fly hook, or Mustad 3366, sizes 4 to 12

Thread – Tan

Tail/throat – White bucktail, tied over eyes and along shank

Wing – Bronze Flashabou over gold Krystal Flash

Overwing – Brown bucktail

Eyes – Lead hourglass eyes, painted red with black pupils

Tying sequence:

1. Place the hook in the vise normally (point down). Tie on the thread in back of the hook eye, and clip the excess.
2. Tie on the dumbbell eyes 1/4 the shank length in back of the hook eye. (See Methods Chapter for specific tying instructions.)
3. Wrap down the hook shank past the dumbbell eyes and tie down a prepared (clip, comb and stack/even) small bundle of white bucktail. Tie down in front of and in back of the lead eyes. Trim the hair butt ends.
4. Turn the hook over in the vise so that the point is up. Tie in a small bunch of gold Krystal Flash in front of the lead eyes. Trim the excess butt ends.
5. Tie in a small bundle of bronze Flashabou and clip the excess.
6. Tie in a bundle brown bucktail (clip, comb, and stack/even) and clip the excess.
7. Make a neat tapered head and complete with a whip finish. Clip the excess thread.
8. Seal with head cement.
9. If needed, paint the eyes red with black pupils.

OLD FASHIONED BASS FLIES

Bass flies from the 1920s and 1930s often-simulated moths with large wings projecting from the sides and simple bodies. This fly from Gaines is an example of that design.

Flies that simulate moths can be made as sinking or floating models. This is a sinking model that allows a slow sink after the cast to make it look like a drowning moth or other large insect. To make this in a floating model, tie a cylinder of foam on the hook shank. With colored foam, this might be all you need, or you can wrap the foam with chenille, floss or yarn. One problem with these effective flies it that the widespread wings do make them tough to cast. They will tend to spin, sail and dive in the air. To counter this, use as heavy a leader tippet as possible to prevent twisting, or use a very tiny swivel between the tippet and leader to reduce line twist. Try this pattern in white and black, in addition to the yellow shown here.

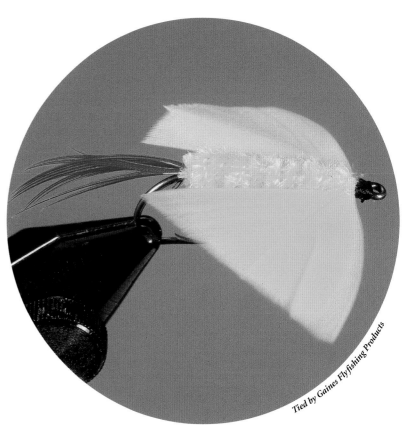

Tied by Gaines Flyfishing Products

Materials Needed

Hook – Long shank hook, 2X, sizes 2 to 6

Thread – Black

Tail – Red dyed turkey fibers or hackle fibers

Body – Yellow chenille

Wings – Yellow dyed turkey or similar feathers, tied spent wing style

Tying sequence:

1. Tie in the working thread at the midpoint, and clip the excess.
2. Wind the thread to the rear of the hook shank and tie in a bunch of red hackle fibers or turkey fibers.
3. Tie in a length of yellow chenille.
4. Wind the thread forward to in back of the hook eye.
5. Wind the chenille forward around the hook shank to the thread and tie off. Clip any excess chenille.
6. Prepare (strip the butt ends) four wing tips for the fly wings.
7. Tie down two of the wings on each side of the hook shank so that the wings flare out to the side. Clip any excess butt ends.
8. Make a neat head, and complete with a whip finish. Clip the excess thread.
9. Seal the head with head cement.

ZONKER

Rabbit fur is a popular soft natural material that makes great flies and creates a lot of action in the water when twitched and jerked. It is particularly good on a slow retrieve.

This fly, is a big fish fly and essential for anyone fishing deep where a baitfish imitation will work. Designed by Dan Byford, Zonkers are flashy flies as a result of the Mylar piping body and tail. They are like the Matuka in that the wing is tied down at both the head end and also at the bend of the hook. The Zonker can be tied weighted or unweighted; with this recipe the standard weighted version. The lead can be left out to make an unweighted version or weight can be added with lead wire (instead of the metal sheeting), although you will lose the beer belly shape of the fly body. Since the pre-cut Zonker rabbit strips are readily available in a variety of colors, this is an easy fly to tie and an effective one to fish. Try it in black, brown and olive in addition to this basic color. Since two threads and two tie down points are used, you can use two bobbins or tie in the red thread and then half hitch it to secure it after tying down the body and before tying down the wing at the rear. This is a weighted, non-beer belly version.

Tied by Chuck Edghill

Hook – 6X long streamer hook in sizes 4 through 12
Thread – Black and red

Weight – Lead wire wrapped around the hook shank
Tail – Silver piping frayed out from the body tubing

Body – Silver Mylar piping
Wing – Natural rabbit strip (Zonker Strip)

Tying sequence:

1. Wrap the hook shank with lead wire and clip any excess.
2. Tie down the red thread at the bend of the hook, and half hitch (if not using a bobbin). Wrap over the lead wire.
3. Measure a length of silver Mylar tubing equal to a length of about 1-1/2 times that of the hook shank. Remove any inner core, and fray out the last ⅓ of the tubing.
4. Slip the Mylar tubing over the hook and the lead wire, position the forward part in back of the hook eye and tie down the tail end with the red thread at the bend of the hook and the junction of the tubing and frayed tail. Half-hitch it to secure it if not using a bobbin. Do not cut the thread.
5. Push the forward part of the Mylar tubing back to be able to tie down the black thread in back of the hook eye.
6. Slide the Mylar piping forward and tie it off with the black thread.

7. Cut or use a Zonker strip that is about twice the length of the hook shank. Tie the strip in at the head of the fly.
8. Form a neat head to the fly and whip-finish it. Clip the excess thread.
9. At the bend of the hook, open a gap in the rabbit fur at the thread location and make several wraps with the red thread to tie down the rabbit strip to the body and hook shank. Secure with a whip finish and clip the excess thread.
10. Seal the two wraps (red, rear and black, at the head) with head cement.
11. Use a paint stick to paint contrasting colors of an eye and pupil on the lacquered head.

MATUKA, OLIVE

This New Zealand pattern has the advantage over other streamers in that the tied-down wing will not wrap around the hook shank or bend to foul the fly. It is another effective minnow imitation.

The Matuka is a New Zealand pattern that has found less favor here than the similarly tied Zonker. As with the Zonker, the wing is secured to the body, although a feather wing is used in place of the rabbit in the Zonker. It is a simple fly, usually tied weighted to get it deep to where big fish live. As a result, it can be tied with a mono weed guard to prevent snagging, which is preferred when fishing snaggy, weedy waters. One advantage of this fly over other feather wing streamers is that the wing will not wrap around the hook bend as a result of it being lashed in place on the body. It can be tied in any color, with black, brown, olive, white, yellow and spruce the most popular colors.

Tied by Brookside

Materials Needed

Hook – Streamer hook, 3X long hook in sizes 4 through 12

Weight – Lead or non-lead wire wrapped around hook shank

Thread – Olive

Rib – Copper wire or oval gold tinsel (If using copper wire, it will add weight and might make the lead wire less necessary)

Body – Olive chenille

Gills – Red chenille or wool yarn (optional)

Wing – Olive dyed grizzly hen

Hackle – Olive dyed grizzly hen (also optional)

Tying sequence:

1. Wrap the hook shank with tight turns of lead or non-lead wire.
2. Tie in the thread at the head of the fly.
3. Spiral wrap the wire with the tying thread, winding several times up and down the hook shank. Coat the wire wrap with head cement to prevent discoloring the body materials.
4. Return to the bend of the hook and tie in the ribbing wire or tinsel, followed by tying down the olive chenille.
5. Wrap the thread forward to a spot 1/2 the shank length in back of the hook eye.
6. Wrap the chenille forward, tie off and clip the excess. Tie down red chenille or red wool, then wrap the thread forward to just in back of the hook eye.
7. Wrap the red chenille forward to the thread, tie off and clip the excess.
8. Select four hen feathers, cupping two feathers on each side

together and measuring so that the feathers are twice the length of the hook shank. Strip the excess feather, tie down with the tying thread and clip the excess hackle stems.

9. Hold the wing parallel to the body, and pull the fibers forward to allow spiral wrapping the ribbing around the body and wing without matting the feathers down.
10. Tie off the ribbing at the head of the fly.
11. Choose a hen hackle, strip the soft end and tie into the fly. Clip the excess stem and then wind the hackle around as a wet fly collar hackle. Tie off and clip the excess hackle. (Optional).
12. Finish by winding the thread through the hackle for additional reinforcement, then complete a neat head and tie off with a whip finish. Clip the excess thread.
13. Seal with head cement.

MYLAR MINNOW

Simple minnow imitations of Mylar tubing are very effective and can be made in a variety of ways. This one has been painted to further enhance the life-like appearance.

Several fly tyers have come up with the idea of using Mylar tubing as the body and tail of the fly to make a one-material fly. This is a simple variation of that in which a tail is added to the fly first and then the frayed strands of the Mylar positioned on top of and around the tail for added flash. The fly can be finished with gills in red permanent marker and painted, or prism, eyes added to make it a more realistic minnow imitation. Many tyers also use a black or blue permanent felt tip marker to darken the back of the Mylar body to make it more like a natural minnow with its camouflage shading. It can be easily tied weighted with a wrap of lead wire, but this is an unweighted version. While Mylar tubing is standard, this same fly can be tied in a more translucent form using materials such as E-Z Body, Corsair and similar translucent plastic tubing.

Tied by Umpqua Feather Merchants

Hook – Standard streamer hook, 2X to 4X long, in sizes 4 through 12

Thread – Red

Tail – Light olive marabou, with a little silver Krystal Flash mixed in

Body – Mylar tubing

Tying sequence:

1. Tie the thread on the hook just forward of the hook bend and clip the excess thread.
2. Tie in a small bunch of olive marabou, followed by a few strands of silver Krystal Flash.
3. Wrap the thread forward up the hook shank to just in back of the hook eye.
4. Prepare a length of Mylar tubing about 1½ times the shank length by removing the internal cord.
5. Place the end of the tubing over the hook shank so that the tubing extends to the right and tie down the end of the tubing just in back of the hook eye. When tied down, the hook will be exposed and the tubing extending to the right. Make sure that the thread wrapping the tubing in place is right against the back of the hook eye.
6. Wrap the thread back to the bend of the hook or previous tie down location.

7. Push the tubing back and over the hook shank, reversing it inside out.
8. With your left hand, position the tubing as you wish (fat or slim by adjusting the pull on the tubing) and then wrap over the end of the tubing with the red thread.
9. Secure with a few wraps, and then make a whip finish and clip any excess thread.
10. Seal the thread with head cement and add eyes and gills as desired.
11. Eyes can be painted on using paint sticks or prism eyes can be added and then sealed with epoxy or head cement. Gills are easy with a permanent red felt tip marker.
12. If desired, shade with felt tip markers or paint to simulate specific baitfish or fry.

RATTLIN' WATER WOLF

Designed for largemouth bass and pike, this fly incorporates a rattle and is another of the fly rodder's equivalent of the bass fisherman's plastic worm.

Since their introduction some years ago, rabbit strips – sometimes called Zonker Strips for the fly tied with them – have been used for a wide variety of flies. In addition, cross-cut Zonker Strips allow winding the strip around a hook shank so that the fur will flare back and make for a bushy, full-bodied fly. This fly incorporates both, and also includes a rattle to attract fish by sound. Originator Greg Webster goes one step further by adding silicone to the skin side of the strip and sprinkling it with fine glitter to add some flash. He does this with a whole rabbit skin, and then cuts his own strips, but you can also add silicone and fine glitter of your color choice to the skin side of commercially available strips when tying this fly. Greg's favorite colors are rusty orange (brownish), black, purple, olive and white/red.

Tied by Greg Webster

Hook – Owner spinnerbait or Gamakatsu stinger hook or similar hook, sizes 1/0 to 3/0

Thread – Orange or brown 6/0 (or color to complement color of fly)

Eyes/weight – Large non-toxic barbells with epoxy stick-on plastic eyes

Rattle – Any appropriate rattle of glass, plastic or aluminum, size to fit on the hook shank

Tail – Rusty orange or brown 1/2-inch wide standard rabbit strip (Zonker strip)

Body – Rusty orange or brown 1/2-inch wide cross-cut rabbit strip

Legs – Dark brown or black rubber legs

Tying sequence:

1. Tie in the thread to the midpoint of the hook shank. Clip the excess thread.
2. Wind forward to ⅛-inch in back of the hook eye and tie in the barbell eyes.
3. Return the thread to the rear of the hook, wrapping over a glass rattle as you do so.
4. Spiral wrap the thread around the rattle up and down the hook shank several times to hold it in place on the back (upper part) of the hook shank.
5. At the rear of the hook shank tie in a tail of a 3-inch strip of rusty orange rabbit fur.
6. Tie in a length of cross-cut rabbit fur and wind the thread forward to 1/8-inch in back of the fly eyes.

7. Tie in several strands of brown or black rubber legs so that they extend on each side of the hook shank.
8. Wind the cross-cut rabbit fur forward around the hook shank. Make sure that the rubber legs protrude on each side of the fly as the strip of fur is wound around and in front of them.
9. Bring the fur strip up to the fly eyes and tie off with the working thread. Clip any excess fur.
10. Wrap to complete the head in front of the fly eyes and tie off with a whip finish. Clip the excess thread.
11. Seal the wraps with head cement.

BEAD CHAIN LEECH

A different way of achieving an up/down undulating leech action is done by tying this fly with an articulated bead chain tail and weight for the eyes to help the fly sink and make a yo-yo action easy with each twitch of the rod.

A black leech is a basic pattern for fish throughout the country. Leeches are found everywhere, even though mostly associated with the tropics or the Northwoods country. The secret of a leech pattern is the up-down action that is completely different from the side-to-side swimming action of baitfish, the jerky scuttling action of crayfish or the erratic twitching action of nymphs and hellgrammites. This is achieved in an original way by using bead chain as some weight, but more importantly as a part of the tail of the leech. That, together with the nickel-plated lead eyes that causes the fly to sink head first, makes this an ideal fly to cast and fish.

Tied by Umpqua Feather Merchants

Materials Needed

Hook – Long shank hook (2X) sizes 8 to 2

Thread – Black

Eyes – Nickel-plated lead eyes, extra small (8 and 6) or small (4 and 2)

Tail – Black marabou tied to small bead chain and bead chain, also black marabou tied to hook

Body – Bead chain tied to the hook shank

Body wrap – Black chenille

Palmered hackle – Black hackle

Tying sequence:

1. Place the end of length of bead chain in fly-tying vise (or small hobby vise if fly-tying vise will be strained) and tie down working thread in the joint between the last and second "ball." Clip the excess thread.
2. Tie down a bundle of marabou, veiling it so that it surrounds the end ball of the chain. Clip the excess marabou.
3. Tie off with a whip finish and clip the excess thread.
4. Seal the wrap with head cement.
5. Place the hook in the fly-tying vise and tie down the working thread in the middle of the hook shank. Clip the excess thread.
6. Wind the thread forward and tie in nickel-plated lead eyes in back of the hook eye.
7. Wind the thread to the rear of the hook shank.
8. Tie down the bead chain and leave a few links forward for tying down later.
9. Tie down a bundle of black marabou to serve as a tail on the hook.
10. Tie down a black hackle by the tip end.
11. Tie down a length of black chenille.
12. Wind the thread forward, wrapping over and between each of the several links of bead chain and finish at the lead eyes.
13. Wind the black chenille forward and tie off with the thread at the eyes. Spiral wind the chenille between the bead chain links. Clip the excess chenille.
14. Spiral wind (palmer) the hackle forward and tie off immediately in back of the lead eyes. Clip the excess hackle.
15. Wind the thread to in front of the eyes and make a small neat head.
16. Tie off with a whip finish and clip the excess thread.
17. Seal the head wraps with head cement.

DEEP WIGGLER

There are many variations of Larry Dahlberg designs of which this is one. It incorporates a jointed or articulated body for more action on the bottom where this fly is fished.

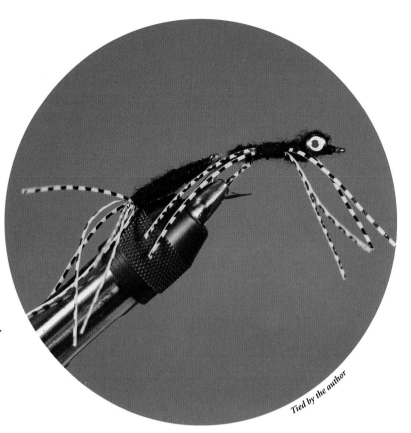

Tied by the author

This is an easy fly to tie, albeit in two parts. It also varies from the original design, which incorporated chopped Flashabou, mixed and applied as a dubbing for the body. This simpler variation uses mohair, Leech Yarn or other sparkly yarn (picked out Antron is ideal) for the body. You can also tie it with cactus chenille for more of a spiky, shiny look. Since this fly is tied in two parts, the standard way of tying is to tie the rear part on a hook and then clip off the point of the hook. To avoid sacrificing hooks this way, you can also tie it on a short length of wire (like spinnerbait wire or other stiff, stainless steel wire), also held in the vise for the first step. The joint – connecting loop – can be made of mono or light wire. Any color can be tied, but black is always good.

Materials Needed

Rear joint

Wire or hook – Long-shank hook, with the hook bend clipped after tying, or a stiff wire with a loop or eye formed in one end

Thread – Black

Tail – Several black or black mottled rubber or Silicone legs

Body – Black mohair, Leech Yarn or cactus chenille, as preferred

Front body

Hook – Regular length hook, sizes 8 to 1

Thread – Black

Joint – Loop of 20-pound mono

Body – Black mohair, Leech Yarn or cactus chenille, as preferred, and to match rear joint

Legs – Black or black mottled rubber or Silicone legs, tied in middle of fly

Eyes – Large lead or non-toxic dumbbell eyes, painted red with black pupil or white with red pupil

Tying sequence:

1. Place a hook or wire into the fly-tying vise and tie on the working thread at the rear of the hook shank. Clip any excess thread.
2. Select a few strands of black or mottled rubber or Silicone legs and tie down at the rear.
3. Tie in a length of black mohair.
4. Wind the thread to the hook or wire eye.
5. Wind the mohair around the hook shank or wire eye to the head and tie off with the thread. Clip any excess mohair.
6. Make a small neat head and tie off with a whip finish. Clip any excess thread.
7. Seal the wraps with head cement.
8. Put on safety goggles and carefully clip the excess wire or hook with wire cutters.
9. Place the front hook in the vise and tie on the working thread at the head of the fly. Clip any excess thread.
10. Tie in lead dumbbell eyes, figure-eighting and crisscrossing the wraps to secure the eyes.
11. Wind the thread to the rear of the fly.
12. Tie in a length of 20-pound mono.
13. Run the mono through the hook or wire eye of the tail, make a small loop and tie the other end of the mono to the hook shank. This will secure the tail joint to the fly. Clip any excess mono.
14. Tie in a length of black mohair.
15. Wind the thread to the midpoint of the hook.
16. Tie in a length of black or mottled rubber or Silicone legs on each side of the hook, to make two legs on each side.
17. Wind the thread forward to the hook eye.
18. Wind the mohair forward around the hook shank, running the mohair between the two legs on each side to separate them and continuing to the head of the fly.
19. Figure eight the mohair around the eyes and tie off with a whip finish. Clip any excess thread.
20. Seal the wraps with head cement.

RATTLIN' CRAWDADDY

Rattle flies are useful when fishing in stained or muddy water, since the noise created helps attract curious fish to the general vicinity of the fly where they can find and hit it.

Rattle flies are not in wide use, but have become increasingly accepted in as fly-fishing frontiers have expanded to warmwater and inshore saltwater. This fly by Greg Webster incorporates a rattle in plastic tubing that is then tied to the fly hook to make this bottom hugging crayfish imitation. It can be tied in olive brown (as with this example) or in crayfish orange, or any other color if desired. To use it effectively and to get the rattles working, work this fly with frequent short twitches so that the rattles in the tube shake back and forth to attract fish. Greg developed it for night fishing for smallmouth bass. The rattle makes it easy for fish to find it in the dark.

Tied by Greg Webster

Materials Needed

Hook – Keel style hook or long-shank spinnerbait hook, slightly bent into downward curve

Thread – Olive brown, or to match fly color

Body – Pearl tubing with inserted rattle, colored olive with permanent felt tip marker

Feelers/legs – Brown, olive or orange rubber legs

Pinchers – Olive rabbit fur

Tail – Olive rabbit fur

Eyes – Large brass or gold bead chain eyes

Tying sequence:

1. Tie in thread in the middle of the hook shank and clip excess.
2. Wind thread to the rear of the hook shank and tie in bead chain eyes, figure-eighting and cross wrapping to hold them in place.
3. Tie in a bundle of rabbit fur and split into two bundles on either side of the eyes to simulate the claws.
4. Slip a large glass rattle into pearl tubing and tie the tube to the rear of the hook shank with thread, with the tubing/rattle pointed towards the rear.
5. Wrap the thread a few turns forward, then fold the tubing/rattle forward and tie down with thread at the mid-point of the hook shank.
6. Tie in several long strands of rubber legs to each side of the tubing at this point.
7. Spiral wind the thread forward, over and around the tubing and hook shank to just in back of the hook eye.
8. Tie down the end of the rattle tubing and clip any excess.
9. Tie in a bundle of olive rabbit fur facing forward in front of the hook eye.
10. Tie in a second bundle of rabbit fur under the fly (hook side). Alternately, glue this bundle in place with the skin side cemented to the pearl tubing.
11. Tie off with a whip finish and clip the excess thread.
12. Seal the thread wraps with head cement.

WIGGLE CRAW

This little fly works more like a lure on retrieve than a fly, but is a great crayfish imitation when fishing shallow waters.

Tied by EdgeWater

Most crayfish imitations are weighted, or at least designed to be fished deep and on the bottom where crayfish are found. This crayfish imitation floats, but is really an underwater fly that will wiggle rapidly on retrieve. In design, it resembles a crayfish fleeing from a predator. Best colors are in the rust or olive, but dark green, orange and even burnt red are also ideal when crayfish of these colors are found in your local waters. It is a great smallmouth fly. You can also tie these in any size, based on what the smallmouth are taking, and the size of the crayfish found where you will cast this.

Hook – Bass hook, 2X long shank, sizes 6 to 2/0

Thread – Brown

Antennae – Two lengths of brown rubber legs

Nose – Bundle of brown bucktail

Weight – Small bb-size split shot, inserted into lip of foam (1/2 for a size 6 or 4 hook, 1-1/2 for a size 2 hook, and 2 for a size 2/0 hook, or as appropriate or desired)

Body – Tan cactus chenille

Legs/claws – Tightly palmered brown saddle hackle

Back – Thin rectangle of thick (4 mm) yellow or tan sheet foam, colored and bared like segmented crayfish body or EdgeWater Wiggle Craw body

Eyes – Black dressmakers pins

Tying sequence:

1. Prepare a length of 4 mm strip foam by cutting 6 mm wide, and tapering the forward lip. Cut it slightly longer than the total hook length. Round the back end with scissors.
2. Use a drill or router bit to cut one or two small depressions, one in back of the other, in the underside of the lip. Glue the bb split shot into these depressions.
3. Use an awl or bodkin to poke a hole at an angle in the front of the foam, just in back of the split shot inserts.
4. Tie on the working thread at the hook bend and clip the excess thread.
5. Prepare (clip, comb and stack/even) a length of brown bucktail.
6. Tie the bundle of bucktail to the hook, tying short.
7. Prepare and tie in two lengths of brown rubber legs as antennae. Tie one on each side of the bucktail, and slightly longer than the bucktail.
8. Wind the thread forward to just about 1/4 inch in back of the hook eye.
9. Tie in a length of tan cactus chenille.
10. Wind the thread back down the shank about ⅓ the shank length.
11. Wind the cactus chenille back down the hook shank and tie off with the thread. Clip the excess chenille.
12. Tie in a length of webby brown saddle hackle. Clip the butt end.
13. Wind the thread down to the hook bend.
14. Wind the hackle around the hook shank to the thread and tie off with the thread. Clip the excess hackle.
15. Push down the hackle and add waterproof glue to the back of the hook (hackle and cactus chenille and hook shank).
16. Insert the hook eye and forward part of the hook shank into the hole poked in the foam lip. Make sure that the hook eye clears for tying the leader tippet.
17. Hold the foam body down over the glue on the back and tie down securely with the working thread.
18. Tie off the thread with a whip finish and clip the excess thread.
19. Seal the thread with head cement.
20. Clip black dressmakers pins to a 1/4 inch length, make a pilot hole with a bodkin in the sides of the foam and glue the black pins into these holes for eyes.

PFEIFFER'S WORM FLY

This is an easy fly fisherman's equivalent of the bass angler's soft plastic worm. It is a one-material fly and easy to tie.

For 50 years, bass fishermen have been taking lunkers with all manner of plastic worms. This fly, tied of one material (exclusive of the hook, thread, and weight) is the fly fisherman's answer to that basic lure. It involves a method of twisting a body material so that when folded, the body material will twist on itself to create a worm-like tail and body. How tight or loose the tail will be is determined by the amount of twist created when making the tail. Make sure that the twist is in the same direction as the original twist of the cactus chenille. Bass fishermen rig (Texas rig) their worms to be weedless, but the same is done with this worm with a double mono weed guard. This is optional, but advisable, since the Worm Fly is weighted and fished on the bottom. Popular colors are black, purple, blue, red, chartreuse, olive and tan.

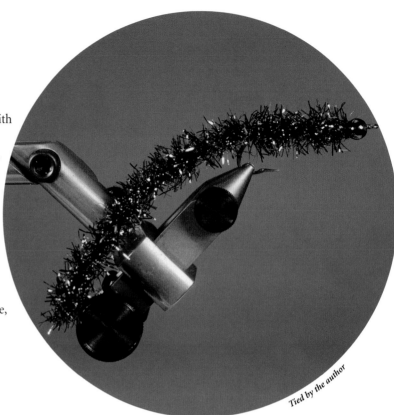

Tied by the author

Materials Needed

Hook – Standard length or long shank hook, in sizes 4 through 2/0

Thread – Black, or to match worm color

Weight – Dumbbell eyes, sized for the size of the fly and the depth fished (another option is a weighted bead or cone)

Tail and body – Black or purple cactus chenille

Tying sequence:

1. Tie in the thread at the eye of the hook and clip any excess.
2. Tie in dumbbell eyes in back of the hook eye, using crisscross and figure eight wraps to hold the dumbbell eye in place. (Alternatively, slide a weighted bead or chain onto the hook before placing the hook in the vise.)
3. Wind the thread to the back end of the hook shank.
4. Cut a length of black or purple cactus chenille about three times the length of the tail that you want on the fly. (This can be varied, depending upon the length of worm fly and tail that you wish.)
5. Tie down one end of the black/purple cactus chenille at the bend of the hook.
6. Hold the cactus chenille at about 2/3rds of its length and twist the chenille. You can do this by hand, or use a small plastic craft turner (like a hand drill) hooked into a bankers clip to hold the material. Twist many times for a tight, twisted tail and a few times for a looser tail.
7. Place a bodkin at the center point of this twist and fold the cactus chenille over on itself. Release the bodkin and the cactus chenille will twist on itself to create the tail.
8. Tie the twisted purple cactus chenille to the rear of the hook shank where the cactus chenille has been folded on itself. This will leave about ⅓ of the total length of chenille loose.
9. Wrap the thread forward to just in back of the hook eye.
10. Wrap the remaining chenille around the hook shank to form the body, then figure-eight it around and in front of the dumb bell eyes. (Or tie up to the bead or cone, if used.)
11. Tie off with the thread in back of the hook eye.
12. Complete a small neat head with a whip finish and clip any excess thread.
13. Seal with head cement.

Note – an alternative to this is to use lead wire on the hook shank, although the dumbbell eyes give more of an attractive jigging action to the fly. Another alternative is to tie with a double mono weed guard.

CONEHEAD WORM

As with Pfeiffer's Worm Fly, this is an effective bass fly that is easy to tie and simple to fish. It is fly-fishing's "black plastic worm."

This fly is a buggy, fuzzy looking fly that can be easily weighted with beads or cone heads. If desired, you can also add lead wire wrapped around the hook shank to get really deep. It is tied with a double-mono weed guard to allow fishing it through slop, snags and weeds. As a result of the fur body and tail, it is heavier to pick up and cast than the cactus chenille used in Pfeiffer's Worm Fly, but still can be cast on a typical 8-weight bass outfit. It can of course, be tied in many colors and several sizes as desired. This one is dark purple, but for largemouth bass, try it in black, red and blue also. For walleye, try a shorter black pattern to imitate a leech. Another variation is to use flexible marine glue to cement a short length of contrasting color rabbit strip to the end. Try red or chartreuse for this.

Tied by Spirit River

Materials Needed

Hook – Regular or long shank hook, sizes 4 through 1/0

Head – Heavy conehead or heavy bead

Weed guard – Double-mono, 20-pound test

Tail – Long strip of black rabbit (Zonker) strip

Body – Continuation of the black rabbit of Zonker strip over a wrapped purple sparkle chenille body

Tying sequence:

1. Bend down the barb of the hook and slide a conehead into place and up the hook shank.
2. Place the hook in a vise and tie in the working thread in the middle of the hook shank. Clip the excess.
3. Tie down two strands of 20-pound test mono and wind over the mono and hook shank to part way around the bend.
4. Return the thread to the rear of the hook shank.
5. Tie in a 4-inch length of purple rabbit strip so that the forward end can later be tied down by the thread at the head of the fly.
6. Tie in a length of purple sparkle chenille.

7. Wind the thread forward to just in back of the conehead.
8. Wind the chenille around the hook shank and tie off at the thread just in back of the conehead.
9. Fold the rabbit strip forward and tie down with the working thread in back of the conehead.
10. Fold the two strands of mono forward, position equally to protect the hook shank and tie off with the working thread. Clip the excess mono.
11. Tie off the thread with a whip finish and clip the excess thread.
12. Seal the thread wraps with head cement.

EELWORM STREAMER

Dave Whitlock, an innovative tyer especially with bass flies, designed this as a fly rodder's answer to the plastic worm and/or the jig and eel bass lures.

There are lots of ways to make long flies that will simulate eels or other slim prey that are often found on the bottom of lakes, ponds and streams. This is one way, while other ways utilize long rabbit strips (Zonker strips), twisted cactus chenille and even velvet tubing available from craft and sewing stores. Most of these are simple, but often require a weed guard as a result of the structure and weeds in which they are fished.

A small horizontal loop tied on the back of the hook shank and under the tail will prevent the tail from twisting around the hook shank on the cast. Popular colors include all those used in plastic worms – black, blue, purple, chartreuse, olive, yellow and brown, but any color in any size can be tied.

Tied by the author

Hook – Standard regular or long-shank bass hook, sizes 6 through 3/0

Thread – Black, or color to match the body and tail

Eyes – Bead chain or lead/lead substitute dumbbell, as desired for weight

Weight – Optional - added lead wire wrapped around hook shank to get really deep

Tail – Four brown dyed grizzly saddle hackles or color as preferred, flanked with two shorter spade or short grizzly saddle hackles, half the length of the tail hackles

Body – Dubbing mix of synthetic (Orlon or Antron) and natural rabbit fur, colors to match tail (Alternately, yarn or stranded dubbing or mohair, in preferred color)

Palmered hackle – Soft dyed grizzly hackle, matching the tail hackle colors

Tying sequence:

1. Tie in the working thread at the head of the hook, in back of the hook eye and clip any excess thread.
2. Tie in bead chain or lead dumbbell eyes, as preferred for the depth desired. Figure eight and crisscross to secure the eyes.
3. If desired, wrap the hook shank with lead wire.
4. Wind the thread to the rear (spiral back and forth over the lead wire if using this option). Coat with head cement to prevent material discoloration.
5. Prepare two pair of long grizzly saddle hackles by trimming butt ends.
6. Tie the saddle hackles on the rear of the hook shank and trim any excess forward part of the hackle.
7. Prepare and tie in one pair of shorter hackles to flank the four-hackle tail. Clip the excess butt ends.
8. Tie in a palmer hackle of soft dyed grizzly hackle by the tip end.
9. Tie in a length of stranded body material (yarn or mohair) or prepare a dubbing of synthetic and rabbit fur.
10. Wind the thread forward to the eyes, or alternatively wrap the thread with the dubbing forward to make the body.
11. Wind the stranded body material forward (if not using dubbing).
12. Palmer spiral wrap the soft hackle or hackles forward around the body and tie off in back of the eyes. Clip any excess hackle.
13. Figure eight the body material or dubbing around the eyes to form a head. Tie off in front of the eyes.
14. Complete the fly by making a whip finish and clip the excess thread.
15. Seal the wraps with head cement.

VELVET EEL

Tied by the author

Subhead - This fly comes to us from Brian Owens of Connecticut, who developed it for saltwater striper fishing. It is equally good for bass, walleye and pike.

This simple fly makes for a fine, flexible eel that is easily fashioned from craft and sewing store materials. The velvet tubing used is readily available there, in colors such as black, white, red and burgundy. Black is the favorite color, but a more life-like eel can be made by using white, then using yellow, olive and brown felt tip markers to color it. Color the belly area yellow and the back dark olive and even brown on top, to closely simulate the color of the natural eelets that are taken by bass and other freshwater species as they return from the sea. For thinner eelets, try using nylon bolo cord. (Also available from craft/sewing stores or parachute cord that is available from general and most hardware/sporting goods stores.) White is best, again colored with permanent felt tip markers.

Hook – Regular or long shank hook, sizes 4 through 1 with nylon tubing, and 2 through 2/0 with velvet tubing

Thread – Black, or color to match eel

Body and tail – Velvet tubing in black or white, or white nylon tubing, tinted to eel color

Eyes – Prism eyes, glued on with Marine Goop

Weight – Cone head

Coloration – Using permanent felt tip markers to color eel shades

Tying sequence:

1. Remove the center strands from a length of velvet or nylon tubing. Use a piece no more than 5 inches long for most eels.
2. Flatten the barb on the hook and thread a conehead onto the hook.
3. Hold the tubing against the hook to judge for the location of hook penetration.
4. Mark the location for hook penetration and run the hook point first through the front end of the tubing and out the chosen hook point location.
5. Place the hook in a fly-tying vise and slightly push the tubing to the rear.
6. Tie on the working thread on the hook shank in back of the cone head to position it against the hook eye. Clip the excess thread.
7. Move the tubing forward to just in back of the conehead, and tie down the end of the tubing with the thread.
8. Tie off the head with a whip finish and clip any excess thread.
9. Seal the head with head cement.
10. Cut the tail at a sloping angle.
11. a. Seal nylon tubing with a clean flame.
12. b. Seal velvet tubing with fabric glue squeezed into the cut opening and clamped overnight. After the glue is cured, trim any ragged edges.
13. Glue prism or doll eyes on the head of the fly using Marine Goop or a similar flexible cement.

CALCASIEU PIG BOAT

This fly combines the best of a bass jig in a fly and is ideal when fishing for southern largemouth bass. Try it for other species as well.

With the chenille body, palmered hackle and rubber leg collar hackle, this fly by Tom Nixon may have been inspired by the Arbogast Hawaiian Wiggler bass lure. It was first fished by Nixon, an expert and innovative tyer, on Louisiana's Calcasieu River, thus the name. This is the original all-black dressing for this fly, but it obviously can be tied in a number of colors or color combinations. Good possibilities for bass are purple, blue (similar to jigs and worms that are used for largemouth), along with white and chartreuse. For more of a worm-like look, you could also tie it with a long tail or rubber skirt for the tail.

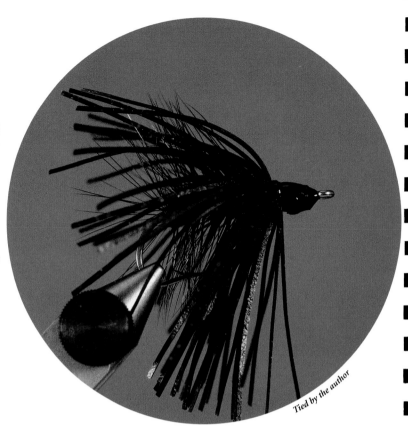

Tied by the author

Materials Needed

Hook – Standard bass hook or regular fly hook, sizes 4 to 2/0

Thread – Black

Body – Black chenille

Palmered hackle – Black saddle hackle

Collar – Black rubber legs, tied collar style (about 60 are recommended)

Head – Black tying thread, with painted yellow eye and red pupil

Tying sequence:

1. Tie in the thread at the midpoint on the hook shank. Clip any excess thread.
2. Wind the thread to the rear of the hook shank and tie in the stripped butt end of a black hackle.
3. Tie in a length of black chenille.
4. Wind the thread to the front of the hook shank, about 1/2 the hook shank length in back of the hook eye.
5. Wind the black chenille forward and tie off with the working thread. Clip the excess chenille.
6. Palmer (spiral wrap) the black hackle forward over the black chenille and tie off at the thread. Clip any excess hackle.
7. Prepare a bundle (enough to make about 60 legs – 60 if tied in at the ends or 30 if tied in at the middle and folded over) of rubber or silicone legs and tie them in with the working thread.
8. If using 60 short legs, tie them in by the ends, pushing the legs around the hook shank for an even collar-like distribution. If using 30 longer legs, tie them in at the middle and tie down with the legs evenly distributed around the hook shank to make a collar.
9. Make a long, even tapered head with the working thread and tie off with a whip finish. Clip the excess thread.
10. Seal the head with head cement or epoxy.
11. Use two sizes of nail heads or painting sticks to make a yellow/red pupil eye on the black head. Seal with head cement, clear finish or epoxy. (Eyes are optional.)

PFEIFFER'S BOTTOM CRAWLER

One of the most effective lures for bass is the hair-or rubber-skirt jig. This Bottom Crawler is the fly fisherman's equivalent of this, in an easy to tie pattern.

Rubber legs are an important part of any bass fisherman's jig, as they are with this fly. This fly has a lot of advantages for any bottom searching fish, and while designed for bass, is equally good for walleye. It has a lot of features that make it a good fly, starting with the jig hook that keeps the fly riding point up. The tail of bucktail has some action and by being split into legs, makes the fly resemble a crayfish. The rubber legs along the body have a lot of action, and make it into a very buggy looking fly. The dumbbell eye gets and keeps the fly deep with any tackle, although it should be fished with a sinking or sinking tip fly line. As with a lot of warmwater flies, it is more of a design than a pattern, and can be tied in any color or with any combinations of colors in the materials used. This one is multicolored.

Tied by the author

Materials Needed

Hook – Standard jig hook, sizes 6 through 2/0, depending upon fish sought

Thread – Black, or to match the color of the materials used

Weight/Eyes – Dumbbell eyes, small for 6 and 4 size hooks, medium for 2 and 1 hooks and large for 1/0 and 2/0 size hooks

Tail – Brown bucktail, tied in two bundles as legs

Body – Olive green cactus chenille

Legs – Yellow rubber or silicone legs

Ribbing – Black size A or D thread to serve as a rib to tie in the rubber legs

Tying sequence:

1. Place the jig hook point down in the vise and tie on the thread at the midpoint of the hook shank. Clip any excess thread.
2. Wrap the thread up to the head of the fly and tie in the hourglass or dumbbell eyes on top of the hook shank at the right angle bend in the jig hook.
3. Wrap the thread to the end of the hook shank and tie on a prepared (clipped, combed and stacked) brown bucktail. This bundle should be about 1½ times the length of the hook shank.
4. Separate the bundle into two legs using the thread and wraps around each leg and hook shank separately. Wrap each leg individually with thread to separate it from the other. Angle the bundles down so that the legs will angle up when the fly is fished point up.
5. Return the thread to the hook shank and tie in a length of olive green cactus chenille.
6. Tie in a length of black A or D rod wrapping thread and wind the tying thread forward to the head of the fly.
7. Wrap the cactus chenille up to and around the lead eyes, then back down to the end of the hook shank, then back up to the eyes to make a thick body. Tie off and clip the excess chenille.

8. Prepare legs of 2- to 3-strips each of yellow rubber or silicone. Make up four to six bundles.
9. Begin to spiral wrap the thread around the hook shank and cactus chenille using the tied-in heavy thread. After two turns, add a bundle of rubber legs to each side of the body as you wrap forward.
10. Continue, adding the other bundles at intervals, with a bundle added to each side to look like legs. Make sure that each bundle is tied down in the middle by the wrap of heavy thread and that the thread does not mat the previously wrapped legs. .
11. Wrap to the head of the fly and tie off the heavy thread with the tying thread. Clip the excess heavy thread.
12. Make a small neat head in front of the cactus chenille wrap.
13. Complete the fly with a whip finish and clip the excess thread.
14. Seal with head cement.

Two alternatives are possible. One is to use short lengths of Zonker strips in place of the bucktail as the legs for more action in still water. The second is to use a short length of marabou or Zonker strip as a single tail.

DRIFTING HELLGRAMMITE

This hellgrammite imitation closely resembles the rolled-up positioning of drifting hellgrammites as they roll downstream through riffles and into pools.

The curve in the caddis nymph hook makes this fly assume a natural position of a drifting hellgrammite, and thus makes it often superior to the straight-body hellgrammite imitations. This fly by Rod Yerger is great for faster river and stream currents and particularly effective during the early part of the season – in May and June. The tying process most closely resembles that of tying trout nymph flies, but it requires only a minimum of materials.

Tied by Rod Yerger

Hook – Mustad 37160 in size 2, or other long shank hook bent to this shape

Thread – Black

Weight – Two strips of lead wire, .030-inch diameter, tied parallel to the hook shank

Tail – Two black goose biots

Abdomen – Dubbed black rabbit fur, picked out and trimmed to shape at sides

Rib – Black V-rib

Thorax – Dubbed black rabbit fur

Hackle – Soft black saddle hackle or schlappen, trimmed at top

Thorax back – Dark mottled turkey tail

Feelers – Two black goose biots

Head – Black

Tying sequence:

1. Tie in the working thread at the mid-point of the hook shank and clip any excess thread.
2. Wind the thread to the bend of the hook, and tie in two black goose biots. Tie in one at a time, crisscrossing and figure-eighting them to get angled separation
3. Tie in a ribbing of black V-rib or similar thin plastic ribbing.
4. Make a dubbing loop and spin some black rabbit fur for the dubbing.
5. Wind the thread forward about 2/3 of the hook shank.
6. Wind the spun rabbit fur dubbing forward and tie off with the thread. Do NOT clip dubbing strand.
7. Wind the ribbing forward and tie off with the thread. Clip any excess ribbing.
8. Tie in a length of dark mottled turkey tail for the thorax back.
9. Tie in a soft black saddle hackle or schlappen.
10. Wind the thread forward to just in back of the hook eye.
11. Tie in two goose biots, using crisscross and figure-eight wraps to separate them.
12. Wind the saddle hackle tightly forward and tie off with the thread. Clip any excess saddle hackle.
13. Trim the top or back of the saddle hackle.
14. Fold the mottled turkey tail over the clipped hackle and tie off with the thread. Clip any excess turkey.
15. Make a small neat head and tie off with a whip finish. Clip any excess thread.
16. Seal the head with head cement.

An alternative to dubbing loop is stranded dubbing such as E-Z Dub.

NIX SHINABOU SHAD

Largemouth and inland stripers in western lakes and reservoirs like shad, with this a typical and ideal imitation of these small forage fish.

Gizzard shad and threadfin shad are favorite food for lake largemouth and stripers. Imitations of them are excellent fly rod offerings. They can be fished shallow or deep, since shad will break on the surface or swim deep in large schools. This is a weighted style with lead eyes, but it can be fished even deeper with split shot or a short leader and sinking line, or weighted with lead wire wraps on the shank to make it sink fast. It can also be tied with prism or plastic eyes for fishing shallow. Try this in different colors, since shad vary as to species and also as to lake and water conditions. In addition to this gray pattern, try the same style in white, cream, ivory, light yellow or very light olive.

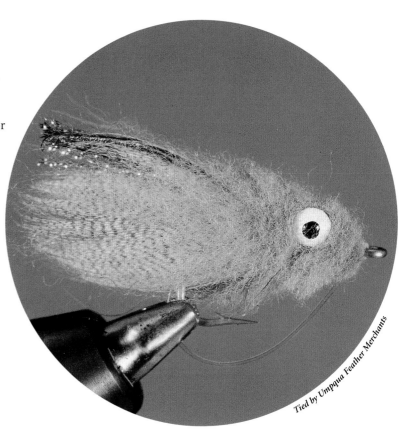

Tied by Umpqua Feather Merchants

Hook – Regular hook, sizes 4 to 1/0	**Outerwing** – Natural mallard flank	trimmed in the front to shape
Thread – Gray	**Topping** – Pearl, silver and peacock Flashabou with peacock herl	**Weed guard** – Single 20-pound test mono loop
Eyes – Lead dumbbell, painted white with black pupils	**Throat** – Red marabou	
Innerwing – Gray marabou	**Head** – Gray lambs wool, spun and	

Tying sequence:

1. Tie in the working thread at the middle of the hook shank and clip the excess.
2. Wind the thread up to about 1/4-the shank length from the hook eye and tie in the lead dumbbell eyes. Figure-eight and crisscross the thread to hold the eyes in place.
3. Wind the thread back to the middle of the hook shank.
4. Tie in a length of 20-pound mono and wind the thread over the mono and hook shank to half way down the hook bend.
5. Wind the thread back up the hook shank about 2/3 the shank length – about 1/3 the length from the hook eye.
6. Tie in a bundle of gray marabou and clip any excess marabou.
7. Flank the marabou with two sections of mallard flank, or one large section folded over the innerwing.
8. Tie on a topping of several strands each of pearl Flashabou, silver Flashabou and peacock Flashabou,

topped by a few strands of peacock herl.
9. Clip the forward excess topping materials.
10. Turn the fly over and tie in a throat of red marabou.
11. Turn the fly back up and tie in a small bundle of gray lambs wool, spinning the lambs wool around the hook shank.
12. Bring the loop of mono forward and tie down under the hook shank at the eye, making sure that the loop protects the point.
13. Tie off the thread in back of the hook eye with a whip finish and clip the excess thread.
14. Seal the thread wraps with head cement.
15. Trim the lamb's wool around the head to shape it, and make sure that the lead eyes show.
16. If the lead eyes are not yet painted, paint them white with a black pupil.

NIX WOOLHEAD SUNFISH

Sunfish usually about the same shape as shad, thus this sunfish pattern from Jimmy Nix. Other than color, it is similar to the Shinabou Shad.

Shad imitations and sunfish patterns are fished in completely different ways under different conditions. Sunfish are ideal for largemouth bass, smallmouth bass, even pike, muskie and pickerel. They are also more typically fished in small ponds and around lakeshores than under the open water conditions when shad imitations are best for feeding stripers and largemouth. You can also use this same design to tie other sunfish such as a light green for a pumpkinseed fly, a light green/yellow for a redbreast or redthroat sunfish, or a darker mostly black fly for a rock bass imitation. This can be tied in a number of sizes to suit your individual fishing requirements.

Tied by Umpqua Feather Merchants

Hook – Regular length hook, sizes 6 to 1

Thread – Olive

Eyes – Lead dumbbell, painted yellow with black pupil

Body – Olive Antron yarn

Ribbing – Copper wire

Tail/wing – Olive grizzly hen hackle

Overwing – Olive wool and olive marabou

Gills – Red marabou

Head – Olive, orange and black lambs wool

Weed guard – Single 20-pound test mono loop

Tying sequence:

1. Tie in the thread at the head of the fly and clip the excess thread.
2. Tie in the lead dumbbell eyes, crisscrossing and figure-eighting the thread.
3. Wind the thread to the midpoint and tie in a length of 20-pound mono for a weed guard.
4. Wind the thread over the mono and hook shank to halfway down the hook bend, then wrap the thread back up to the rear of the hook shank.
5. Tie in a pair of olive grizzly hen hackles short, but leave the forward part of the feather in place.
6. Tie in a length of copper wire.
7. Tie in a length of olive Antron yarn.
8. Wind the thread forward to in back of the eyes.
9. Tie down the front part of the tail/wing and clip the excess forward of this tie.
10. Wind the Antron yarn around the hook shank and through the hackle feather fibers, just as you would thread through a feather when making a Matuka.
11. Tie off the yarn and clip the excess.
12. Wind the copper wire forward, following the path of the yarn.

13. Tie off the wire and clip the excess.
14. Turn the hook over and tie in a short bundle of red marabou for the gills.
15. On top of the gills (really the under part of the fly) tie in a small bundle of orange lambs wool. Clip the excess.
16. Turn the hook back and tie in olive marabou for a topping wing. Clip any excess.
17. Tie in a second topping of olive wool and clip any excess.
18. Tie in a bundle of olive lambs wool for the head. Clip any excess.
19. Tie in a bundle of black or dark brown lambs wool and spin it around the hook shank.
20. Bring the 20-pound mono loop forward and tie down under the hook shank, so that the loop protects the hook point. Clip the excess mono.
21. Tie off the head with a whip finish and clip the excess thread.
22. Trim the head of the fly (lambs wool) to shape and so that the eyes show.
23. If not yet painted, paint the lead eyes yellow with black pupils.

SHIMMER BLUEGILL

Flat-sided sunfish and perch imitations can be made in many ways, of which this is one of the simplest and most popular.

Once it was thought that every fly required a body wrapped or wound onto the hook shank. With warmwater patterns, this is not true, since often the wing materials will hide any part of the hook shank, making a body wrapping superfluous. This fly does have a body wrap of thread, but only to hold the single mono weed guard in place. The wing of the fly is made up completely of Shimmer, a synthetic stranded material with a lot of flash in it. Early similar patterns were tied with multi-colored bunches of marabou, and achieved a similar effect. You can tie the same fly with less flash using other types of stranded materials such as Poly Bear, Aqua Fiber, Neer Hair and others, or you can make it with more flash using Krystal Flash, Crystal Splash, Flashabou or similar materials. The tying steps will be the same. Fish this as a slowly twitched pattern in bass hot spots.

Tied by McKenzie

Hook – Regular hook, sizes 2 to 2/0
Thread – Orange
Wing – Yellow Shimmer
Topping – Medium blue Shimmer

Shoulder – Long yellow dyed grizzly saddle hackle
First collar – Short length of red Flashabou, tied in front of wing
Second collar – Orange cross-cut

rabbit strip, one wrap
Eyes – Plastic, yellow with black pupil
Weed guard – Single loop of 20-pound monofilament

Tying sequence:

1. Tie down the working thread in back of the hook eye and clip any excess thread.
2. Wind partly down the hook shank, and at midpoint tie down a length of 20-pound mono.
3. Continue to wind around the hook shank and mono until part way around the hook bend.
4. Reverse thread direction and wind back up the hook shank about 2/3 of its length.
5. Prepare and tie in a length (about three times the hook length) of yellow Shimmer.
6. Prepare and tie in a length of medium blue Shimmer, equal to in length to the yellow.
7. Prepare matched dyed yellow grizzly hackles, and tie one on each side of the yellow wing.
8. Prepare a collar of a short, thick bundle of red Flashabou and tie down immediately in front of the wing. Push this collar down and around the hook shank while securing it to make it surround or veil the hook.
9. Clip any excess material in front of the working thread.
10. Tie in a short length of orange cross-cut rabbit fur and wind the thread forward several turns.
11. Tie in stemmed plastic eyes.
12. Wind the thread forward to in back of the hook eye.
13. Make one turn of the rabbit fur in front of the eyes. Make sure that the fur flows to the back of the fly and that the eyes will show through the rabbit fur.
14. Tie off the rabbit fur with the working thread and clip any excess rabbit fur.
15. Bring the mono loop forward and tie off under the hook shank. Clip any excess mono.
16. Make a neat head and complete with a whip finish. Clip any excess thread.
17. Seal the head with head cement.
18. (Alternatively, complete the head and then glue plastic or prism eyes to the head or immediately in back of the wrapped head. If using prism eyes, epoxy should be used to seal and protect them.)

SHIMMER PERCH

Specific perch imitations are seldom seen, but this one is a good one for bass, pike and walleye.

One of the favorite foods for walleye is perch, and this is an ideal fly. It is tied similar to the Shimmer Bluegill, but with different colors to more closely simulate a perch. You can also tie it in yellow, olive, purple and orange marabou. Marabou was used for earlier similar patterns like this long before the availability of appropriate synthetics. For shallow pike or bass, tie it unweighted and fish it with a sinking tip or sinking line to help the fly suspend at the right depth. For deep walleye, deep summer bass or deep pike, tie it weighted with a wrap of lead wire on the hook shank or large lead dumbbell eyes in place of the plastic eyes used here.

Tied by McKenzie

Hook – Regular hook, sizes 2 to 3/0

Thread – Yellow

Belly wing – Red Flashabou

Wing – Dark blue-green Shimmer

Topping – Yellow Shimmer

Shoulder – Long brown dyed grizzly saddle hackle

Collar – Brown cross-cut rabbit strip

Eyes – Plastic, yellow with black pupil

Weed guard – Single loop of 20-pound mono

Tying sequence:

1. Tie in the working thread in back of the hook eye and clip any excess.
2. Wind the working thread to the rear, and at midpoint tie in a length of 20-pound mono for the weed guard.
3. Continue to wind the thread to the rear, part way around the hook bend and then wrap up again to a spot about 2/3 of the shank length.
4. Tie in a length (about three times the hook length) of red Flashabou on the underside of the hook shank.
5. Tie in a length equal to the Flashabou of dark blue-green Shimmer on top of the hook shank.
6. Tie in a topping of an equal length of yellow Shimmer.
7. Clip any excess materials forward of the working thread.
8. Tie in a short length of brown cross-cut rabbit strip.
9. Wind the thread forward slightly and tie in the stemmed plastic eyes.
10. Wind the thread forward of the plastic eyes.
11. Make one or two wraps of the cross-cut rabbit fur in front of the plastic eyes. Tie off with the working thread. Clip any excess rabbit fur.
12. Bring the single mono loop forward, and make sure that it protects the hook point and tie off with the thread. Clip any excess mono.
13. Make a neat head and tie off with a whip finish. Clip any excess thread.
14. Seal the head wrap with head cement

Alternatively, glue eyes on the head after completing the rest of the fly and sealing it, or use lead dumbbell eyes for added weight to get the fly deep.

LITE BRITE MINNOWS – BABY BASS

Some of the simplest flies are made with just one or two materials and some innovation in tying and use of materials. This is one of them.

Bill Black of Spirit River claims that he can outfish bait and soft plastics with these simple minnows that can be tied and colored in any fashion to imitate any baitfish. This involves a dubbing technique of tying using chopped up Lite Brite, a flashy material designed for dubbing. You can use any fine material to do this, including other synthetic dubbing materials, or chopped Flashabou, Krystal Flash, and Crystal Splash. The secret of this is in the coloration of it after it is tied onto the hook and completed. You can also tie these with a bead or cone head for weight to make it work in an up-down action like a Clouser. Without weight, as with this example, they can be fished shallow or deep, depending upon line choice.

Tied by Spirit River

Materials Needed

Hook – Long shank hook, sizes 2 to 10	**Tail** – Light brown marabou or rabbit fur	**Body** – Mix of gold and pearl-green Lite Brite
Thread – Gray	**Underbody** – Gray yarn	**Eyes** – Prism eyes, gold with black pupil

Tying sequence:

1. Tie on the working thread at the midpoint of the hook shank. Clip any excess thread.
2. Tie in a length of thin gray yarn.
3. Wind the thread to the rear of the hook shank.
4. Wind the yarn to the rear of the hook shank and tie off with the working thread. Clip any excess yarn.
5. Tie in a prepared tail of a short bundle of light brown marabou.
6. Mix a small portion of gold and pearl-green Lite Brite.
7. Make a dubbing loop, and secure the thread to the hook shank with several turns.
8. Wind the thread to the front of the hook shank.
9. Wax the dubbing loop thread and add the mixed Lite Brite dubbing. Twist the dubbing loop to secure it.
10. Wind the dubbing loop around the hook shank and tie off at the head of the fly. Clip any excess dubbing or Lite Brite.
11. Tie down a small neat head and tie off with a whip finish. Clip any excess thread.
12. Seal the head with head cement.
13. Use scissors to trim the body to the shape desired – basically a slim minnow shape.
14. Use a black permanent felt tip marker to draw a black lateral line along the side of the minnow on the side of the hook shank.

BENDBACK

One way to make for an effective fly that also has weedless capabilities is to use Bendback hooks as with this pattern.

There are many ways to tie Bendbacks, but they are all simple since the flies usually do not have any body to them. The wing material chosen hides, and somewhat protects, the hook point. Bendback hooks are available from the major manufacturers or you can make your own by using pliers – carefully – to slightly bend the shank in back of the hook eye. Remember to leave enough room to tie the wing desired.

Tied by Spirit River

Hook – Long shank hook bent to shape or a Bendback hook, sizes 6 to 1/0

Thread – White

Wing – White Ultra Hair or Super Hair topped with tan Ultra Hair or Super Hair

Eyes – Self-stick prism eyes, silver

with black pupil

Head – White, coated with epoxy to protect the eyes

Tying sequence:

1. If needed, prepare a long shank hook by bending the hook shank up about 1/4 inch from the hook eye, or use a Bendback hook.
2. Tie in the working thread in back of the hook eye and clip any excess thread.
3. Wind the thread back to the angled bend (not the hook bend) and tie down a prepared length of white Ultra Hair or Super Hair about twice the length of the hook shank.
4. Tie in a prepared length of tan Ultra Hair or Super Hair on top of the white.
5. Clip any excess wing material forward of the working thread.
6. Make a neat rounded head with the thread.
7. Tie off the head with a whip finish and clip any excess thread.
8. Add self-stick prism eyes to each side of the head.
9. Seal the eyes in place with a coating of epoxy to protect the eyes.
10. Place the fly on a rotator until the epoxy is cured.

EGG-SUCKING LEECH

Leeches are common throughout the country, and more so in the northern and north-central states where they are commonly used as bait for walleye. This pattern takes advantage of leeches as fish food, as the leeches feed on fish eggs.

Leeches commonly seek out fish eggs so that a leech with an egg stuck to the front end is not the strange mix that it might initially seem. They can be most commonly found feeding this way when local fish are spawning. This fly, with the olive body and red egg head, is designed to imitate a leech eating a fish egg. It is a common and popular fly for a number of species, even though it started as a trout/salmon pattern. It originated in Alaska, then gained acceptance in the West, now is used almost universally and gaining popularity in warmwater fly-fishing. To simplify the fly, you can think of it as a woolly bugger with a pink wrap of chenille added to the front end. For best results, fish it in a drift that will take it through deep pools and into quiet eddies or with slow, twitching strips through still-water ponds and lakes. It has lead in this pattern to take it down, but can be tied without this for fishing shallower or with split shot on the leader in place of the lead in the fly. While shown in olive with a red egg, it can also be tied with a body of any dark color and an egg of any bright fluorescent color.

Tied by McKenzie

Materials Needed

Hook – Standard streamer hook, 2x to 3x long, sizes 2 through 10
Thread – Olive

Weight – Lead wire
Tail – Olive marabou
Body – Olive chenille

Hackle – Olive, palmered over the body
Egg – Red chenille

Tying sequence:

1. Tie in the thread at the rear of the hook shank and clip the excess.
2. Wrap lead around the body as desired. For an up/down action to the fly, tie it only at the front end.
3. Spiral wrap up and down the hook shank with the thread to secure and cover the lead wire.
4. Tie in the tail of olive marabou.
5. Tie in the palmering olive hackle by the tip end, and then tie in the olive chenille body.
6. Wrap the thread forward to a point about 1/4 inch in back of the hook eye, or a spot leaving enough room to add an egg of red chenille.
7. Tie in a short length of red chenille, then wrap the chenille forward and then back again. Tie off with the working thread and clip any excess chenille.
8. Wrap the olive body chenille forward and tie off at the thread. Clip any excess.
9. Palmer wrap the hackle forward and tie off at the thread, after making a few final turns of hackle around the hook shank at the thread position.
10. Clip the excess hackle.
11. Complete with a few whip finish wraps and clip any excess thread.
12. Seal the whip finish with head cement.

CLOUSER'S CRAYFISH

Crayfish are a favorite food of smallmouth bass, and also taken by carp. Some panfish and perch also take small ones.

Crayfish patterns are legion, and can be tied small or large, with or without weight or rattles, and with short claws or long claws. They are also tied in a variety of colors, since crayfish vary in color depending upon their species, waterway in which they are found, and the time of the year. Spawning crayfish often become an orangish-red or brownish-red color. This fly is for small hooks for those times when you want a small crayfish for river fishing smallmouth or even sight fishing carp. You can also mix material colors slightly to tie this same pattern in different colors.

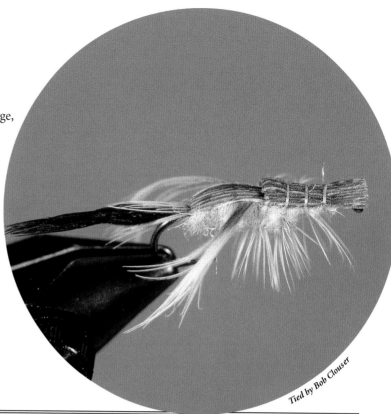

Tied by Bob Clouser

Materials Needed

Hook – Long shank (3X) regular hook, sizes 6 to 10

Thread – Olive

Tail – Natural hen mallard hackle fibers

Body – Pale gray yarn

Rib – Gray thread

Back – Dark turkey quill

Palmered hackle (legs) – Ginger hackle

Claws – Natural hen mallard hackle fibers, clipped out of center quill to make the two claws

Tying sequence:

1. Tie in the working thread at the rear of the hook shank and clip the excess thread.
2. Prepare and tie down a small bundle of natural brown hackle fibers. This bundle is clipped from the center of a hackle tip, with the tip ends only tied down. The remaining hackle fibers are left in place to become the claws.
3. Clip and tie in a long narrow strip of turkey quill, with the length of the quill extending behind the hook.
4. Tie in a length of gray yarn.
5. Wind the thread forward to the midpoint of the hook and tie down a length of gray thread. (Note – use a pair of hackle pliers to hold this thread tension tight during subsequent tying operations. This thread will tie down the back, claws and legs.)
6. Wind the olive working thread the rest of way forward to in back of the hook eye.
7. Hold the hen hackle fiber center quill up to wind the gray yarn forward, leaving the gray thread ribbing in place at the midpoint.
8. Tie off the gray yarn at the head of the fly with the olive thread. Clip any excess yarn.
9. Tie down a ginger hackle by the butt ends with the gray thread in the center of the hook. Clip any excess butt hackle ends.
10. Continue to spiral wind (palmer) the ginger hackle around the body until reaching the head of the fly. Tie off the hackle with the working thread and clip any excess tip hackle.
11. Fold the turkey quill over the hook and over the hen mallard quill. Tie down with the gray thread.
12. Continue to spiral wrap the gray thread around the body and turkey quill, taking care to avoid matting the hackle.
13. Tie off the gray thread with the olive thread at the head of the fly. Clip any excess gray thread.
14. Fold the turkey quill up for clearance and tie off the fly with a whip finish. Clip any excess thread.
15. Seal the wraps with head cement, fold the turkey quill down and clip just beyond the hook eye.

BILL'S FOAM CRAWDAD JIG

This is another way to tie a neat little crayfish that is ideal for everything from smallmouth to walleye to panfish.

The simplicity of this fly makes it hard to beat. The claws, body and tail are all one piece of foam. It is called a jig by originator Bill Skilton, even though it is tied with lead or non-lead dumb bell eyes on a straight hook. It can also be tied on a true jig hook with the dumb bell eyes or on a jig hook with a molded on lead head. Since it only uses several materials, it is a quick and easy fly to tie. Fish it right on the bottom using a short leader and sinking or sinking tip fly line to keep it in the strike zone as long as possible. The following varies slightly from Bill Skilton's tying directions, but this is slightly easier and eliminates the ribbing around the body as on the original design. Shown here upside down from the way in which it will be fished.

Tied by Bill Skilton

Hook – Hook size 10 to 2, 2X long shank	dumbbell eyes	**Claws, back and tail** – USA-FLIES had shell foam or similar foam sheeting, colored with permanent felt tip pens
Thread – Brown	**Antennae** – Several strands of brown bucktail	
Weight – Lead or non-lead	**Legs** – Brown hackle	

Tying sequence:

1. Tie in the working thread at the front of the hook shank and clip the excess thread.
2. Tie in the dumbbell or hour glass eyes and secure with figure eight wraps.
3. Wind the thread to the rear of the hook shank.
4. Tie in several (up to ten) lengths of stacked (evened) brown bucktail. Clip any excess.
5. Tie in a length of brown hackle.
6. Remove the hook from the vise and remount with the point up.
7. Prepare a piece of foam that is about twice the hook length. Make a cut about one-third the length of the foam down the center of the rectangle. Trim and taper these two lengths of cut foam and cut lengthwise part way through the center of each to make the claws. Do NOT remove the claws from the main strip of foam.
8. Tie down the foam on top (hook point side) of the hook shank at the bend of the hook.
9. Fold the foam back and wind the thread forward to the midpoint of the hook shank.
10. Wind the hackle around the hook shank and tie off with the thread. Clip any excess hackle.
11. Fold the foam over the hook shank and tie down with the thread.
12. Wind the thread forward one spiral wrap around the hook shank and then tie down the foam with the thread.
13. Continue the above, making one spiral wrap around the hook shank and then one around the hook shank and the foam to segment the body or carapace.
14. Fold the foam over the dumb bell eyes and tie down with thread.
15. Push the eye of the hook through the foam and trim the foam to complete the tail.
16. Color the foam back and claws with permanent felt tip pens.
17. Apply Softex to the foam body and finish any necessary trimming of the claws.

WOOLLY BUGGER

The general shape and action of the Woolly Bugger allows it to be fished for almost anything, and to be tied in any color and a variety of ways.

Woolly Buggers are basic searching or explorer flies that may, and probably do, imitate a lot of different things to different fish species. With the long marabou tail, and often-dark body, it can imitate a leech, hellgrammite, crayfish, sculpin, little mad tom catfish, and in small sizes, even some stonefly nymphs. It is a variation of the older Woolly Worm that is similar except for the short red yarn tail in place of the marabou. It works equally well in rivers and on ponds and lakes. It is an ideal fly to use on new water or as the first fly fished to test the waters. You can continue fishing with the Woolly Bugger or then switch to flies that might be more fun to fish, more of a challenge or even more productive. It can be tied in any color, using the same colors for body and tail or even contrasting colors in the tail. Typical colors that seem to be best for most warmwater species are black, olive, orange and brown. A variation of this basic pattern is to add some flash material such as Krystal Flash, Crystal Splash or Flashabou to the marabou tail or to use cactus chenille for the body.

Tied by the author

Materials Needed

Hook – Streamer hook, 2X to 4X long, in sizes 4 through 12

Weight – Optional – Lead or non-lead wire wrapped around the body

Thread – Color to match the fly color – black, gray, olive or brown

Tail – Marabou to match the fly color – black, gray, olive or brown

Flash – Bright Krystal Flash, Flashabou or Crystal Flash (optional)

Body – Chenille to match the fly color – black, gray, olive or brown

Hackle – Soft saddle hackle, to give action to the fly, in colors to match the fly body – black, gray, olive or brown

Tying sequence:

1. Tie in thread at the bend of the hook shank.
2. If adding weight, wrap the lead or non-lead wire around the hook shank as desired. (Tie forward for a jigging action, along the entire hook shank for more weight.) Spiral wrap the thread up and down over the wire to secure it, and add a coating of head cement so that the wire will not bleed through and stain the body materials. Return the tying thread to the bend of the hook.
3. Tie in the marabou tail fibers. The tail should be about as long as the hook shank. Clip any excess butt ends.
4. Tie in the palmering hackle by the tip end, and then tie down the end of the chenille body. Wrap the thread forward to just in back of the eye.
5. Wrap the chenille forward in tight wraps over the hook shank or lead wire base. Tie the chenille off and clip any excess chenille.
6. Wrap the palmering hackle forward in a spiral wrap and tie off with the tying thread in back of the eye. Clip any excess hackle.
7. Wrap a neat head with the tying thread and tie off with a whip finish.
8. Seal with head cement.

EPOXY MINI MINNOW

Tiny minnows are a staple of many gamefish. This example is an easy imitation to tie and one that is very durable as a result of the epoxy body.

The use of epoxy has become far more popular in recent years. The heaviest use has been in saltwater flies, but it is also useful for making bodies of warmwater minnow imitations. There are many ways to use epoxy, with this simple body coating one of the easiest and one that makes for a durable fly. One important point in tying these flies is that at the present time, all epoxies will slightly yellow in time. It would not adversely affect this small yellow minnow imitation, but keep that in mind before tying more of a pattern than you can use in a season or two. Fish these in the shallows or anywhere that minnows congregate. These can be tied in any size and are ideal for virtually all game fish, and especially good for walleye, bowfin, pike, pickerel, muskie, crappie, smallmouth bass, largemouth bass, rock bass, drum, inland stripers and perch. They can be tied in any size for the species sought, and with variety of materials using this basic body-coating technique. Any color is possible, with this example in yellow.

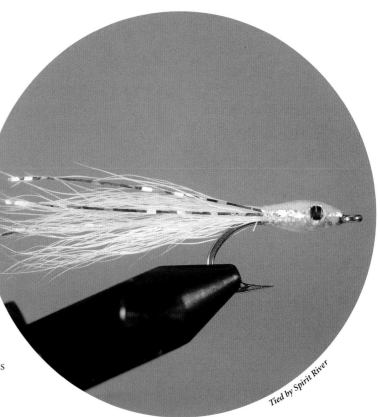

Tied by Spirit River

Materials Needed

Hook – Regular length hook, sizes 12 to 2/0

Thread – Clear monofilament

Tail/body – Length of white bucktail, overtop of which is tied an equal bundle of yellow or chartreuse bucktail

Flash – Holographic Fly Flash or similar holographic flash material

Underbody – Wrap of holographic Fly Flash or silver tinsel

Body coating – Five-minute epoxy

Eyes – Prism eyes under body coating

Tying sequence:

1. Tie thread in at the head of the hook and clip any excess thread. Wind back up to the head of the fly.
2. Tie in a length of holographic Fly Flash or tinsel.
3. Wind the holographic Fly Flash down and then back up the hook shank to create a silver body.
4. Prepare (clip, comb and stack/even) a small bundle of yellow bucktail.
5. Tie the bucktail in at the head of the fly, with the length of the bundle about two times the shank length and the butt tied in with the tips facing forward. (It will be folded back later.)
6. Prepare (clip, comb and stack/even) a small bundle of white bucktail.
7. Tie this bundle at the head of the fly, also about twice the length of the hook shank and facing forward to be later folded back.
8. Prepare and tie down two to three strands of holographic Fly Flash on each side of the body/wing, with the Fly Flash also facing forward.
9. Wind the clear mono thread evenly over the body to the rear of the fly.
10. Fold over the white bucktail and tie down at the rear of the hook shank.
11. Fold over the yellow bucktail and tie down at the rear of the hook shank.
12. Fold the holographic Fly Flash back along each side and tie down with the thread.
13. Tie off with a whip finish and clip the excess thread.
14. Add prism eyes to each side of the head of the fly.
15. Prepare (measure and mix) a small puddle of five-minute epoxy and use a bodkin to thoroughly coat the body, including the wrap at the rear of the hook shank and covering the eyes.
16. Place the finished fly on a fly rotator and allow to turn for a few minutes to prevent the epoxy from sagging.

BLACK GNAT

Black wet flies like this show up well against the sky, which is often how fish are looking at them. This is a great fly for any panfish or insect-eating warmwater fish.

Perhaps as a misnomer, this fly is called a gnat, even though true gnats are so small that they could never be imitated with even the smallest hook sizes. While often fished as a trout fly, this is also excellent as an early season and midsummer wet fly for bluegills, other sunfish, perch and even river smallmouth. As a black fly, it might be suggestive of ants, crickets, and bottom-hugging nymphs, flies or wasps. For panfish and bluegills, find a likely area, and fish it on a sinking tip line or with a split shot 18 inches up on the leader, and retrieve slowly so that the fish get a good look at the fly.

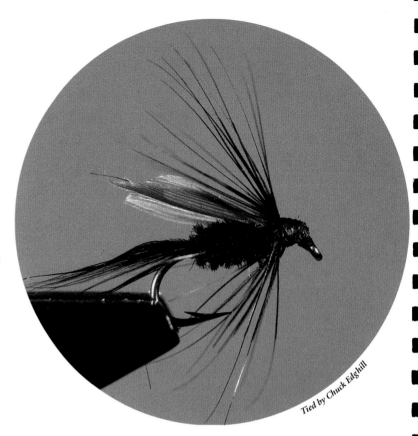

Tied by Chuck Edghill

Materials Needed

Hook – Wet fly hook, sizes 6 to 12

Thread – Black

Tail – Black hackle fibers

Body – Black yarn or black chenille

Wings – Slate mallard wing quill sections

Hackle – Black hen hackle

Tying sequence:

1. Tie in the thread at the midpoint of the hook shank and clip any excess thread.
2. Wind the thread to the bend of the hook and tie in a tail of black hackle fibers.
3. Tie down a strand of chenille or yarn.
4. Wind the thread forward to just in back of the hook eye, leaving enough room for the hackle and wing.
5. Wind the chenille or yarn around the hook shank to make the body and tie off with the thread in back of the hook eye. Clip the excess yarn or chenille.
6. Select and prepare matched section of slate gray quill feathers and tie them down to the hook with the concave side facing each other. (For more wing visibility, tie with the convex sides facing each other.)
7. Clip the excess quill material from in front of the tie down point.
8. Prepare and tie down by the butt end a black hen hackle feather.
9. Wind the hackle feather around the hook shank, with the hackle flared to the rear. Tie off and clip the excess hackle.
10. If the hackle has not flared back enough, wind around the head with thread to push the hackle into a swept back angle.
11. Complete the head with a whip finish and clip the thread.
12. Seal with head cement.

MCGINTY

This bee pattern is particularly good as a panfish and bluegill fly and a must for anyone going after these species.

The McGinty is one of those flies that will work everywhere, at any level of the water column; even through it imitates a bumblebee with the alternate bands of yellow and black chenille. While probably few bumblebees fall into the water, this fly works as another of the colorful attractor patterns. Obviously, it is best as an imitative fly during the summer months when worker bees are out. It is particularly good around lowlands and pastures with flowers that are frequently visited by bees. Try it in weighted styles also, with a little lead wire wrapped parallel to the hook shank or wrapped around the hook shank for an even faster sink rate.

Tied by Holly Flies

Hook – Standard wet fly hook, sizes 8 to 12

Thread – Black

Tail – Mixed dyed red hackle fibers and barred teal flank fibers

Body – Bands of black and yellow chenille

Wings – White-tipped mallard secondary wing quill sections

Hackle – Brown

Tying sequence:

1. Tie in the thread at the bend of the hook, and then clip the excess thread.
2. Tie in the tail, first with the red hackle, over that is tied the teal fibers.
3. Tie in the yellow chenille, followed by the black chenille.
4. Wrap the thread forward, followed by one wrap of black chenille wrapped over the yellow.
5. Tie off the black chenille and wrap the thread forward again, followed by one wrap of the yellow chenille wrapped over the black.
6. Tie off and clip the yellow chenille, then wrap the thread forward, followed by a wrap of the black chenille.
7. Tie off the black chenille and clip the excess.
8. Tie in a brown throat or collar hackle, tying in the fibers or tying in the hackle and then wrapping it around the hook shank. Clip the butt fibers or the excess hackle.
9. Prepare the white-tipped wing quills and tie in place, then clip the excess butt ends.
10. Tie a neat head, then tie off with a whip finish and clip the excess thread.
11. Seal with head cement.

BLOODY MARY

This is another popular panfish fly that incorporates elements of both attractor flies and imitative flies.

With the biot tail, soft hackle and ribbing of peacock herl, this fly has elements of a buggy looking imitative design. With the bright bead head and red body, it looks like an attractor. This fly has all the right things for a fly for panfish, bluegills, perch and crappie. The bright bead head helps to attract fish, while getting the fly down fast. It also allows giving the fly an up-down jigging action as you bounce it through a school of bluegill or snake it through a brush pile for crappie. You can use the same basic design to make other flies that look completely different but vary only in the body color. In addition to the red shown here, try yellow, bright blue, orange, light green and white.

Tied by Spirit River

Hook – Long shank hook, 2X, sizes 8 through 16	**Body** – Red Flex Floss or other floss	**Hackle** – Soft Partridge or speckled hen
Thread – Black	**Ribbing** – Peacock herl	**Head** – Bright brass or gold bead
Tail – Brown biots	**Thorax** – Peacock herl	

Tying sequence:

1. Carefully bend down the hook barb and slide a bright gold or brass bead onto the hook and up in back of the eye.
2. Place the hook in a vise.
3. Tie in the working thread at the midpoint of the hook shank and clip the excess.
4. Wind the thread to the rear of the hook shank and tie in two brown biots. Crisscross wrap slightly to separate and angle the biots.
5. Tie in a length of peacock herl.
6. Tie in a length of red Flex Floss or other red floss.
7. Wind the thread forward, over the tag ends of the biots, peacock and floss to a point about 1/6-inch in back of the bright bead.
8. Wind the Flex Floss forward to make a smooth tapered body and tie off at the thread. Clip any excess floss.
9. Spiral wrap (palmer) the peacock herl forward around the body.
10. Make a few additional turns of peacock herl around the hook shank in front of the body and tie off with the working thread. Clip any excess peacock.
11. Tie in a soft partridge hackle by the butt and clip and excess of the butt end.
12. Wind the hackle several times around the hook shank and tie off with the thread. Clip any excess hackle.
13. Make a small neat wrap against the back of the bead and tie off with a whip finish. Clip any excess thread.
14. Seal the wraps with head cement.

BODY BUG

This little wet fly is as much a jig as it is a wet fly, but ideal for getting deep for panfish.

The barbell eyes on this little panfish fly get it down deep for mid-summer fishing. Greg Webster designed this with weight for deep fishing. It resembles more of a jig and while Greg does not tie it this way, can be tied on a small jig hook that will make the fly ride hook point up. Another alternative is to tie this fly on a prepared molded jig head, either painted or unpainted, adding the materials otherwise as above. Greg ties his Body Bugs in one uniform color for each fly, with favorite colors black, chartreuse, and silver.

Tied by Greg Webster

Materials Needed

Hook – Size 10, 2X long hook, (alternatively a jig hook with or without a molded lead head)

Thread – Chartreuse or to match body color

Eyes – Non-toxic small barbell eyes with stick-on prism eyes

Tail – Chartreuse Krystal Flash on top of short chartreuse marabou tail

Body – Chartreuse Body Stuff (Angler's Choice) or V-rib or Larvae Lace or similar body material

Head – Bright chartreuse dubbing or dazzle dubbing, on front of hook and figure-eighted around the eyes

Tying sequence:

1. Tie in the thread in back of the hook eye and clip the excess thread.
2. Tie in small non-toxic barbell or hourglass eyes. Figure-eight and crisscross to tie securely.
3. Return thread to the rear of the hook shank and tie down a short bundle of chartreuse marabou.
4. Tie down a slightly longer bundle of chartreuse Krystal Flash on top of the marabou tie down point.
5. Tie in a length of chartreuse body material (Body Stuff, V-rib, Larvae Lace or thin yarn) and wind thread forward to the barbell eyes.
6. Wind the body material forward and tie off in back of the barbell eyes. Clip any excess material.
7. Tie down a length of prepared chartreuse dubbing, or dub to the waxed thread to wind in place.
8. Wind the thread or the dubbing material around the hook shank, in front of the eyes and figure-eighting around the eyes.
9. Tie off the head material and clip any excess.
10. Complete the fly with a whip finish and clip the excess thread.
11. Seal the head with head cement.

OLIVE NYMPH

Many patterns like this have tails, but this tailless variety seems to work extremely well, while being extremely easy to tie. It is a great fly for any of the smaller warmwater species.

As a small boy, I was introduced to trout fishing and to this fly at the same time. I soon learned that it is not only good for trout, but also for panfish such as bluegill, pumpkinseed, redbreast sunfish, and similar popular warmwater species. I knew it first as a gray nymph, but it can be tied in a variety of colors, including olive, tan, brown, black, cream, yellow, brownish orange and white. As a suggestive, imitative type of fly, it could be any of a number of aquatic insects, nymphs, or even terrestrial food washed into a pond or stream. I like it best tied with mohair or Leech Yarn, either of which gives it a very buggy look for a simple fly. In recent years, I have also done well with it tied as a bead head design. It is the same fly, just with the weight of a metal bead head on the front end that helps to get it down, and gives it a jigging action when twitched or retrieved. A more standard version of this favorite fly has a badger guard hair tail.

Tied by Spirit River

Hook – Standard wet fly style, sizes 8 through 16	**Body** – Olive mohair or Leech Yarn
Thread – Olive	**Hackle** – Olive or olive dyed grizzly

Tying sequence:

1. Tie in the thread at the mid-point on the hook shank and clip off any excess thread.
2. Tie in the body material and wrap the thread forward to just in back of the hook eye.
3. Wrap the body material up to the thread, then down to the bend of the hook, then back up to the thread again. Tie off and clip the excess body material.
4. Choose an olive, olive dyed, or gray grizzly hackle, trim the butt end and tie down to the hook shank. Trim any excess and wind the hackle around the hook shank flared back wet fly style.
5. Tie off with the thread and clip any excess hackle.
6. Wrap a neat head and complete the fly with a whip finish. Clip the excess thread.
7. Seal the head with head cement.

RED ANT

Unlike the McMurray Ant, which is a floater, this fly sinks and drifts with the current. Red is popular although it can be tied in black also.

Ants eventually sink, and that is where this pattern comes into play for taking sunfish, perch, and even carp and smallmouth. Other useful variations of this red ant are a brownish-red cinnamon ant and a black and red (red thorax and black abdomen) ant. It can also be tied in white on a longer hook shank with a longer white abdomen to simulate a termite fallen from a rotten log next to the shore. These ants (or termites) are harder to follow when fishing, since they do not float on the surface, as do most other terrestrials. A long rod/short line is best using a dapping technique that allows good control to the drift of the fly or a very slow retrieve and the ability to react to the slightest strike.

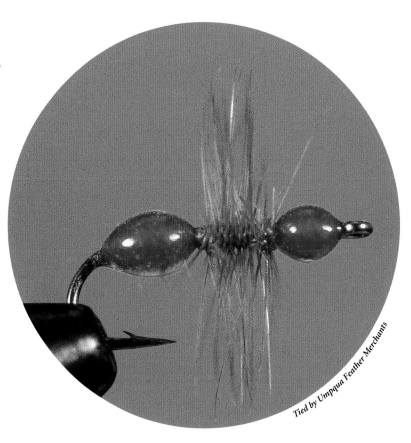

Tied by Umpqua Feather Merchants

Hook – Standard wet fly hook, 1X or 2X heavy hook, sizes 10 through 18

Thread – Red

Thorax – Light brown or brownish red floss

Abdomen – Light brown or brownish red floss

Hackle – Brown or ginger hen hackle

Tying sequence:

1. Tie in the thread at the bend of the hook and clip any excess thread.
2. Tie in floss and wrap the thread forward to the mid-point of the shank.
3. Wrap the floss back and forth to build up a neat tapered and rounded body or abdomen. Tie off and wrap slightly forward over the floss to preserve the thin waist of the fly. Do not cut the floss.
4. Tie in a hackle and clip the excess from the butt area.
5. Wrap the hackle around the waist (mid-point of the shank) several times. (Since ants only have six legs, do not try to use the entire hackle fiber or make the fullest hackle possible.) Tie off the hackle with the tying thread and clip any excess hackle.
6. Wrap the thread forward to just in back of the eye, but do not wrap over the floss.
7. Wrap the floss around the hook shank to build up a shorter and slightly smaller thorax of the ant forward of the hackle that simulates legs.
8. Clip any excess floss, make a small neat head and tie off with a whip finish. Clip excess thread.
9. Seal the abdomen, thorax, and head with head cement, taking care to avoid getting head cement on the hackle legs.

SAN JUAN WORM

The San Juan worm is the fisherman's answer to bait fishing with worms, and an established but simple-to-tie fly for many species.

The San Juan Worm is the famous fly developed for fishing the San Juan River in New Mexico, but is also great as a warmwater fly for everything from suckers to perch and bass. Numerous worms live on the bottom of rivers, ponds and lakes. Some are small, but some are far larger than you would expect. In addition, worms are washed into rivers and lakes during rain and high waters, at which time fish actively seek them. And of course, worms are the favored bait for early season spin-fishermen trying for anything that will hit. The San Juan Worm is the simplest of flies, and can be tied in any color desired, although the red/orange/maroon colors are usually favored as a result of their close resemblance to the natural. This one is tied maroon to simulate a natural night crawler.

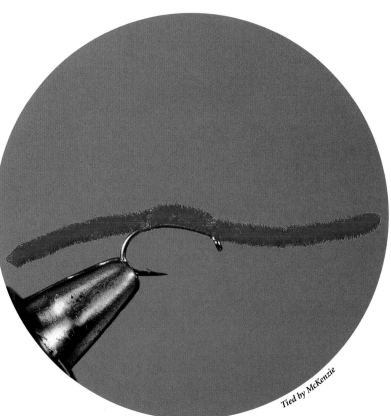

Tied by McKenzie

Materials Needed

Hook – Any wet fly hook or a curved caddis larva hook in sizes 6 through 12

Thread – Maroon or dark red, to match the worm color

Body – Vernille or Ultra Chenille in maroon or dark red (other colors also possible) Note that regular chenille will not work as well, since the worm requires burning and tapering the chenille ends to make it look more natural (Whether the fish care or not is something else!)

Tying sequence:

1. Secure the tying thread in back of the hook eye and wrap evenly to the bend of the hook. Clip excess thread.
2. Tie down a length of Vernille or Ultra Chenille to extend in back of the hook bend by one- to one-and-one-half inches.
3. Wrap the thread forward to just in back of the eye of the hook, making spaced wraps over the chenille as you do so to secure it to the hook shank.
4. Tie off the thread in back of the hook eye using a whip finish, tying on the bare hook shank under the forward part of the chenille. Clip the excess thread.
5. Seal with head cement.
6. Use a cigarette lighter to gently singe each end of the chenille, and use your fingers to roll the end to taper it. (Take care to not burn yourself.) The flame will also prevent the chenille from unraveling.

GRUBBY GERT

This little panfish and bluegill fly is simple to tie and easy to use. It can be tied in many colors and even using different materials.

Some twenty years ago, Tom Eggler, owner of Gaines Fly Fishing Products, developed this as one of a series of panfish flies that they were experimenting for the company. It is a slow sinking fly and with the calf tail/wings and chenille body, makes for an effective panfish, crappie, bluegill and perch fly for mid-summer fishing. Tom also has series of similar flies tied with different materials. All have a chenille body, but use rubber legs, marabou, or hackle for the tail and wings. Try it with a sinking tip line or even as a trailer at the end of 18 inches of mono behind a top-water popping bug.

Tied by Gaines Fly Fishing Products

Hook – Standard hook, sizes 4 through 12
Thread – Black or color to match

body
Tail – Bundle of yellow calf tail
Body – Dark green chenille

Wings – Yellow calf tail
Head – Dark green chenille

Tying sequence:

1. Tie the working thread at the midpoint of the hook shank and clip the excess.
2. Prepare (clip, comb and stack/even) a bundle of yellow calf tail and tie in place.
3. Tie down a bundle of dark green chenille.
4. Wind the thread forward to a point about 1/4 the shank length in back of the hook eye.
5. Wind the dark green chenille forward to the thread and tie off. Do not clip.
6. Prepare (clip, comb and stack/even) a bundle of yellow calf tail and tie onto the hook shank at this point. Push the bundle down to separate it into two wings, then tie securely with the wings separated and extending at an angle to each side.
7. Wind the thread forward to just in back of the hook eye.
8. Wind the chenille forward to the thread and tie off with the working thread. Clip the excess chenille.
9. Make a neat head and complete with a whip finish. Clip the excess.
10. Seal the head with head cement.

SIMPLE ONE

Originally tied by the author some forty years ago, this is a simple generic fly that works well in various colors and sizes for all warmwater species.

The author originated this style of tying some 50 years ago in an effort to make a simple fly that would work well in a variety of situations. It was originally designed as a saltwater fly for Chesapeake Bay stripers, but soon proved it's worth as a fly for bass, and later on when tied in larger sizes, even for pike. On small hooks it is a great fly for crappie and can be used weighted for walleye. This is the unweighted version, with the weighted version best when tied with dumbbell eyes to help create a jigging action on retrieve. This is a basic white, but it can also be tied in any color and either with or without the body included here.

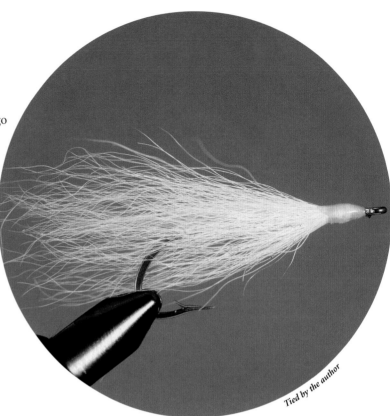

Tied by the author

Materials Needed

Hook – Long shank hook in sizes 12 through 2/0, depending upon fish sought

Thread – White, or black if tying flies of different wing colors

Body – Silver tinsel or silver Mylar (optional)

Wing – White calf tail for small flies; white bucktail for larger flies

Tying sequence:

1. Tie in the thread in back of the hook eye and clip the excess thread.
2. Tie in the tinsel or Mylar body material.
3. Wrap the tinsel to the bend of the hook and then back up to the head of the fly.
4. Tie off the tinsel or Mylar with the working thread and clip any excess tinsel.
5. Clip and comb a length of white calf tail or white bucktail and position as a wing on top of the hook shank in back of the head. Wrap in place with two turns of working thread.
6. Clip any excess wing material in front of the tying point.
7. Push down on the wing to distribute the wing material around the hook shank so that it veils the hook as an encircling wing.
8. Wrap with thread to make a neat head.
9. Tie off with a whip finish and clip any excess thread.
10. Seal with head cement (small flies) or with epoxy (large flies). If using epoxy, place the fly on a rotator until cured.

ZIMMER/SWOPE SHAD FLY

Shad are a saltwater fish that run into fresh waters to spawn each spring on both the Atlantic and Pacific coasts. They are a popular fly rod fish, with this effective fly one of dozens available.

During the popularity of shad fishing in the mid-Atlantic area some 40 years ago, many of us fishing for both hickory and American shad developed our own shad flies. Most were simple, as is this one developed by friends Joe Zimmer and Irv Swope for fishing tributaries of the Susquehanna River in Maryland. Most flies like this have emulated in color the bright (often fluorescent) colors used for the popular red/white/yellow (and other colors) lead shad darts cast by spin fishermen. A red wing/yellow body is described here, but other effective colors are all white, all yellow, all chartreuse, all red, red/yellow, purple/green, yellow/purple, etc. While designed specifically for shad, this is also an effective pattern in small sizes for perch, smallmouth, sunfish, bluegill, crappie, and other panfish. For fishing in snaggy water for these species, these can also be tied weedless, with a single or double mono weed guard.

Tied by the author

Materials Needed

Hook – 2X long shank hook in sizes 4 to 8 for shad, smaller or larger for other species
Thread – Black
Body – Yellow chenille

Ribbing – Silver tinsel or silver Mylar
Wing – Red calf tail
Head – Black

Tying sequence:

1. Tie in the thread at the middle or tail end of the hook shank. Cut off any excess thread and wrap to the hook bend.
2. Tie in the silver tinsel or Mylar ribbing.
3. Tie in the yellow chenille body material.
4. Wind the thread forward to just in back of the hook eye.
5. Wind the chenille forward around the hook shank and tie off with the working thread.
6. Spiral wrap the ribbing forward and tie off at the same point, in back of the hook eye.
7. Cut, comb and prepare a bundle of red calf tail and position it as a wing over the hook shank. The wing should be no longer than the hook shank.
8. Tie down the wing of calf tail and clip any excess calf tail in front of the tie-down point.
9. Wrap area with thread to make a smooth, tapered head.
10. Complete with a whip finish and clip any excess thread.
11. Seal with head cement.

CARL'S HOT RED SHAD FLY

This wingless fly is designed for shad, but makes an excellent small fly for any of the panfish or sunfish species.

While shad on both coasts are saltwater fish, they ascend into freshwater rivers each spring to spawn, thus the inclusion of flies for them here. Carl Blackledge, from Santa Rosa, Cal., has developed a wide range of shad flies for fishing along the West Coast. This is just one of his many patterns that often incorporate fluorescent materials in red, chartreuse, and hot pink along with a chrome bead to provide weight and flash at the head of the fly. The wingless pattern of this fly makes it ideal as a small, weighted, fast sinking fly for fishing crappie, panfish, bluegill, perch and other small species. It is a great fly for helping kids get an introduction to bluegill fishing with a fly rod.

Tied by Carl Blackledge

Hook – Size 6 for American shad, 8 for hickory shad, sizes 12 through 2 for other species

Thread – White

Tail – Bundle of white wool

Underwrap – Chrome or silver tinsel or Mylar

Body – Red Edge Bright, or similar red plastic fly-tying lace material

Collar – Red chenille

Head – Chrome bead

Tying sequence:

1. Bend down the barb of the fly hook, using flat nose pliers.
2. Slide a chrome bead onto the hook and up to the hook eye.
3. Tie in the thread at the rear of the hook shank. Clip any excess thread.
4. Clip and tie down a small bundle of white wool. The bundle must extend along the hook shank to provide a level base for the body.
5. Tie down the underwrap of chrome or silver tinsel.
6. Tie down the body material of red Edge Brite or similar red plastic lace material.
7. Wind the thread forward to a spot about 1/3 in back of the hook eye.
8. Wind the underwrap of tinsel forward and tie off with the thread.
9. Wind the body material of red Edge Brite forward and tie off with the thread.
10. Tie in a short length of red Ultra Chenille. Wind the thread forward to just in back of the chrome bead.
11. Wind the chenille a few turns forward and tie off with the thread.
12. Make a few wraps with the thread and complete with a whip finish. Clip the excess thread.
13. Seal the whip finish with head cement.

CONNECTICUT RIVER SHAD FLY

This is an old simple fly that is nothing more than a bright streamer, but which still accounts for a lot of shad – and other fish as well.

This is an old Atlantic Coast shad fly that was first fished in the Connecticut River. It was also fished with a red glass bead on the leader in front of the fly. Today, we would use a small red fluorescent plastic bead on the leader. This fly is slightly different from others in that it is tied with the silver tinsel body extending part way around the bend of the hook, rather than stopping at the end of the hook shank. As with most shad flies, fish this on a cross or quartering downstream cast, then allow the fly to swing in the current until straight downstream. Then twitch it a few times before making the retrieve and casting again. For panfish and other species, fish it on a slow, twitching retrieve with a sinking or sinking-tip line.

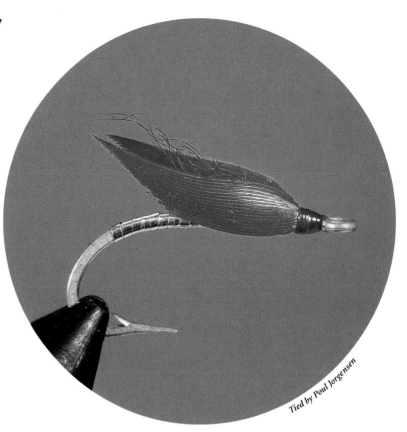

Tied by Poul Jorgensen

Hook – Hook in sizes 2 through 6, 2X to 3X long

Thread – Black
Body – Silver tinsel

Wing – Red duck flight feather, tied full but short, about the length of the hook shank

Tying sequence:

1. Tie in the thread just in back of the hook eye. Clip any excess thread.
2. Tie in the tinsel.
3. Wind the tinsel down the hook shank and part way around the bend, then back up the shank again. Tie off with the working thread.

4. Clip and prepare two portions of matching red quill section. Tie down with the working thread on top of the hook shank. Clip the excess quill section.
5. Wrap the thread to make a smooth tapered thread.
6. Tie off with a whip finish and clip any excess thread.
7. Seal with head cement.

SHEWEY SHAD SHAFTER

John Shewey lists this as a top West Coast shad fly in his book, Northwest Fly Fishing, Trout And Beyond.

John Shewey, a fly-fishing expert from the northwest, ties this fly of his design using fluorescent materials. It is a simple fly of two materials, not counting the thread and dumbbell eyes. Typically, West Coast shad fishermen use this fly and others like it, casting long sinking or sinking tip lines to fish the heavy currents found in West Coast shad rivers. As a neat bright fly, it is also good in appropriate sizes for bluegill, panfish, perch and crappie.

Tied by John Shewey

Materials Needed

Hook – Regular hook sizes 4 and 6, or smaller sizes down to size 10 for panfish

Thread – Yellow

Weight – Bead chain, medium lead dumbbell or hourglass eyes

Tail – Fluorescent chartreuse marabou mixed with

chartreuse Krystal Flash

Head/Body – Chartreuse cactus chenille wrapped in back, front and around the eyes to make a head and body

Tying sequence:

1. Tie in the thread at the midpoint on the hook shank, and clip any excess.
2. Wind the thread forward and tie in the lead eyes on top of the hook shank and a little in back of the hook eye.
3. Wind the thread to the midpoint of the hook shank and tie down the fluorescent chartreuse marabou bundle.
4. Tie in a little chartreuse Krystal Flash to mix with the marabou tail.
5. Clip the excess marabou and Krystal Flash.
6. Tie in a length of chartreuse cactus chenille and wind the thread forward to the hook eye.
7. Wrap the cactus chenille forward, winding it around and in front of the lead eyes to completely encircle them.
8. Tie off in back of the hook eye and clip the excess cactus chenille.
9. Complete with a whip finish and clip the excess thread.
10. Seal the wrap with head cement.

CALIFORNIA SHAD FLY

Subhead - In the late 1950s and 1960s, many shad flies were developed in California. This is one of many patterns for fishing for this increasingly popular springtime game fish.

American shad were introduced to California's Sacramento River on the West Coast in 1871. They were taken there from Hudson River stock by railroad in milk cans, and enough survived to make the stocking a success. These fish are now springtime targets in rivers from Alaska down through southern California. They became increasingly popular with the advent of spinning in the mid-1950s, as this tackle allowed casting small shad darts. They also became popular with fly fishermen with the advent of sinking line and shooting heads that allowed fly anglers to get the fly deep to the fish. This fly is just one of many bright patterns developed during this period. Flies like this are also excellent for perch, crappie and panfish.

Tied by Poul Jorgensen

Materials Needed

Hook – Size 4, 2X long hook
Tail – White hackle fibers
Butt – Orange/red chenille

Body – Oval silver tinsel
Hackle – White hackle
Collar – Orange/red chenille

Head – Orange/red thread

Tying sequence:

1. Tie the thread onto the hook shank just in front of the hook bend. Clip any excess thread.
2. Tie in the tail of white hackle fibers.
3. Tie in the butt of red chenille.
4. Wind the thread forward a few turns, enough to make one or two turns of chenille to form the butt.
5. Wind the chenille for one or two turns and tie off.
6. Clip any excess chenille.
7. Tie in a length of oval tinsel.
8. Wind the thread tightly and evenly forward to about 1/4 the shank length in back of the hook eye.
9. Wind the tinsel forward over the thread base and tie off at the thread position. Clip the excess tinsel.
10. Tie in a white hackle feather by the butt.
11. Wind the hackle around the hook shank to make a collar wet fly style hackle. Tie off and clip any excess.
12. Tie in a short length of red chenille and wind the thread forward to the hook eye.
13. Wind the red chenille one or two turns around the hook to form a collar. Tie off and clip any excess.
14. Tie a neat tapered head and tie off with a whip finish. Clip any excess thread.
15. Seal with head cement.

Conclusion

Tying flies for any species of fish is a fascinating and rewarding hobby. For warmwater species we can develop new patterns, learn more about the forage and food of the fish and how to best imitate that bait, and gain an absorbing ancillary fishing hobby for any time of the year.

Learn fly-tying and you will become a better angler. You will learn that a fly that cost you only a few cents is worth throwing into the roughest cover to try for a bass, pike or crappie. Forgetting for the moment the amortized cost of tools, materials and supplies, it is far easier to convince yourself to cast to a snaggy spot from which you might not get your fly back if you know that it only took a few minutes of your time at the bench rather than a few bucks per fly from a shop.

Fly-tying, particularly for warmwater species, also often involves materials available from craft and sewing shops in addition to fly shops and fly-fishing catalogs. As a result, you learn more about materials that have not yet been explored for fly-tying. It teaches you that flies of synthetic materials hold up better when pike fishing than those of natural products; that small simple wet flies and nymphs for trout do just as well for sunfish; that you can mix and match materials and colors in these patterns to adjust to your fishing situations. We also learn about the food of the fish we seek.

Tying flies also gives us a greater understanding of what makes an effective fly. This constantly developing knowledge also helps when fishing strange locations where we might have to visit a local shop and buy a few flies for local conditions to back up our basic boxes.

Fly-tying starts as a hobby and can become a compulsion. It mirrors art when you design your own patterns and care deeply about how they will look in addition to how they will catch fish. It has the base elements of a science when dealing with the qualities and properties of materials used and the entomology of the insects studied to fish forage. .

Fly-tying is what you make of it, and as with a lot of things in life, you and your fishing life get from it what you put into it. This book covers the basics. From this you will be able to tie many types of patterns, to perfect most techniques and to evolve steadily in your experience and abilities. Hopefully, your fly-tying will lead you to more fun on the water as you catch more fish on flies you have created.

Boyd Pfeiffer

Bibliography

The following books are only a few of the many dozens available on fly-tying and warmwater flies. Even though most fly-tying and pattern books have a heavy emphasis on trout, many will also include flies for warmwater and saltwater species. Rather than list an entire library, those books included here are designed to help with future fly-tying projects, to aid in learning or perfecting advanced techniques and suggesting more ways to tie specific warmwater patterns. They are all excellent and recommended for any reader interested in progressing in warmwater fly-tying.

Brooks, Joe. BASS BUG FISHING, New York, NY, A. S. Barnes and Company, 1947

Bruce, Joe. FLY FISHING FOR SMALLMOUTH BASS, Woodbine, MD, K & D Limited, 1997

Bruce, Joe. FLY FISHING FOR PANFISH, Woodbine, MD, K & D Limited, 1997

Ellis, Jack. BASSIN' WITH A FLY ROD, North Conway, NH, Mountain Pond Publishing, 1994

Keith, Tom. FLY-TYING AND FISHING FOR BASS & PANFISH, Portland, OR, Frank Amato Publications, Inc., 1989

Leeson, Ted and Schollmeyer, Jim. THE FLYTIER'S BENCHSIDE REFERENCE TO TECHNIQUES AND DRESSING STYLES, Portland, OR, Frank Amato Publications, Inc., 1998

Livingston, A. D. BASS ON THE FLY, Camden, ME, Ragged Mountain Press, 1994

Livingston, A. D. TYING BUGS AND FLIES FOR BASS, Philadelphia, PA, J, B. Lippincott Co., 1977

Mackenzie, Gordon. HAIR-HACKLE TYING TECHNIQUES & FLY PATTERNS, Portland, OR, Frank Amato Publications, Inc., 2001

Malo, John. FLY FISHING FOR PANFISH, Minneapolis, MN, Dillon Press, Inc., 1981

Meyer, Deke. TYING BASS FLIES – 12 OF THE BEST, Portland OR, Frank Amato Publications, Inc., 1995

Morris, Skip. THE ART OF TYING THE BASS FLY, Portland, OR, Frank Amato Publications, Inc., 1996

Morris, Skip. TYING FOAM FLIES, Portland, OR, Frank Amato Publications, Inc., 1994

Muma, John and Muma, Jim. OLD FLYROD LURES, Belleville, IL, Great Lakes Initiatives, 2001

Murray, Harry. FLY FISHING FOR SMALLMOUTH BASS, New York, NY, The Lyons Press, 1989

Pfeiffer, C. Boyd. BUG MAKING, New York, NY, The Lyons Press, 1993

Pfeiffer, C. Boyd. FLY FISHING BASS BASICS, Mechanicsburg, PA, Stackpole Books, 1997

Pfeiffer, C. Boyd. SHAD FISHING, Mechanicsburg, PA, Stackpole Books, 2001

Reynolds, Barry and Berryman, John. BEYOND TROUT – A FLYFISHING GUIDE, Boulder, CO, Johnson Books, 1995

Reynolds, Barry and Berryman, John. PIKE ON THE FLY, Boulder, CO, Johnson Books, 1993

Reynolds, Barry; Befus, Brad and Berryman, John. CARP ON THE FLY, Boulder, CO, Johnson Books, 1997

Ryan, Will. SMALLMOUTH STRATEGIES FOR THE FLY ROD, New York, NY, The Lyons Press, 1996

Skilton, Bill. MY FLY PATTERNS, MATERIALS AND TECHNIQUES, Boiling Springs, PA, privately printed, 2002

Stewart, Dick. BASS FLIES, Intervale, NH, Northland Press, 1989

Stewart, Dick and Allen, Farrow. FLIES FOR BASS &PANFISH, Intervale, NH, Northland Press, 1992

Talleur, Dick. MODERN FLY-TYING MATERIALS, New York, NY, The Lyons Press, 1995

Tapply, William G. BASS BUG FISHING, New York, NY, The Lyons Press, 1999

Waterman, Charles F. BLACK BASS & THE FLY ROD, Mechanicsburg, PA, Stackpole Books, 1993

Whitlock, Dave. L. L. BEAN FLY FISHING FOR BASS HANDBOOK, New York, NY, The Lyons Press, 1988

Williamson, Robert. CREATIVE FLIES – INNOVATIVE TYING TECHNIQUES, Portland, OR, Frank Amato Publications, Inc., 2002

Wilson, Terry and Wilson, Roxanne. BLUEGILL – FLY FISHING & FLIES, Portland, OR, Frank Amato Publications, Inc., 1999

Index

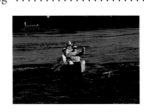